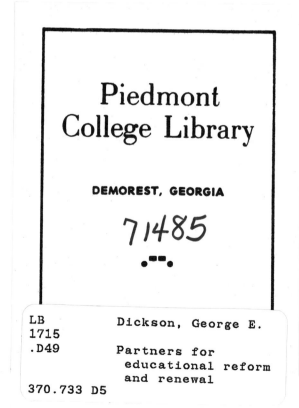

Partners for Educational Reform and Renewal

Competency-Based Teacher Education, Individually Guided Education and the Multiunit School

George E. Dickson

and

Richard W. Saxe

et al.

The University of Toledo

McCutchan Publishing Corporation
2526 Grove Street
Berkeley, California 94704

1/26/78 Berbert Tyler 11.25

*To our partners in educational reform—colleagues,
teachers, school administrators, students, parents,
consultants, project staff—with sincere gratitude
for their vigorous efforts and unfailing support
in this endeavor to make a difference in education.*

Contents

Preface

Books about education seem to come in four varieties. Most popular are those that criticize the subject but provide precious little in
terms of concrete suggestions for doing something about the criticism so expansively provided. Then there are books on educational
theory that provide thoughtful insights on educational development
but do not indicate how theory can be translated into practice.
Books on educational methods and curriculum are popular fare because they deal with how to organize and teach our traditional subject matter with minor concern for relating that subject matter to the
needs and goals of society. In recent years there have been books on
specific educational innovations that attend to a particular concern
about education, give the impression that doing one thing differently
will make *all* the difference, but fail to relate that innovation to the
total process of educational change.

It is difficult to find a book that goes beyond an argument for a
massive reorganization of our educational effort. Alvin Toffler in his
popular *Future Shock* has placed that argument into perspective. He
states that the "present curriculum is a mindless holdover from the
past" and "imposes standardization on the elementary and secondary
schools."[1]

> Attempts by the present educational leadership to revise the physics curriculum or improve the methods for teaching English or Math are piecemeal at best. . . . We need more than haphazard attempts to modernize. We need a systematic approach to the whole problem.[2]

Toffler makes it clear that our schools are facing backward, toward a dying system, rather than forward to an emerging new society. His final words on the subject are that "education must shift into the future tense"[3] and its prime objective must be to increase the speed and economy with which the individual can adapt to continual change.

What the Tofflers of the world request from the education profession is an end of simplistic approaches to complex issues. Foray after foray against the forces of change have convinced some educators that the quick and simple one-concept programs make no impression. No one innovation has been our Rosetta Stone to unlock the mysteries of the unknown. Inevitably, educators have been forced to realize that there can be no substitute for massive, comprehensive, arduous effort to study our problems, amass our total talent and resources, and begin to apply them in a systematic, self-conscious (evaluative), disciplined effort to redirect and revitalize our sagging educational institutions. Those who do not know this have not yet recovered from a Rip Van Winkle concoction downed before Sputnik, before all the myriad innovations and changes of the fifties and sixties.

The time seems ripe for a book that tries to "put it all together," or at least to put some things together. There is a need for a description of an effort that attempts to come to grips with complexity by developing change strategies which recognize and encompass the various phenomena. This book describes such an attempt. It is an account of the development and implications of an educational reform-renewal strategy for a region, a city, and their educational institutions. It concerns a systems approach and modeling in developing, organizing, and operationalizing the educational change effort. The basic organizing elements in the system are the development of multiunit schools, individually guided education, and competency-based teacher education. We attempt to inform the reader about these elements and how they can be effectively linked in any area with its schools to create the climate for and support of a strategy for massive educational change. This is a book about how it was begun and is being done in the Toledo, Ohio, area. Our experiences can be utilized to suggest how to do it elsewhere. We do not suppose that our plans and operations should be exactly imitated in other locations, but our specifications and blueprints are available as guides to action. We know that others will substantially modify and improve them. In any real-world change process nothing ever stands still, is truly complete, or inflexible. We offer a program for change that has possibilities for constantly becoming—self-renewing—in the never-ending process of educational renewal. We think we can help others adapt to and even direct continual change.

Notes

1. Alvin Toffler, *Future Shock* (New York: Random House, 1970), p. 410.
2. Ibid., p. 411.
3. Ibid., p. 427.

Contributors

(In order of their first contribution)

George E. Dickson is Dean of the College of Education, University of Toledo, Professor of Higher Education, and CBTE Project Director.

Richard W. Saxe is Associate Dean, Professor of Educational Administration, and Assistant Project Director.

Leo D. Leonard is Associate Professor of Educational Theory and Sociological Foundations and facilitator of the Toledo Archdiocese competency-based program.

Joan Inglis is Director of Field Experiences and Associate Professor of Elementary and Early Childhood Education.

William Wiersma, Jr., is Director of the Center for Educational Research and Services, Professor of Educational Research and Measurement, and Assistant Director of the CBTE Project.

Castelle G. Gentry is Chairman of Educational Media and Technology, Associate Professor of Educational Media and Technology, and systems process coordinator for the CBTE program.

Edward J. Nussel is Director of the Division of Educational Foundations, Professor of Educational Theory and Sociological Foundations, and a facilitator in the CBTE Project.

John F. Ahern is Associate Professor of Elementary and Early Childhood Education and a CBTE facilitator.

Richard Ishler is Assistant Dean and Professor of Elementary and
Early Childhood Education.

Thomas C. Gibney is Director of the Division of Curriculum and
Instruction, Professor of Elementary and Early Childhood Education, and a CBTE facilitator.

John Schaff is Professor of Secondary Education.

Stephen Jurs is Assistant Professor, Educational Research and Measurement.

Eugene Wysong is Professor of Guidance and Counseling.

Richard Hersh is Chairman of Secondary Education, Associate Professor of Secondary Education, and process coordinator for the
CBTE program.

Hughes Moir is Chairman of Elementary and Early Childhood Education, Associate Professor of Elementary and Early Childhood Education, and process coordinator for the CBTE program.

Howard Coron is Associate Professor of Education and Director of
Student Teaching and the Teaching Performance Center, New
York University.

1/ A Strategy for Educational Reform and Renewal

George E. Dickson
Richard W. Saxe

This book is an attempt to come to grips with educational complexity by developing change strategies that recognize and encompass current phenomena in education. We think that total abandonment of present schools, personnel, and facilities is both unwise and impossible, and that the best approach to broad educational improvement is a process that can be applied within the existing educational system. Our primary efforts will center around suggestions of "how to do it" within the present educational system.

The "it" we describe is a program of competency-based teacher education with multiunit schools that employ individually guided education. Such a program will likely be associated with the development of competency-based curriculum in cooperating public and private schools. However, competency-based education for schools is not the focus of this book. Competency-based education for schools will be considered only to the extent necessary to describe relationships to competency-based teacher education. A complete discussion of these elements follows in chapters 2, 3, and 4. In this chapter we deal with the prior issue, "why?"

In one sense, the "why" is so well documented that we could merely refer to the statements of a host of critics and rest our case.[1] All will agree that the schools are in trouble to some degree. The degree is a matter of dispute. Some maintain that the schools are beyond salvation and should be abandoned in favor of other educational arrangements.[2] Others believe that, with reform, the schools can continue to serve.[3]

The reason for our efforts to bring about a change at this particular time is the clear evidence that the schools have been unable to keep pace with the changing needs and values of an expanded client population. Different types of children with different needs now attend schools for longer periods than at any previous time. Technological improvements and new knowledge have come into being but seem paradoxically to have complicated the task of the schools.

The preceding comments are familiar, and they are certainly sufficient to support a general demand to improve education. However, we need to add some explanation of the thinking behind our particular project. Our efforts at changing teacher education are intended to be comprehensive. This is essential because of the obvious lack of impact (failure) of countless, specific, segmented projects. Moreover, we at the University of Toledo acknowledge the responsibility of being partners with public and private (those that wish to join us) schools in this task. As institutions are presently organized, the university has a primary role in both preservice and inservice teacher education. It also controls the theoretical introduction to administrative positions. Perhaps small, private institutions can disavow this close affiliation, but a large state-supported university is directly linked through its college of education to the success or failure of identifiable public schools.

We must pursue a field-based program to change teacher education. This permits our public and private school partners to have more control over the training of their own replacement teachers. More important, it ensures that our program will be meaningful in relation to the pressing problems of public schools.

The need to be competency based is tied to our concern about the explicit and implicit goals of education and to the new desire and need to be accountable for our efforts. We shall be clear about our objectives, for only in this way can we demonstrate our success or partial success in accomplishing them.

The continued insistence on a multiunit approach—an alternative organizational structure to the self-contained classroom—reflects our conviction that more and different kinds of persons should be directly involved in helping pupils learn. This permits the use of specific talents of different individuals, but also represents our belief that learning is a social process involving more than one professional working with a group of pupils assisted by various technological devices. An additional justification for our insistence on some form of differentiated staffing is tied to the need to be accountable. The presence of additional adults (aides, volunteers, student teachers, interns, teachers, specialists) is a way of opening the class or school to the profession and to the community. It requires and creates trust and responsibility from all concerned.

Closely related to the idea of maximizing individual talents of teachers is our insistence that a viable program be flexible enough to accommodate the individual differences of learners. This is accomplished by individually guided education (IGE) in the elementary schools, which is made possible by alternative means of reaching teacher competencies, in varying lengths of time, in the teacher education institution.

Other aspects of our design are necessary correlates of the elements mentioned. For instance, it is not crucial, but efficient, that the program be organized into modules. The management information system is an important technological adjunct that adds to the probability of becoming accountable. An individualized and particularized program is mandated by the presence of pupils with diverse needs and abilities.

All these characteristics of our program are delineated in subsequent chapters. We identify them at the outset since they are the justification for the particular form in which our change effort is cast. In addition to these elements (competency based, field centered, multiunit, IGE) that are of particular concern to our program design, other important activities help to direct efforts to bring about comprehensive change.

STRATEGIES FOR CHANGING EDUCATION

It is admittedly difficult to come to grips with a complex problem. The problem must be analyzed so that its parts are well known, which also makes apparent the ability or inability of any of these parts to mesh effectively with each other in the operational whole. The next effort involves the search for and addition of new data to the total situation. Further analysis should result in the development of an organizational theme around which a change strategy can be fashioned. The strategy finally adopted must involve the whole problem and not simply concern itself with one or a few of the facets needing attention.

Systems Theory and Analysis

A systems approach is essential to decision making in our highly complex world. The use of systems theory and analysis will enable us to see education and the activities of educators as a whole, to recognize how the various functions of educational organizations and operations depend on one another, and, finally, to understand how a change in any one part affects all components of the system.

The systems approach begins by considering all potential programmatic plans in terms of broad goals and their more specific objectives, plus the interdependent activities needed to achieve the product desired. A system has been defined as "a set of components organized in such a way as to constrain action toward the accomplishment of the purposes for which the system exists."[4]

The components of a system are:

(1) Goals or objectives capable of being measured in operational or behavioral terms;

(2) Statements of criteria (processes affected by and within the system) to determine how the objectives will be met and when they have been reached;

(3) Development of strategies or alternatives for meeting the objectives;

(4) Statements of resources needed for various alternatives or strategies;

(5) Means of evaluation or assessment strategies to determine the "best" procedures for obtaining the objectives; and

(6) The development of evaluation procedures as a repetitive process using feedback mechanisms and cycles of evaluation that permit strategy readjustments to ensure that the system is moving toward its objectives.

This is the general process involved in the utilization of systems theory and analysis. As Meals has ably stated, "Systems analysis calls upon the educator today to see his activity as a whole—not only the whole child but also the curriculum and the media and the teacher and the management system for putting these and other resources together in a functional system."[5]

Designing

The systems approach becomes a design process in which a series of functions are performed that result in the achievement of particular objectives. Designing is a systematic planning process that allows us to deal with the nature and needs of the individual and society, provides us the opportunity to apply our educational theories, and enables us to exercise our professional judgments in systematic fashion. We can design systems and subsystems. Subsystems become the principal processes or operations within a larger system, and have their own objectives plus the processes and components for achieving these objectives.

Whether applied to whole systems or to subsystems, designing becomes a process of exercising the six components or elements listed above. In education, designing usually refers to curriculum or instructional program development. It makes little difference whether the change contemplated is the development of a teacher education program or an elementary education subject area; the design process involving systems theory entails the same comprehensive effort to achieve curricular goals. The educational change efforts described in this book are operational examples of the curriculum design process.

Modeling

The use of systems analysis and designing involves modeling, i.e., the use of model theory. The concept of modeling in systems theory is based on the mathematical concept of set. A mathematical set has been defined as "a carefully defined collection of discrete elements which may be symbols, ideas, or physical objects."[6]

The idea of set appears simple, but its use is one of the most powerful strategies in educational change efforts because "the unit of a collection of symbols" can be "associated completely with the concept and not with the discrete actualities themselves."[7] This means that in modeling we do not need to confine our thinking to the individual items that make up a set, but can instead concern ourselves with the collection of items and how such a collection may be more interestingly conceived in our developing model.

The basic types of models are iconic, analogue, and formal symbolic. *Iconic* models are pictorial or physical representations of various parts, or the totality, of any system under consideration. *Analogue* models involve the use of flow charts, verbal descriptions, or diagrams to portray the various elements in a model. A formal *symbolic* model is a mathematical representation of set using symbols of logic or mathematics. Educators typically use analogue models in their modeling process.

The development of a curriculum model makes possible the collection of particular elements as well as their interconnections "as a system which calls for stating or setting forth the purpose of a system; explaining or describing the nature of the essential qualities of the collection, indicating the boundaries or extent of the system; and specifying distinctly the outline or form of the collection under consideration."[8] Modeling enables the basic purpose of systems analysis to occur: the process of decision making. Modeling allows an entity to be broken down into its basic components and their relationships for initial examination, reexamination, assembly, reassembly—the processes (decision making) necessary to achieve the purposes of the system.

A basic systems design model is illustrated in Figure 1-1. An educational program is essentially an effort to process input to achieve output or a product with necessary feedback mechanisms

Figure 1-1. Simplified Analogue Model

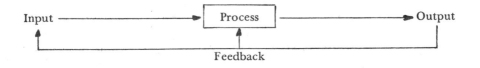

available to either change or improve input or process for the further development of output. Figure 1-1 is a simplified analogue model for the development of any educational program involving systems analysis. More complicated models are elaborations of this basic model.

Utilizing Unifying Themes and Organizing Elements

Consistent with the educational change strategies of systems analysis designing and modeling is the need to employ overarching, unifying themes and their organizing elements that sharpen and consolidate such themes to accomplish the basic purposes of the systems approach. Systems theory requires broad information that can be utilized to identify a system's purposes, structures, and major functions. This information is usually expressed as a "mission statement," which attempts a definitive description, brief but sufficient, of the matter under consideration. From such a statement flow detailed system objectives, design criteria, strategies or activities for meeting the objectives, resources needed, evaluation procedures, and feedback mechanisms. The brief statement of a unifying theme may not appear at first glance to encompass all these, but it establishes the basic concepts around which a system will be organized and operated.

Unifying themes and organizing elements are a popular technique employed by governments, business, industry, and a variety of organizations in establishing the goals, parameters, and potential activities for problem solutions and the achievement of desired results. President Franklin D. Roosevelt effectively used a unifying theme of three words, "the New Deal," to establish and characterize an entirely new and different approach by the federal government to the affairs of its citizens and institutions. Around this unifying theme were created a whole series of organizing elements, e.g., the Social Security Administration, the Civilian Conservation Corps, National Reconstruction Administration, and other elements of the New Deal program. More recent government examples of unifying themes have been "the Great Society" and "a Generation of Peace." Such terms suggest systems designed to accommodate the problems and operations of social change.

Similarly, attempts to develop change strategies for educational systems necessitate the formulation of unifying themes and their organizing elements. In education, however, the problem has been that often the themes are limited, too much concerned with the past, and attempt only a partial thrust for educational change. For example, "the right to read" attempted a confrontation with the problem of children learning how to read more effectively but did not address itself to larger educational concerns that also affect the ability to read. Many themes have been announced by educational organizations, government agencies, and private foundations. Most have been discarded, misused, or replaced by yet another theme calling for educational efforts to deal with modern complexities. Educational themes have seldom been comprehensive enough to deal with the complexities of society today. Such a theme, we submit, is competency-based education for teachers and its organizing elements of individually guided education and multiunit schools. These terms suggest a strategy for a comprehensive reorganization of the educational system, from primary school through teacher education.

Implementing and Operationalizing

The ultimate step in a change process is putting into operation and trying out what has been devised. Much effort and important resources go into the development, designing, and modeling of any new educational system. However, the final analysis of whether the system produced can be operated successfully can only occur with model implementation. Until a potential user of information has internalized it through personal experience, all that has been written on "how to do it," with suggested procedures, rationales, et cetera, is likely to remain just that: suggested procedures, rationales, etc. Implementing and operationalizing are the crucial problems—finding ways for potential users of new theories and processes to become actually involved with them.

The basic implementation question is: "Where does one begin and what strategy will likely lead to the desired end?" Obviously, no implementation-development effort in any particular institution or locale can be exactly like that in another. What works in one place can be tried in another setting but there is no guarantee that success will occur in the new environment. In any change process every institution will need a slightly different treatment or strategy.

Implementation-operationalization must be *individualized*. Concepts and procedures may be borrowed, but it would be futile to copy exactly other program designs or plans. Implementation strategy first calls for the realization of one's individuality and the necessity of program development appropriate for that individuality.

All persons who are to be identified with implementation-operationalization must become involved in the process. No one can be conveniently left out. People are more likely to support and react positively to programmatic efforts in which they have personal identification and responsibility. A successful strategy involves all concerned not only with the major change effort but also with the development of the process.

Simply to involve others in a change effort is, of course, not in itself a guarantee of eventual programmatic success. Involvement means asking those who implement to participate in goal setting. This risks changing systematically developed designs and models, but that is what change is about. Systematic continuous feedback is necessary; no program creation should be considered ideal or ultimate.

Implementation requires personal latitude along with the necessary structure to facilitate completion of the task. Individuals rarely work well in organizational vacuums. Programmatic change is most likely to occur when a system enables a complete consideration of every component involved in the change process.

Educators must learn that "disseminating" (telling) is not synonymous with "implementing." Many good ideas and programs in education have been widely disseminated but never implemented. Talking and reading about change in education does not accomplish the change. The first step in implementation-operationalization strategy goes beyond dissemination.

A "REAL-WORLD" FUTURE FOR EDUCATIONAL CHANGE

Educators contemplating educational change must shift their thinking into the future tense of society by employing change strategies such as those briefly outlined above. This calls for drastic change, for the most part, in past and present curriculums, and for the realization that we must now be engaged in preparing those who come to us for education to deal with the future. Our present standardized approach to elementary, secondary, and teacher education was never designed for the future. It is not even adequate for the present.

Efforts to achieve educational change cannot be piecemeal. We have around us the debris of single educational innovations devised and abandoned. Toffler puts it well: "We need more than haphazard attempts to modernize. We need a systematic approach to the whole problem."[9] That systematic approach requires the utilization of all the change strategies that are needed to handle complexity. Only in this way will the present program be basically reformed.

SUMMARY

In this chapter we have proposed that competency-based, individually guided education, with multiunit schools, is well suited to current needs. We briefly introduced some activities of a comprehensive change strategy: systems theory, designing, modeling, unifying themes, operationalizing. In Chapter 2 we describe our particular unifying theme: competency-based teacher education.

Notes

1. See, e.g., Goodman, Holt, Kohl, Kozol, Illich.
2. See Ivan Illich, *Deschooling Society* (New York: Harper & Row, 1971).
3. See R. Saxe, ed., *Opening the Schools* (Berkeley: McCutchan Publishing Corp., 1972).
4. Kathryn V. Feyereisen, A. John Fiorino, and Arlene T. Novak, *Supervision and Curriculum Renewal: A Systems Approach* (New York: Appleton-Century-Crofts 1970), p. 38.
5. Donald Meals, "Heuristic Models for System Planning," *Phi Delta Kappan* 48 (January 1967): 200.
6. Joseph E. Hill, *How Schools Can Apply Systems Analysis* (Bloomington, Ind.: The Phi Delta Kappa Educational Foundation, 1972), p. 13.
7. Ibid., p. 14.
8. Ibid., p. 15.
9. Alvin Toffler, *Future Shock* (New York: Random House, 1970), p. 411.

Suggested Readings

Hill, Joseph E. *How Schools Can Apply Systems Analysis.* Bloomington, Ind.: The Phi Delta Kappa Educational Foundation, 1972.
Immegart, Glenn L., and Francis J. Pilecki. *An Introduction to Systems for the Educational Administrator.* Reading, Mass.: Addison Wesley, 1973.
Mansergh, Gerald G., ed. *Systems Approach to the Management of Public Education.* Detroit: Metropolitan Detroit Bureau of School Studies, 1969.
Miles, Matthew B., ed. *Innovation in Education.* New York: Bureau of Publications, Teachers College, Columbia University, 1964.

2/ Considering the Unifying Theme: Competency-Based Teacher Education

George E. Dickson

Teacher education has a direct relationship to what happens to children in a classroom, and both are subject to the reciprocal influence of the needs and goals of society. Because of this logical and psychological connection, competency-based teacher education (CBTE) will be and should be associated with competency-based education (CBE) in schools. The arguments advanced on behalf of competency-based education for teachers are equally valid for their pupils. The same changing social conditions that cause us to advocate CBTE will bring about CBE. In our opinion, real change and reform in teacher education will result in an educational revolution in elementary and secondary education.

OVERVIEW OF TRADITIONAL PROGRAMS

Reform and improvement in teacher education are subjects about which much has been said and written but little achieved. Most teacher educators are basically conservative by nature. From their efforts and the products of their programs, the general evidence indicates implicit satisfaction with the status quo. Examination of programs of teacher education today reveals them to be much as they were at mid-century. Such programs emphasize knowledge about subject matter, teachers, and teaching acquired mainly from general psychological principles, studies in philosophy and social science, and practical experience. We are still seeking dependable knowledge about teaching behavior. However, even if we had all such knowledge, we would still have the problem of how to prepare teachers, how to use such knowledge and practice, and how to induce institutional changes in teacher education programs.

At least forty years of study in the field of teacher education have attempted to answer the question of how the behavior of an individual preparing to teach can be made to conform to desirable patterns. The results of this concern are represented in most teacher education programs by professional preparation (providing teaching experiences and skills, teaching pedagogical concepts and principles, and developing professional attitudes) and by academic preparation, which involves the knowledge (with some concern for teaching) of various subject areas. Educational patterns for providing knowledge of subject matter are known and applied. More difficult has been the problem of how to develop teaching skill, provide pedagogical concepts and principles, and establish professional attitudes. Present teacher education instruction relies principally on the apprentice approach (practice teaching) and long used instructional modes (lecturing, reading assignments).

If the way college and university professors instruct young adult students could be based on sound principles of learning that are equally relevant for children, there would be no problem. But we all know this is not the case; university teaching styles are not closely related to principles of learning. Certainly our colleagues in the arts and sciences would themselves ridicule the notion of using their lecture style as a model for teaching children. This is only one instance in which the overall educational system is inconsistent, but it is an important instance to which we shall return frequently.

A principal difficulty, then, is that most teacher education programs operate without prior comprehensive conceptualization derived from research findings and societal concerns. Few programs concern themselves with the role of the learner, the changing role of the teacher in a changing society, and the kinds of skills and attitudes a teacher needs in order to continue to grow as a teacher and as a person. In present programs teacher education conceptualization is most often found in terms of particular courses needed to meet someone's standards or, more often, state department of education certification requirements. Most programs are designed without a research or theoretical base.

We now know better than to expect teachers to be prepared to teach by a process related only accidentally to their subsequent actual teaching. We always knew better, but now we *really* know better. Major breakthroughs have been made in the analysis of teaching behavior and the conception of such behavior as a complex of skills that can be identified and practiced systematically under specified conditions.

A review of teacher education goals will invariably find them stated vaguely, in general terms. Such statements from catalogs of American universities and colleges do not really give us the direction for designing program components, nor the means to determine when the goals are achieved. Some college teacher education programs actually operate year after year without *any* specified objectives. General goals are necessary as broad guidelines for any program, but only by operationalizing them into more specific behavioral objectives can program components be designed to achieve objectives and to evaluate the effectiveness of a program by explicit criteria.

Many current teacher education programs have introduced educational innovations, e.g., micro-teaching, interaction analysis, simulation, and team teaching, but these have been used in an appended, piecemeal fashion. Innovations offer program potential, but despite their addition to existing curriculums, the net result is that the total program does not change significantly. Innovative program components need to be considered in terms of how they relate to the total system and how the goals of that system are to be achieved.

New teacher education programs call for new functions and new roles on the part of teacher educators. Present departmental organizations in colleges and universities often act to constrain the development of new faculty functions. Components of teacher education programs are often determined by departmental tradition.

Conventional teacher education programs typically lack programmatic evaluation processes that can determine the degree to which program objectives are met. Even when program objectives are clearly specified, there is a tendency to shy away from evaluation of a program monitoring nature. Inadequate program evaluation makes data-based program decision making most difficult.

SIGNS OF CHANGE

Teacher education is currently being forced to operate in a more open system, with a wide range of organizations and individuals directly and indirectly involved. It is becoming more client oriented, with its clients extending beyond the usual boundaries. Teacher educators are finding that they must be responsive to their students, school administrators and teachers, parents, children, and to the community at large.

Teacher educators can no longer ignore the forces that are creating the need for change. Attitudes toward education at all levels are causing a reconsideration of content and method—as well as the extent to which the public is willing to fund professionals who seem unresponsive to the new scene. Accountability in education has become a national policy. Educators are expected to accept responsibility for their performance as shown by the accomplishments of learners.

Preservice and inservice teacher education students consistently charge that teacher education programs lack "relevance." Through their educational organizations, teachers have secured a greater voice in matters of program planning, certification, and self-regulation within the profession. The end of the teacher shortage now finds us with sufficient numbers of teacher personnel but with a need for preparing most teachers for changed roles, and some persons for new roles.

STRATEGIES FOR CHANGE

The demands of society, mirrored in current educational change efforts, have engendered confusion, uncertainty, and self-analysis, as well as excitement and hope in terms of the options available to teacher educators as they seek new directions. Two broad strategies for the design and operation of teacher education programs are available, and in competition. H. Del Schalock of the Teaching Research Division of the Oregon State System of Higher Education has identified them as the *experienced-based* strategy and the *performance-based* strategy.[1]

Experience-Based Strategy

The experience-based strategy describes most existing teacher education programs, which require a specified number of courses and course hours in specific areas of study, plus a student teaching requirement. The present standards of the National Council for the Accreditation of Teacher Education express this concept by recommending: (1) course work in general studies, (2) course work in the content of the teaching specialty, (3) humanistic and behavioral studies, (4) teaching and learning theory with laboratory and clinical experience, and (5) a practicum experience.[2] Such specifications are classifications of experience in which students are to engage. As Schalock points out,[3] they do not specify what is to be learned from such experience nor do they indicate what prospective teachers need to know or should be able to perform in order to be qualified to teach. Transcripts reveal only how many credit hours students have taken in certain classes.

Performance-Based Strategy

The authors maintain that change in teacher education is more likely to occur with a strategy based on performance, where the outcomes are clearly specified. This means that the knowledge, skills, attitudes, and competencies that prospective teachers are expected to have on completion of a teacher education program are specified, and that the criteria that are evidence for the realization of these outcomes are known. This type of teacher training is classified as performance or competency-based teacher education.[4] The competencies to be acquired by the student and the criteria to be applied in assessing the competencies are made explicit, and the student is accountable for meeting these criteria. The teacher competencies to be so specified are those involved in the particular teacher skills, understandings, attitudes, and behaviors that promote the various types of growth (intellectual, physical, social) in children.

Three types of criteria are used to determine the competencies of the teacher: knowledge criteria, performance criteria, and product criteria.[5] Knowledge criteria are used to determine his cognitive understandings. Performance criteria are employed to assess his teaching behaviors. Product criteria are used to assess his ability to teach by examining the achievement of the pupils he has taught.

The trend today in American teacher education is toward an emphasis on performance and product. There is a great difference between "knowing" and "doing" and teachers must now not only give evidence of what they know but what they can do.

ESSENTIAL ELEMENTS OF CBTE

The major and most far-reaching effort to implement the competency-based strategy has been the Model Elementary Teacher Education Programs, sponsored by the U.S. Office of Education.[6] Nine of these developmental research programs were funded in a Phase I design effort. An additional program was added during the Phase II feasibility studies, which looked into the matter of program design time and cost factors. These ten model teacher education programs, over two million words in technical research reports, are the foundation of the literature on competency-based education. In the opinion of the authors, these model designs and the subsequent cooperative work of the model directors and their colleagues, from 1967 to the present, have been the most significant events in the design and development of competency-based teacher education.

Application of Systems Theory

The systems approach is fundamental to competency-based teacher education curriculum development. Systems theory or systems analysis, as indicated in Chapter 1, is a process of applying scientific thinking to a major endeavor; its use in teacher education indicates a concentration on *process*. The systems approach begins with the broadest statement of the problem (system) and then uses systems analysis procedures to determine and define the system's parts as functions, as well as the interrelationship among those functions. For example, the basic position of the Ohio model building effort was that the changing demands of society, increasingly complex technologies, children with different needs, and variable economic support levels for education necessitated more deliberate planning for teacher education. The systems approach offered the goal-oriented procedures to effect this deliberate planning.

When teacher education is conceived in terms of a system:

(1) The role of the teacher must be designed (and his education developed) in the context of various related educational roles (such as team leaders and regular teachers in team teaching situations, educational technologists, teacher aides, supervisory and administrative personnel, etc.);

(2) The role of the teacher must be considered in relation to all the elements of the learning environment (classrooms and their equipment, books, theories of teaching, etc.);

(3) The distinction between preservice and inservice training is eliminated as teaching is more and more viewed as a continuing, developmental process;

(4) The education of teachers becomes goal-oriented, based on the development of competencies required to facilitate pupil learning.

With this rationale in mind, a teacher education system has as its *purpose* the development of teachers who have certain knowledge, skills, and attitudes that promote children's learning. Its *processes* are the readings, discussions, activities, etc., that provide the necessary knowledge, skills, and attitudes. Its *components* are the instructional and managerial elements involving courses, schedules, learning modules, and time factors necessary to organize and operate the instructional process designed to achieve the program's purposes. The *products* of a teacher education system are the teachers who graduate from it. Success is determined by the degree to which graduates have achieved the system's objectives in terms of the specified knowledge, skills, and attitudes. Evaluation ascertains the degree to which this occurs. Information obtained from evaluation is constantly fed back into the system to make needed changes in the purposes, or components, of the entire program. As corrections are made, the entire cycle becomes repetitive; the total process is ongoing and regenerative.

A simple way of looking at such a system is to view the entire procedure as one of input, process or operation, output, and feedback. (The relationship among these components was shown in Figure 1-1.) The purpose of a system is realized through processes in which the components of the system interact to produce a predetermined output. Purpose determines the processes required, and the process suggests the components that will make up the system. Thus the systems approach forces a total consideration of teacher education—its goals, its processes, its components and subsystems, and the relationship of all of these to each other.

An overview of the systems analysis approach is provided by Le Baron.[7] Step 1 is the total conceptualization of the system or the "problem universe." Step 2 consists of defining the subsystems within the total system. Step 3 involves the stating of the objectives of the system. Step 4 requires the developing of alternative procedures for achieving the objectives. Step 5 asks the system planner to select and implement the best alternative. Finally, in step 6, the system becomes operational. All these steps have feedback relationships among them as well as from step 6 back to step 1. Systems designing is the process of moving through all the steps (except step 6—operation) at a general level for overview purposes and then returning to the first step and those that follow to develop the details based on the overview. This process enables each subsequent specific action to be related to the basic goals of the project and to be evaluated on that process.

The model teacher education program described in this book uses a systems approach that began with the conceptualization of the total educational program, including its needs and broad objectives, considered the potential components of such a program, stated the specific objectives for each component, and then designed the instructional procedures—called modules—to achieve the objectives. The analytical process of the systems approach demanded a consideration of teachers from a product-oriented perspective, accompanied by reference to educational theory and research on teacher behavior, effectiveness, and the learning process. Systems theory called for precise development of goals and objectives, because the design of all processes and components of a system depends on objectives that clearly state criteria to determine the system's effectiveness. The approach forced our model designers to look at educational innovations and new practices in respect to their relationship to specific program goals and objectives. Educational innovations were not added to the program design at random. The systems approach required that the components of the program be derived directly from the objectives. This entire process has been well analyzed in a paper written by M. Vere DeVault, Bruce Joyce, and Mary A. Golladay. These authors define competency-based teacher education in terms of four interrelated storage and retrieval systems:

1. A *competency specification* subsystem that specifies teacher competencies in behavioral terms.
2. An *evaluation* subsystem that relates assessment devices to specified competencies.
3. An *instructional* subsystem that consists of instructional modules designed to achieve specified performances.
4. A *management* subsystem that comprehensively and effectively combines the competency specification, the assessment devices, and the instructional modules in the education of particular teachers.[8]

These authors properly indicate that a CBTE system involving the four subsystems "has the capacity to diagnose teacher competencies, relate these diagnoses to instructional modules that facilitate competency development, monitor progress toward competency through the application of the assessment subsystem, and create continuous re-diagnosis data for use by both learner and instructor."[9]

The basic concepts and thinking behind the use of systems theory are neither new nor mystical. An analytical, logical process is employed that approximates scientific thinking. A different way of approaching the designing and developing of a teacher education program is required, but this process is not difficult to apply. What *is* required is a full understanding of the system called "teacher education" and its relationship to the whole of education. It is essential that we note that we cannot reject all current teacher education practices merely because we have not begun in this fashion. Many current practices will surely be retained; certainly the entire traditional program cannot be retained.

Personalization and Individualization

Competency-based teacher education programs are sometimes criticized as being nonhumanistic. Although we reject this charge, we acknowledge the concern as valid. For programs to be both humanistic and relevant for students they must be personalized. "Personalization" requires a variety of strategies that individualize and make more personal the learning-teaching process. The word personalization has a meaning beyond the term individualization. Individualization generally refers to providing educational opportunities for a student to engage in learning activities at his own rate, sometimes independently, sometimes with others. Individualization has many instructional forms, and some of these tend to be abstract and to lack humanness. Personalization of instruction, on the other hand, is the attempt to particularize instruction by being more concerned with the diverse interests, achievements, and activities of each learner.

The systems approach to the development of competency-based teacher education requires a continuous, regenerative effort to design, develop, and operationalize a teacher education program. Personalization requires that *all* persons, including students, who have any role in the programmatic effort be involved. Each student's program will vary to some extent on the basis of his interest, specialization, background of knowledge, skills, and personal learning style. Personalization requires a continuing relationship among the college faculty, the students, and other involved persons throughout the program's development and operation.

The student in particular is expected to interact continuously with the instructional staff, whether they are college faculty or school personnel. Interaction should result in definition and negotiation of the competencies to be developed by the student, the context in which such competencies will be demonstrated, and the criteria by which they will be judged. The concept of personalization assumes that not all students are alike and recognizes their individual differences. Consequently, the basic objective is to provide a program of teacher education that will achieve broad competence for prospective teachers but at the same time will single out and promote teacher individuality. The utilization of faculty, cooperative teachers, and other instructional personnel is also guided by the concepts of personalization and individualization.

The merit of personalization is that students will know exactly what they want to do and what they can do. They are then held accountable for demonstrating the competencies they have participated in defining and which they have contracted to achieve. This calls for assessment procedures considerably different from those presently in practice. In competency-based teacher education, assessment is "criterion referenced" in terms of the three previously mentioned classes of criteria—knowledge, skills, and products. When seeking the products of a teacher's behavior in assessing competency, competence is assessed in specific situations where specific objectives are achieved and should not be thought of as abstract or generic. This achievement of situation-specific competence will occur in real life educational settings, with real pupils working toward real objectives. The practice will result in teachers with markedly different styles of teaching who can produce predictable educational outcomes. Competency-based teacher education attempts to prepare prospective teachers who will provide a personalized and individualized learning environment for children. We find it only reasonable that a teacher education program should reflect a similar learning environment.

Competency-Based Criteria

Competency-based teacher education requires and commits us to the use of competency-based criteria for teacher preparation. Once specified, these criteria hold prospective teachers (students) and inservice teachers accountable for their performance. Achievement requires certain acquired knowledge, demonstrated performance, and predictable products.

The competencies for entering the teaching profession have not been clearly defined. Examination of various state department of education certification requirements and the catalogs of teacher education institutions indicates that competence is stated in terms of courses or credits required, time served, and a teacher practice requirement, usually in the form of student teaching. These become the ill-defined objectives of teacher education, which do not specify teacher education processes let alone required teacher performance. Although many teacher education programs require a full college quarter of all-day student teaching, there are no specific performance expectancies for this experience and no means are suggested to measure the effects of training on the student's performance as a teacher or his specific qualifications to enter the teaching profession.

A competency-based teacher education approach assumes the use of previously stated assessment criteria—knowledge (what a prospective teacher should know), performance (what a prospective teacher can do), and products (what a prospective teacher can achieve in learners). There has been no lack of concern for knowledge criteria in traditional teacher education programs; knowledge of subject matter and general teaching or methodological concepts have become the primary basis for the assessment of broad teacher education objectives. Emphasis is now shifting, however, to assessment procedures that emphasize performance criteria. These criteria need to be as systematically derived and explicitly stated as any criteria for assessing knowledge. The ability to attain specified objectives with learners (product criteria) represents another kind of competence that will be required of a teacher candidate.

Criteria assessments can be accomplished and described systematically. When a prospective teacher has the appropriate *knowledge,* can *perform* in a stipulated manner, and can *produce* anticipated results with learners, he has met competency-based criteria requirements. In the present state of competency-based teacher education development it has been far easier to state knowledge and performance criteria than product criteria.

Competency-based teacher education programs cannot exist without rather precise statements of the specific competencies to be achieved and the definite procedures for assessing competence in terms of the criteria developed. These conditions require that certain procedures be observed. Decisions on what knowledge, behavior, and products are to serve as a criteria base must be made in collaboration with appropriate knowledge, behaviors, or product outcomes. Teacher education institutions are no longer the sole or even the major determinants of program focus or requirements. All educational groups involved in teacher education must become part of the system in determining the basis for competence assessment.

The use of competency-based criteria means that CBTE programs put more emphasis on exit requirements than on entrance requirements; it also requires that program achievement, and not time spent in the program, be held constant.

Instructional Modules

The principal instructional element in a competency-based teacher education program is the instructional module, which may be defined as a set of learning activities intended to facilitate the student's achievement of a specified behavioral objective or set of behavioral objectives. Basically, a module consists of the following elements:

(1) A specific objective or set of objectives in behavioral terms;

(2) A pretest designed to assess the student's level of achievement relative to the objective or objectives, prior to any instructional experiences;

(3) A series of instructional activities designed to help the student meet the objective or objectives;

(4) A posttest designed to assess the student's level of mastery relative to the objective or objectives.

The development of instructional modules is a teachable process which can reflect individual styles. However, certain information about module elements needs mentioning. The behavioral objective, or objectives, is derived from a competency, or competencies, specified in knowledge, performance, or product criteria. Such competencies, in behavioral objective form, are empirically based and made public in competency-based teacher education programs. Pretesting and posttesting situations should emulate as much as possible the real world of teaching, thereby placing greater emphasis on the utilization of performance and product criteria. Instructional modules provide students and faculty with opportunities for individualization, personalization, team teaching, and a variety of instructional activities not possible in usual college courses. Module development procedures have been well explained in two instructional materials handbooks,[10] and various module examples are available from institutions that offer competency-based teacher education programs.

Management Information and Evaluation Subsystem

Teacher education currently suffers from a lack of systematic evaluation. It is one thing to plan a course of training for teachers, but quite another to determine how future teachers will behave once they are responsible for their own teaching. Unfortunately, present teacher education programs have not required the collection, sorting, and frequent retrieval of large amounts of data for evaluative purposes. Competency-based teacher education focuses unusual attention on evaluation; if programs are to realize their objectives, it is essential that modern technology be employed in management and evaluation.

Viewed as a complex system, competency-based teacher education requires a program management subsystem for successful operation. A concurrent need is systematic program evaluation, to determine the validity of CBTE assumptions and to provide data for the continuous decision making necessary for development. Evaluation requires: (1) clear determination of objectives, (2) careful planning of means to accomplish the objectives, and (3) ongoing revision and improvement of the chosen means. The program can be evaluated at any time and becomes, in effect, self-correcting.

The basic purpose of management is problem solving. Good management ensures the well-being and smooth functioning of the entire system through the integration of all system parts into goal-achieving combinations and behavior. The basic concepts employed in the Ohio model are successive approximation, continual assessment, and management by objectives. Teacher education usually operates from a base of limited resources and demands pragmatic approaches to its reform and renewal; therefore the concept of *successive approximation* is employed in the acquisition and development of personnel, materials, space, equipment, and time as we move toward more ideal CBTE instructional and management systems. Since we are successively approximating the ideal, there must be *continual assessment* (evaluation) of objective data from the CBTE effort for continual decision-making processes. CBTE in operation requires that learners master, at prescribed levels, prerequisite behaviors before continuing on to successive behaviors—a process that requires *management by objectives*. Management by objectives likewise applies to instructional program and management system development. Just as changes in the instructional system occur in the process of bringing it closer to approximating the ideal, so also will the management information system be improved.

As with any system, a management-evaluation system consists of inputs, processes, and outputs. *Inputs* involve organizational problems that are concerned with discrepancies between program objectives and program performance. *Processes* are the coordination and control operations through which organizational problems are raised and potential solutions are generated and assessed. *Outputs* are the organizational solutions designed to reduce the difference between the intended objectives and the actual performance.

The development and operation of a management-evaluation subsystem requires an operational statement of its goals, policies and rules, system models, system components, means of assessment, and the means for system revision. The operational definition of components refers not only to the functions of each component, but also to the relationships among them. In a logical, sequential order, the components of a management-evaluation subsystem are analysis, synthesis, implementation, information handling, and evaluation.

Analysis identifies management needs, tasks, and goals, as well as variables and constraints. *Synthesis* develops alternative solutions, examines these from various standpoints, and selects the most appropriate solutions. *Implementation* is acquiring and allocating all resources on the basis of operational objectives, providing direction to all personnel involved, scheduling all resources necessary, and operating the field test or solution. *Information handling* concerns data collection and its statistical or other treatment for program or management revision, including the proper distribution of such information. *Evaluation* involves procedures and their validation for determining whether instructional and management system goals have been met. Evaluation is a decision-making process; it determines whether to continue, terminate, further evolve, or modify the ongoing activities. From these efforts come the refinement of present activities or the generation of new tasks. Thus CBTE program development and management are not static but regenerative.

The increased attention to management-evaluation systems procedures calls for additional personnel—e.g., program systems analysts, computer programmers, media specialists, systems technicians, counselors, and accountants—in teacher education operations. Such personnel are available on most university campuses but have been little used in typical teacher education activities. CBTE ensures that the neglected areas of program evaluation and management will receive far greater attention than has been the case in the past.

OTHER FACTORS

The fundamental components of CBTE programs have been broadly presented. Some factors, such as competency-based criteria, behavioral objectives, instructional modules, and evaluation procedures, are of special importance; a more detailed discussion of these elements will be presented in subsequent chapters. The remainder of this discussion will deal with other matters important to CBTE considerations.

The Preservice-Inservice Continuum

Competency-based teacher education calls for continuity of preservice and inservice teacher training. A teacher is never fully educated; his intellectual and practical development must be nourished regularly. Consequently, the concept of a fixed three- or four-year program for teacher education is discarded, and concentration is focused on a more balanced and integrated approach to continual teacher growth. The competency-based curriculum is deliberately designed for growth in given knowledge, teaching performances, and student outcomes, because possible hierarchies of learning from the simple to the complex in the various content and skill areas are made more explicit. Competency-based approaches are consciously designed for self-renewal; as content and processes become obsolete, the system is continuously redesigned. Competency-based design strategy calls for timely delivery of instruction when the teacher needs it, not restricted to vacations, weekends, after-school sessions, or to formal instructional classrooms. The attempt is to make education as explicit and as public as possible, with alternative objectives and instructional routes from which the next steps of growth can be selected. This curriculum approach also includes the technology that enables the various partners in the teacher education enterprise to maintain anticipatory design activities, permitting the program to continue delivering instruction based on changing needs. Under these conditions continuity in teacher education is a necessity.

Instructional Partnerships

Multi-institutional organizational patterns and interdisciplinary study are prominent in competency-based teacher education. *Multi-institutional organizational patterns* refers to the fact that teacher education must be the business not only of colleges but also public schools, certain educational and governmental agencies, educational industries, educational professional organizations, teacher education students, and the community. This concept greatly extends the cooperative base for teacher education planning and operations. The objective is to maximize the resources available to teacher education programs and to involve more closely those concerned in the decision-making processes.

Various kinds of partnership relationships can be developed; for example, the use of consortia is becoming more widespread. Teacher education programs are becoming more *interdisciplinary*; teaching tasks call for such a range of sensitivities, information, and skills that only an interdisciplinary approach is feasible.

A CONCLUSION

The entire effort by the U.S. Office of Education model programs in CBTE has been to prescribe and delineate needed changes in teacher education. Society has changed the goals of education; however, most educational institutions—especially colleges and schools of education—appear still uninformed of the new goals. The needs and natures of learners have changed, but our schools are still organized and operated for pupils of an earlier, simpler time. Curriculums have not kept pace with social, economic, cultural, and technological changes. That educators have not kept up with societal change is not unusual or unexpected. It is not a simple matter to keep educational goals and practices consistent with society's needs, but the need remains to reduce a major aspect of societal strain and achieve the development of a more appropriate fit between society and education. This is a crucial objective of a modern society. The authors are fundamentally concerned with teacher education because it is here that educational forces seem most resistant to change, but it is also the place where we believe that the greatest educational breakthroughs can be realized and exploited.

The evolving, changing, regenerative nature of teacher education has been mentioned. Teacher education programs of the future must have the built-in capacity to reform and renew themselves. The method of program development called competency-based teacher education can make possible the consideration of teacher education as evolving, changing, and regenerating. In all of the model efforts, our concern for educational change has been the central guiding principle: change is contemplated for both the teacher education process and its products. If the process can be transformed, we expect to realize very different products. If the behavioral objectives established by and for our products are achieved, we expect teacher education operations of a vastly different nature. The education of teachers as it now exists must be fundamentally changed.

SUMMARY

In this chapter we have compared traditional—experience-based—teacher education with innovative—competency-based—programs. Some major elements of CBTE were presented and additional concerns for continuous education and partnerships in teacher education were described. More detailed exposition of the basics of CBTE—behavioral objectives, criteria and modules—appears in the following chapter.

Notes

1. H. Del Schalock, "Alternative Strategies and Foci for Teacher Education" (Paper presented at the Twenty-third Annual Conference on Teacher Education, Austin, Texas, October 25-27, 1970); idem, "BEPD, NCERD, and Teacher Education That Makes a Demonstrable Difference" (A working paper prepared for a 1972 BEPD task force, Monmouth, Ore.: Teacher Research, Division of the Oregon State System of Higher Education, May 14, 1972), p. 9; idem, "BEPD, NCERD, and Teacher Education That Makes a Demonstrable Difference," in *The Power of Competency-Based Teacher Education: A Report*, ed. Benjamin Rosner (Boston: Allyn & Bacon, 1972), pp. 114-22.

2. National Council for Accreditation of Teacher Education, *Materials for Institutional Accreditation* (Washington, D.C.: The Council, 1970), pp. 3-6.

3. H. Del Schalock, "Alternative Strategies and Foci for Teacher Education."

4. There are nice semantic distinctions between performance-based and competency-based but these need not concern us here.

5. Some writers now use the term "consequence" for "product" criteria in referring to the outcomes a teacher is expected to bring about in pupils.

6. D. W. Allen and J. M. Cooper, *Model Elementary Teacher Education Program*, University of Massachusetts Model Project (Washington, D.C.: Government Printing Office, 1968); M. Vere DeVault, *Wisconsin Elementary Teacher Education Project*, University of Wisconsin Model Project (Madison: School of Education, University of Wisconsin, 1969); G. E. Dickson, *Educational Specifications for a Comprehensive Elementary Teacher Education Program*, University of Toledo Model Project (Washington, D.C.: Government Printing Office, 1968); W. Robert Houston, *Behavioral Science Elementary Teacher Education Program*, Michigan State University Model Project (Washington, D.C.: Government Printing Office, 1968); J. Hough, *Specifications for a Comprehensive Undergraduate and Inservice Teacher Education Program for Elementary Teachers*, Syracuse University Model Project (Washington, D.C.: Government Printing Office, 1968); C. E. Johnson, G. F. Shearron, and A. J. Stauffer, *Georgia Educational Model Specifications for the Preparation of Elementary Teachers*, University of Georgia Model Project (Washington, D.C.: Government Printing Office, 1968); B. R. Joyce, *The Teacher Innovator: A Program to Prepare Teachers*, Columbia University Teachers College Model Project (Washington, D.C.: Govern-

ment Printing Office, 1969); H. D. Schalock, *A Competency-Based, Field Centered, Systems Approach to Elementary Teacher Education,* Oregon Model Project (Washington, D.C.: Government Printing Office, 1968); H. C. Southworth, *A Model of Teacher Training for the Individualization of Instruction,* University of Pittsburgh Model Project (Washington, D.C.: Government Printing Office, 1968); J. W. Sowards, *A Model for the Preparation of Elementary School Teachers,* Florida State University Model Project (Washington, D.C.: Government Printing Office, 1968).

7. Walt Le Baron, "Systems Analysis and Teacher Education," in *Competency Based Teacher Education: 1, Problems and Prospects for the Decades Ahead,* ed. M. Vere deVault, Dan W. Andersen, George E. Dickson (Berkeley: McCutchan Publishing Corp., 1973).

8. M. Vere DeVault, Bruce Joyce, Mary A. Golladay, "Organizing Resources for the Support of Competency-Based Teacher Education," mimeographed (Madison: University of Wisconsin, July 1, 1972), p. 9.

9. Ibid., pp. 9-10.

10. Robert L. Arends, John A. Masia, and Wilford A. Weber, *Handbook for the Development of Instructional Modules in Competency-Based Teacher Education Programs* (Syracuse, N.Y.: Center for the Study of Teaching, Syracuse University, January 1971); Robert W. Houston et. al., *Developing Learning Modules* (Houston, Texas: College of Education, University of Houston, 1971).

Suggested Readings

Andersen, Dan W., James M. Cooper, M. Vere DeVault, George E. Dickson, Charles E. Johnson, and Wilford A. Weber. *Competency Based Teacher Education.* Berkeley: McCutchan Publishing Corp., 1973.

Burdin, Joel, and K. Lanzillotti, eds. *A Reader's Guide to the Comprehensive Models for Preparing Elementary Teachers.* Washington, D.C.: ERIC Clearinghouse on Teacher Education and the American Association of Colleges for Teacher Education, December 1969.

Rosner, Benjamin, ed. *The Power of Competency-Based Teacher Education: A Report.* New York: Allyn & Bacon, 1972.

Houston, W. Robert, and Robert B. Howsam, eds. *Competency-Based Teacher Education: Progress, Problems and Prospects.* Chicago: Science Research Associates, 1972.

3/ Behavioral Objectives, Criteria, and Modules

George E. Dickson
Leo D. Leonard

Our discussion to this point has dealt with a general strategy to improve teacher education and the rationale supporting that strategy. In this chapter we will discuss three elements basic to the development of a competency-based education program: behavioral objectives, criteria, and modules.

In explaining the roles of objectives, criteria, and modules it makes no difference whether we describe them as applied to a population of preservice teachers or elementary school pupils. We shall do both to demonstrate the merit of this process approach.

BEHAVIORAL OBJECTIVES

Behavioral objectives are planning statements that teachers can use to both develop and assess their teaching. They are the building blocks of competency-based education. A behavioral objective is much like a road map; it can tell the teacher where he is going, suggest ways of arriving at the destination, and help the teacher know when he has completed the trip.

Objectives are stated in terms of the behavior the teacher wishes to bring about in the student. In terms of difficulty an objective can be termed appropriate if at the end of a module of instruction a large (usually predetermined) percentage of the students have mastered the objective. A number of writers have suggested elaborate procedures for developing objectives. Basically, however, all writers agree on four essential elements a behavioral objective must contain:

1. The objective must be stated in *terms of the student.*
2. The objective must *state the behavior* the student is to perform.
3. The objective must list the *conditions* under which the behavior is to be performed.
4. The objective must list the *criteria* the student must achieve in order to successfully accomplish the task.

Here is an example of an objective that contains all four elements: The student will demonstrate his comprehension of basic addition principles by correctly solving 70 percent of the addition problems on a 100-item teacher-made test to be administered at the end of a course of study. This objective is stated in terms of the student's behavior—it designates that the student is to solve problems in addition. It outlines the conditions—a teacher-made test given at the end of a course. The objective specifies the criterion for successful completion—70 percent correct responses on a 100-item test.

Another example of a behavioral objective is: The student will list the four components of the basic teaching model and illustrate how a feedback loop from performance assessment (the fourth component) results in adjustments in the three remaining components. This task is to be accomplished as an end-of-term examination and will constitute half the student's term grade.

Here is another: Following a course in the concept of science as an explainer of phenomena, the student will, when presented phenomena for which he has no immediate answer, reject myth and superstition as an explainer of those phenomena.

For more information and sample objectives, a complete listing of source books and objective banks is found at the end of this chapter under Suggested Readings. Many CBE projects are now preparing "banks" of objectives that they are willing to share with others.[1] It has been our experience that both objectives and modules must be custom designed for a given situation. However, the objectives and modules developed by others are helpful resources.

By developing a number of objectives for a course of study, the teacher has a plan of action. He can then gear his instruction so the pupils will learn the concepts needed to solve the problems that will be given them at the end of the course.

A Short History of Behavioral Objectives

The idea of writing specific planning statements that outline desired pupil behavior most recently received new emphasis from the *Taxonomy of Educational Objectives* by Benjamin Bloom and associates.[2] Although it was not unusual for teachers to use some type of goal or objective, Bloom suggests that educational objectives should be stated in behavioral form and that teaching should be arranged so that student performance could be observed and described behaviorally. In this, he builds on Tyler's earlier insistence upon behavioral objectives.[3]

Bloom also noted that pupil behavior could be classified by levels, from simple to complex. He and his colleagues developed a classification system to describe learning, divided into three domains, and categorized into elements. The first domain is the *cognitive,* in which the concern is to label those elements of learning that involve the logical, rational thought process. The least complex classification in this domain is knowledge, followed by comprehension and then by application. The more complex levels are analysis, synthesis, and evaluation, in that order.

The second domain of learning is called *affective.*[4] This domain is concerned with the development of values and the expression of emotion. The categories in this domain are, from simple to complex: receiving, responding, valuing, organizing, and characterizing a value or a value complex. All these classifications for both domains are defined in Tables 3-1 and 3-2, which also illustrate the different levels of learning and corresponding "action verbs." Bloom developed a number of action verbs to describe appropriate pupil behavior for each level of learning in each domain. By using these verbs, the teacher is able to write objectives that should allow students, given appropriate instruction, to perform at the desired learning level.

Table 3-1. Cognitive Domain: Learning Levels and Corresponding Action Verbs

Element	Level of learning	Action verbs
Knowledge	Remembering previously learned material	Defines, describes, identifies, labels, lists, matches, names, outlines, reproduces, selects, states
Comprehension	Ability to grasp the meaning of material	Converts, defends, distinguishes, estimates, explains, extends, infers, generalizes, gives examples, paraphrases, predicts, rewrites, summarizes
Application	Ability to use learned material in new and concrete situations	Changes, computes, demonstrates, discovers, manipulates, modifies, operates, predicts, prepares, produces, relates, shows, solves, uses
Analysis	Ability to break down material into its component parts so that its organizational structure may be understood	Breaks down, diagrams, differentiates, discriminates, distinguishes, identifies, illustrates, infers, outlines, points out, relates, selects, separates, subdivides
Synthesis	Ability to put parts together to form a new whole	Categorizes, combines, compiles, composes, creates, devises, designs, explains, generates, modifies, organizes, plans, rearranges, reconstructs, relates, reorganizes, revises, rewrites, summarizes, tells, writes
Evaluation	Ability to judge the value of material (statement, novel, poem, research report) for a given purpose	Appraises, compares, concludes, contrasts, criticizes, describes, discriminates, explains, justifies, interprets, relates, summarizes, supports

The third, or *psychomotor,* domain refers to muscular or physical activity. The emphasis is on motor skill, manipulation of materials and objects—any act that requires neuromuscular coordination. Learning in this domain involves individual body control and acting. The psychomotor domain has not yet been completely classified. Its concern with the physical behaviors of bending, throwing, lifting,

Table 3-2. Affective Domain: Learning Levels and Corresponding Action Verbs

Element	Level of learning	Action verbs
Receiving	Student's willingness to attend to particular phenomena or stimuli (classroom activities, textbook, music, etc.)	Asks, chooses, describes, follows, gives, holds, identifies, locates, names, points to, selects, sits erect, replies, uses
Responding	Active participation on the part of the student	Answers, assists, compiles, conforms, discusses, greets, helps, labels, performs, practices, presents, reads, recites, reports, selects, tells, writes
Valuing	The worth or value a student attaches to a particular object, phenomenon, or behavior	Completes, describes, differentiates, explains, follows, forms, initiates, invites, joins, justifies, proposes, reads, reports, selects, shares, studies, works
Organization	Bringing together different values, resolving conflicts between them, and beginning to build an internally consistent value system	Adheres, alters, arranges, combines, compares, completes, defends, explains, generalizes, identifies, integrates, modifies, orders, organizes, prepares, relates, synthesizes
Characterization by a value or value complex	The individual has a value system that has controlled his behavior for a sufficiently long time for him to have developed a characteristic "life-style"	Acts, discriminates, displays, influences, listens, modifies, performs, practices, proposes, qualifies, questions, revises, serves, solves, uses, verifies

running, etc., allow it to be eliminated from this brief discussion. However, a complete CBE program will certainly include some psychomotor behavioral objectives.

Some Misconceptions

Despite the convenience of categorizing learning into such levels, it is a mistake to assume that these classifications are mutually exclusive. In learning situations the cognitive and affective domains cannot be separated. Bloom separated the domains merely for illustrative purposes, and it is certainly more convenient to discuss the domains and write objectives for each of them separately than to attempt to deal with them both in the same taxonomy.

For example, if a child touches his finger to a hot stove, he has passed through a number of levels in *both* domains. He has received the stimuli, he has comprehended the effect of the heat, he has responded to the stimuli by removing his finger, and he has analyzed and evaluated the situation so that in the future he will apply the concept just learned by not touching a hot stove! This experience, perhaps coupled with the similar experiment of putting his fingers near a fire, allows him to organize a set of values around the advantages and disadvantages of fire and extreme heat. Over time, similar experiences can develop a value complex and cause him to control his behavior regarding the proper uses of fire and heat.

Individuals are constantly undergoing this kind of process both in and out of the classroom. The advantage of the taxonomic domains is that they help the teacher plan and assess what stimuli the student will receive, and help the student develop ways of responding and organizing a value system so that, whatever the stimulus, it can be incorporated into an appropriate value complex.

By isolating the domains on paper, teachers can study the behaviors that are appropriate to each category. In addition to planning and assessing curriculum, the list of behaviors helps diagnose where the pupil is at any point in the learning program. These are the functional reasons for the separation of the domains in the professional literature.

Early in the history of the behavioral objective movement, critics mistakenly assumed that, because many objectives were written for the cognitive domain, teachers using the behavioral objective approach were exclusively concerned with teaching cognitive skills. The fallacy of this reasoning was that critics were not aware that even objectives written for the lower levels of the cognitive taxonomy required some corresponding affective responses from the student. Teachers probably initially wrote behavioral objectives at the lower cognitive levels because they are easier to write, and at this level evaluation of performance is primarily direct and content oriented. It is easy to evaluate students when they are asked to define, give examples, compute, solve, or identify. It is considerably more difficult to write and evaluate materials that ask the student to reconstruct, appraise, synthesize, or modify. However, teachers are now writing objectives that ask for behaviors at all levels of both domains.

Another misconception is that unless the teacher has written objectives in a given lesson that include both domains at all levels, he is somehow remiss in his planning. Since the two domains are not really separate, objectives can be written at the higher levels of the cognitive domains (analysis, synthesis, and evaluation) and the teacher will receive adequate feedback of a student's cognitive and affective positions on a given topic. Needless to say, this is not intended to suggest that affective objectives are any less important, nor that we need not be as clear about our affective intentions as we are about cognitive intentions.

Suppose that at the conclusion of an advanced music class the teacher presents the students with several musical styles and asks them to compose a piece. Each student can choose the form in which he will write, and he must integrate the elements of the style he has chosen into his work. This synthesis project will provide the teacher with indirect evidence of the student's values. The teacher can see the student's choice of musical style, his preference in instrumentation, etc. There are times when this indirect evidence is not enough, and the teacher may wish to write objectives and plan instruction so that both domains can be precisely evaluated.

One other misconception is the notion that students necessarily obtain knowledge first, comprehension second, application third, etc. Learning is not always this discrete and well coordinated. Students often begin to evaluate with almost no knowledge and without being able to apply the data; for this they may be considered prejudiced and misinformed. Regardless of the teacher's careful planning and good intentions, students are constantly evaluating information as it is given to them. The taxonomy and behavioral objectives help limit feedback from the student until he has had sufficient information to handle more complex tasks.

However, instruction need not begin with students working primarily on the knowledge level. To arouse interest, some lessons begin by having students demonstrate misconceptions, such as in the Oliver-Shaver social studies materials.[5] Other teachers ask for continual analysis and application of material as students acquire basic knowledge. These approaches all recognize that basic knowledge is necessary before any substantive analysis or value change can be made by the student.

The most common classification scheme for behavioral objectives uses the concept of cognitive, affective, and psychomotor domains. There are other ways to classify objectives. One is by subject areas and topics within a subject, a typical organizational pattern used in schools, colleges, and universities. The Ohio Elementary Model utilized this format in its original program design effort. Another method is the sequential arrangement of learning objectives, from the simple to the complex. A third classification procedure is to use levels of behavioral objectives, beginning with knowledge objectives (cognitive domain), performance objectives (teacher behaviors with students), and product or consequence objectives (changes in pupils and growth of pupils as a result of teachers' effective performances).

All procedures can also include a statement of expressive objectives, which are teacher experiences that need not be stated behaviorally. An example of an expressive objective is, *The student will visit an inner city school.* Finally, in any classification of behavioral objectives there can be terminal and enabling objectives. A terminal objective is a final instructional goal or criterion of performance. Enabling objectives are necessary learning tasks and demands to achieve a terminal objective. In all classification methods, the cognitive, affective, and psychomotor domains are represented.

Impact of Objectives

The use of objectives in writing curriculum has created a new dimension in education. Whether or not one agrees with the underlying principle of measuring changes in pupil behavior and assuming that this constitutes learning, the mere existence of the idea of behavioral objectives and levels of learning has forced educators to consider these three questions: How do pupils learn? What methods and materials most efficiently produce learning? What outcomes can be expected once learning has taken place? This implies that educators are (1) reexamining methods in terms of how children learn, and (2) concerned with promoting pupil growth and change. If it is true that these two concerns were always paramount, the use of behavioral objectives has merely accelerated that quest.

Objectives have also had an impact because they have moved from a *content* orientation toward a *concept* orientation. Conceptual learning involves the development and analysis of ideas, and their application and relation to objectives and problems outside the classroom. In order to ensure that students are able to comprehend, analyze, apply, and integrate concepts into their own value system, objectives at increasing levels of learning complexity are needed. Behavioral objectives can be written that merely classify learning in the more traditional content approach to teaching, but the greatest advantage of these objectives has been in *operationalizing* concepts.

Table 3-3 is an example of a completed competency-based lesson format, taken from an intermediate science program that uses a

Table 3-3. Sample of a Portion of a Module

Generalization: Matter and energy.

Concept: Heat energy.

Subconcept: Expansion and contraction of solids, liquids, and gases.

Instructional objective: The student should be able to describe how materials usually expand when heated because heating increases the activity of the molecules while cooling slows down the activity and causes the materials to contract.

Teacher techniques: Discuss examples of expansion and contraction from daily experiences. Use filmstrip or transparency to supplement and initiate further discussion.

Learning activities: Place a balloon over the the top of an empty bottle. Observe and explain why the balloon expands when the air in the bottle is heated. Study the rise and fall of the red liquid in a thermometer when it is placed in hot water and in cold water. Report what has happened to the liquid in each experiment.

Resource materials: Filmstrips (Encyclopedia Britannica, no. 11790): Hot and Cold: Heat and Temperature; Making a Thermometer; Heat and Matter; Heat and Work; How Heat Travels.

number of behavioral objectives for students to accomplish as they master the concept of heat energy. The abstraction heat energy is made more workable by writing a subconcept, "the expansion and contraction of solids, liquids, and gases." This subconcept can then be used to develop a number of instructional objectives. The teacher asks himself what a student must be able to do in order to demonstrate his understanding of expansion and contraction. He may list a number of behavioral objectives that would fulfill his requirement, for example:

Given a test situation, the student will describe in writing how materials usually expand when heated. He will explain how heating increases molecular activity while cooling slows down activity, causing contraction. He must give at least two examples of this principle to have mastered this objective.

Once the students have met the requirements contained in this objective, they are considered to have mastered the concept.

A competency-based approach also allows the teacher to develop a number of appropriate teacher techniques and learner activities. In this instance the teacher might use a combination of methods, such as discussing the concept of expansion and contraction, demonstrating to the students, and perhaps completing the course of instruction with filmstrips and transparencies. The students could then carry out certain lab exercises where they actually cause materials to expand and contract.

PLANNING FOR INSTRUCTION IN CBE

Instructional planning with specific objectives and appropriate teaching techniques and learning activities provides the teacher with a written instrument to refer to for assessing the scope and sequence of instruction. The lesson on heat energy described above includes a number of components in current curriculum planning. The discussion that follows will list these elements.

Using Concepts in Curriculum Planning

The current trend in competency-based education is to develop either subject matter or cross-subject matter concepts. Once the concepts have been developed and sequenced, curriculum makers search for curriculum material to teach these principles.

Of all the processes in the CBE model, the most difficult task for curriculum developers and teachers is that of developing concepts for instruction. It is hard to determine what kinds of terminal behaviors, skills, or values are to be desired in the students. It is even more difficult to develop concepts from these. It is also hard to sequence the concepts from simple to complex. Once all this is done, the task still remains of developing appropriate goals and objectives to operationalize the concepts. Probably the easiest task is the selection of appropriate teaching techniques and student activities.

Among the first attempts at using concepts in planning curriculum was the Kettering Model High School Program. One of these programs was conducted in the mid-1960s at Roy High School in Roy, Utah, which developed a competency-based program in social studies. This was followed by a more comprehensive effort in the Clark County schools of Las Vegas, Nevada, consisting of several academic subjects. Currently a number of school systems are developing curriculum guides, modules, or smaller units of instruction based on the CBE model.

The Catholic Diocese of Toledo, Ohio, is a comprehensive example of a competency-based approach to curriculum design, and will be discussed in more detail in Chapter 6. The diocese developed a competency-based curriculum for all subject areas, grades one through eight, that will do away with traditional grade levels when the program is in full operation. In place of grade levels, there will be a highly individualized program of continuous progress.

CBE planning and operational efforts are widespread in teacher education. Of the original ten elementary model institutions mentioned in Chapter 2, the universities of Georgia and Toledo continued development and implementation of their CBE design programs. Other institutions showing considerable progress in CBE are Brigham Young University, Livingston University, Southwest Minnesota State College, University of Houston, and Weber State College. Many other institutions are engaged in pilot projects or otherwise limited operations using CBE concepts.

Concepts allow for individualized instruction by requiring the teacher to move from content to ideas. Once the teacher begins to think of the ideas he wants the students to work with, the door is open for the use of multi-materials to convey these ideas to the students. It isn't long before students and teachers discover which materials are appropriate for different groups of students. Textbooks and descriptive content have become merely the vehicles to promote the learning and analysis of ideas.

Table 3-4 illustrates how social studies at the secondary level have changed from memorizing political statements and data to helping students acquire a conceptual base of understanding social change.

Using Objectives in Planning Instruction

Behavioral objectives are a key factor in competency-based education. Whether the teacher is committed to a traditional content

Table 3-4. Sample of Partial Module for Political Science

Generalization: Political ideals, values, attitudes, and institutions develop and change over time.

Concept: Social change.

Subconcept: Contact between cultures or the interaction of new ideas or material goods within a culture often results in a modification of knowledge, attitudes, and skills of the people.

Instructional objectives: The student will describe orally in small groups how contact between cultures or the interaction of new ideas or material goods within a culture often results in a modification of knowledge, attitudes, and skills of the people.

Teacher techniques: Use student-selected groups, collages, pictures without captions, and games like Twenty Questions. In introducing different cultures, societies must have had material goods, clothing, foods, and homes, e.g., American Indian, early Egyptians, Greeks, and Chinese societies. Show examples of changing attitudes and skills. Assign readings about these cultures from the many sources at your disposal.

approach to learning or sees content as a vehicle to promote the comprehension of concepts, behavioral objectives play a major role. They are vital because they translate the abstractions of the concept (or the information in the content) into discrete, observable, measurable behavior.

In Chapter 1 competency-based education was described as a system which, at one level, addresses itself to overall goals, needs, and resources. At the level of implementation, the system becomes a competency-based model, a skeletal framework that helps the teacher write objectives, select appropriate activities, and develop appropriate assessment techniques to measure change in pupils. As stated earlier, objectives call for appropriate activities, and the conditions and criteria in the behavioral statement give the teacher clues for evaluating student performance. Neither objectives, activities, nor concepts in any way inhibit pupil or teacher creativity. As adapted in Toledo for use in public and private schools and in college instruction, CBE has focused on preservice and inservice teachers—together with students and parents—as they develop objectives appropriate for a particular population.

THE SOURCES AND DERIVATION
OF BEHAVIORAL OBJECTIVES

Using behavioral objectives in instructional planning requires creativity and skill on the part of educators. It is obvious that teachers
must have a thorough understanding of the subjects they teach, of
children, and of our society. To understand the concepts of one's
field of study is a sophisticated undertaking, and to translate these
concepts into teachable objectives and find suitable activities and
methods requires skilled practitioners. To write competency-based
curriculum, teachers must have the sociological skills to recognize the
cultural needs and differences of their students and to plan materials
and instruction accordingly. They also must be able to translate
concerns of the community into teachable learning objectives.

At this point it must be clearly indicated that an instructional
program that devises and uses behavioral objectives does not "jes'
grow," like Topsy. Any program conceptualization process requires a
strong theoretical base. This base is constructed from two sources:
(1) the broad goals of education and (2) fundamental program
assumptions. The goals of education reflect for any particular time
and place a society's philosophical and social values and psychological concepts about individual growth and the learning process.
The mission of any educational program should be well stated by its
broad goals. Program assumptions determine the nature and potential
content of an educational program. They can be stated as facts,
hypotheses, or expressions of values, and as such they have much to
do with final program organization, management, and operation. To
indicate more clearly how statements of goals and assumptions are
vital to the development of behavioral objectives for program
process, we will examine the derivation of behavioral objectives for
the Ohio Model Elementary Teacher Education Program.

The goals of education and of teacher education should certainly
be congruent. The experiences that pupils have in classrooms are
dependent on teacher behaviors in those classrooms. Although little
has been written to indicate clearly the comprehensive goals of
teacher education, much has been written about the broad goals of
education. An early expression of such goals was the Seven Cardinal
Principles of Education[6] developed in 1918, which were followed by

other excellent statements.[7] Recognizing the lack of comprehensive goal statements on teacher education, the Ohio model developers first adopted and then modified (for teacher education purposes) a statement on educational goals by the Committee on Quality Education for the State of Pennsylvania,[8] which represented the best thinking of a distinguished group of behavioral scientists from all over the country. For our purposes they were further reviewed for teacher education goal legitimation or modification by a national blue ribbon committee of prominent educators. Ten broad goals of teacher education resulted from this effort, each beginning with the phrase, "Each teacher should be prepared to employ teacher behaviors which will help every child"—

1. Acquire the greatest possible understanding of himself and an appreciation of his worthiness as a member of society.
2. Acquire understanding and appreciation of persons belonging to social, cultural and ethnic groups different from his own.
3. Acquire to the fullest extent possible for him mastery of the basic skills in the use of words and numbers.
4. Acquire a positive attitude toward school and toward the learning process.
5. Acquire the habits and attitudes associated with responsible citizenship.
6. Acquire good health habits and an understanding of the conditions necessary for the maintenance of physical and emotional well-being.
7. Acquire opportunity and encouragement to be creative in one or more fields of endeavor.
8. Understand the opportunities open to him for preparing himself for a productive life and enable him to take full advantage of these opportunities.
9. Understand and appreciate as much as he can of human achievement in the natural sciences, the social sciences, the humanities, and the arts.
10. To prepare for a world of rapid change and unforeseeable demands in which continuing education throughout his adult life should be a normal expectation.[9]

These ten statements were our starting point in the process to develop more specific enabling objectives.

In creating program assumptions for the Ohio model elementary teacher education program, we began with the belief that existing programs of teacher education were not adequate to prepare future teachers for the changing conditions in American life and schools. We agreed with Don Davies of the U.S. Office of Education, who described these changing conditions as the following:[10]

1. Moving from a mass approach to an individual approach in education;

2. Moving from an emphasis on memorizing to an emphasis on learning how to think, how to learn, as well as to an emphasis on the noncognitive, nonintellectual components of life;

3. Moving from a concept of a school isolated from the community to a concept of a school that is in and of the community;

4. Moving from a fear of technology to utilizing machinery and technology for educational purposes;

5. Moving from a negative to a positive attitude toward children who are different;

6. Moving from a provincial perspective of the world and education to a multicultural perspective;

7. Moving from a system characterized by academic snobbery to one that recognizes and nurtures a wide variety of talents and fields;

8. Moving from a system based on serving time to one that emphasizes performance.

We were proposing to prepare teachers and the children they teach for a world of rapid change, which would obviously require a continuing educational process for *all* persons (students, teachers, and administrators) in *all* types of educational institutions involved with teacher preparation. This process could not be restricted by long-held beliefs about the conduct of teacher education programs or elementary schools. If new directions in teacher education are to produce new teachers with different skills and abilities, the schools in which these teachers practice should reflect such difference and innovation. The discussion of the historical development of the Ohio model in Chapter 5 includes these and many other assumptions.

Having acquired broad basic goals of teacher education and general assumptions about the process and results of teacher education, the Ohio model developers now had to transform these goals and assumptions into relevant behavioral objectives for further program development. To accomplish this, we made another major assumption, that is, that there are five conditions of life and education of major importance to teacher education. These conditions, which we called "contexts," were identified as instructional organization, educational technology, contemporary learning-teaching process, societal factors, and research. Using information gathered about these contexts and our general assumptions about teacher education, we began to refine the ten broad general goals. The result of this effort was the development of major subject areas (including topics for each subject area) for each context and the creation of behavioral objectives for each topic.

The contexts and their major subject areas and topics are listed in Chapter 5, Tables 5-1—5-5. For illustrative purposes, the first subject area and its topics for the first context are reproduced below:

Context: Instructional Organization
Subject: Necessary Training for Instruction
Topics:
1. General Education
2. Curriculum Development and Evaluation
3. Academic Disciplines and Skills—Methodology
4. Evaluation Techniques for Multi-Sized Group Instruction
5. Curriculum Techniques for Multi-Sized Group Instruction
6. The Administration of Individually Guided Education
7. Internship

Each topic became a source for the production of behavioral objectives. For example, eighty-three behavioral objectives were prepared for Topic 5, Curriculum Techniques for Multi-Sized Group Instruction. They began by defining the meaning of individually guided education and ended by requiring the student to participate in a school situation involving individually guided education so as to demonstrate competent management of the function or functions assigned to him as a teacher. The first behavioral objective stated: "The student will identify individually guided education as a teaching technique that utilizes a combination of:
a. large groups
b. small groups
c. pictorial activities
d. independent study."
Examples of final behavioral objectives for the topic were:

Given a simulated teaching situation that requires individually guided education on a one-to-one basis, the student will perform the functions of the teacher and accomplish the objectives of the teaching situation.

Given the instruction to participate as an intern in an ongoing school situation involving individually guided education within a large group, the student will demonstrate competent management of the function assigned to him by the inservice teacher and the unit leader.

Obviously, a potential leader must acquire a certain amount of knowledge and demonstrate teaching performance developed from this knowledge in learning how to use individually guided education in school classrooms. The results of such newly learned abilities must be assessed—again through the use of behavioral objectives—by examining the efforts of pupils who are instructed by the student teacher.

The development of behavioral objectives forces a step-by-step, logical consideration of the learning or teaching process. The use of behavioral objectives with each student necessitates more individualized instruction. No student is able to avoid addressing himself to each behavioral objective in a sequential pattern of instruction.

A further advantage of behavioral objectives is that they make it easier to measure student performance; one can assess students before and after instruction to measure growth. By pretesting (i.e., before instruction), students who can already perform the required skill will advance to more difficult tasks or to other projects. In the same manner, testing student behaviors at the end of instruction identifies the behavioral level at which he began to have difficulty in learning. This kind of diagnosis allows for remediation geared to the learning needs of the individual.

Using behavioral objectives requires skills, the ability to diagnose needs, and the talent and experience to decide what curriculum is best for the students at any given point in time. The structure provided by competency-based education facilitates teachers at any instructional level in working with their colleagues and others in the community to develop and assess the effectiveness of behavioral objectives, activities, and evaluation.

THE INSTRUCTIONAL MODULE

Behavioral objectives alone are, of course, insufficient as a guide to a learning situation. They must be combined with potential learner activities designed to ensure that the objectives are being mastered, with appropriate materials and evaluation techniques to ascertain when each objective has been accomplished in the behavior of the student. In this form they become *modules*.

On first appearance, a learning module resembles a lesson plan or group of lesson plans comprising a unit. There are, however, substantial differences between these formats and modules. The underlying concepts of a module are that the time it takes to complete a module is flexible, and that the skills to be acquired are necessary for all students to learn. This is contrary to the typical lesson plan or unit, which has a fixed time designation; a lesson usually takes a portion of time within a class period in one day, and the unit is designed to last two weeks or so. It is not expected that all students will achieve mastery of the content. This viewpoint is represented by state regulations of so many clock hours of instruction per pupil and pupil attendance for so many school days per year in each subject, implying, for example, that evidence of a student's understanding of algebra could be supplied by proof that he had spent 180 days in an algebra class.

A module recognizes that each student is a unique individual, with different learning rates and skills that he brings to any learning situation. In common practice, competency-based instruction is organized into a number of learning modules that use Bloom's taxonomic categories, from the simple to the complex. There is no fixed grade or time level. Instead, a continuous progress approach provides the student with an opportunity to move through the material at his own pace and, where possible, to select the learning materials most appropriate to his own needs. In a sense, achievement is held constant and time varies.

Unlike some units, all modules contain preassessment exercises to enable students who have demonstrated competencies required by the objectives to bypass further instructional activities for those objectives. Furthermore, module postassessment puts greater emphasis on knowledge and skill demonstration in relation to specific behavioral objectives than have usual instructional procedures. The advantages of individualization, independent study, self-pacing, and a variety of means of instruction is readily apparent in the use of modules.

The Elements and Format of a Module

To fulfill the foregoing conditions, a module must contain the following elements:

1. *Topic statement.* This need only be a sentence or phrase listing the subject matter area to be taught.

2. *Rationale.* A brief discussion of the reason for learning the material and its value to the student.

3. *Concept statement and prerequisites.* They define the scope and sequence of the concepts in relation to other concepts in the subject area. The statement discusses the prerequisite skills a student should have before entering the module. It may discuss how the student will apply the skills learned in the module, and it may tell what *related* skills the student needs to have in order to master the concept in this module.

4. *Concept.* This is an abstraction or idea used to represent a class or group of things that have certain things in common.

5. *Behavioral objective.* A statement of intent that describes in performance terms the desired outcomes of the instructional program.

6. *Pretest.* The pretest should be administered to all students and should contain items that measure the student's grasp of the behavioral objective before instruction has even begun. The assumption is that students already possessing the required skills outlined in the objective will have the opportunity to progress to the next level of instruction or work with the teacher in designing an individualized program that applies the skills associated with those contained in the module.

7. *Suggested teacher techniques.* This is a list of one or more appropriate methodologies the teacher may use to implement the objective.

8. *Suggested student activities.* This relates to the tasks the students will perform as necessary practice before fulfilling the requirements contained in the behavioral objectives.

9. *Multimedia resources.* Resources and a variety of *optional* materials are listed here which the teacher could use when teaching the module.

10. *Posttest and evaluation.* In this section, the teacher imple-

ments the conditions and criterial statements in the behavioral objective into some form of student assessment. This may take the form of a written examination, spot checking student work, or verbal and other kinds of appropriate responses.

11. *Remediation plans.* Since a competency-based model is so explicit in its planning and statement of intent about student behavior, it is imperative that students failing to meet this requirement as measured on a posttest be given the opportunity for remedial instruction. This tutorial program may be self-instructional or highly individualized. The goal in a competency-based model is to have a variety of media available for those needing remedial help.

12. *General reassessment potential.* This term refers to the need for continual reassessment of the elements in the module. In other words, the teacher must continually check to be sure the techniques and activities are appropriate to the objective. The teacher should be able to make quick assessment of any conflicts that may exist in the module. An inappropriate activity that does not help implement the objective can be discarded and another more appropriate activity can be substituted.

Although there are twelve elements to a module, in general practice developers organize written descriptions of modules under these headings:

1. Subject or topic statement
2. Prerequisites
3. Objectives (terminal and enabling behavioral objectives)
4. Preassessment procedures
5. Instructional activities
6. Postassessment procedures

These constitute the fundamental parts of a module; all elements can be incorporated within them.

The following examples of instructional modules from the Ohio Model Elementary Teacher Education Program indicate consideration for module elements and format. In the interests of brevity, preassessment and postassessment instruments and teaching materials are not provided.

UNIVERSITY OF TOLEDO

Elementary Education 312:324

Module 3

1. *Department/Context:* Contemporary Learning-Teaching Process

2. *Subject/Topic:* Basic Behavioral Operations

3. *Title:* Behavioral Objectives

4. *Prerequisite(s):* None

5. *Objectives:*
   General Objectives: The student will learn to write, revise, and use behaviorally stated terminal performance and enabling objectives in the three domains, at two levels of the taxonomy.
   Behavioral Objectives:
   a. Given a list of statements, the student will be able to label each statement as either an educational goal or a behavioral objective, without error.
   b. Given a list of objectives, the student will be able to identify the audience, behavior, conditions, and degree with less than 10 percent error.
   c. Given a list of objectives, the student will be able to discriminate between those which are inadequate in terms of audience, behavior, conditions, and degree (ABCD) with 90 percent accuracy.
   d. Given a list of objectives, the student will be able to rewrite those which are not stated in behavioral terms so that they include audience, behavior, conditions, and degree (ABCD) without error.
   e. Given descriptions of each of the cognitive, affective, and psychomotor domains, the student will be able to match each with its name, without error.
   f. Given a list of objectives, the student will be able to identify each as a cognitive objective, an affective objective, or a psychomotor objective, without error.
   g. Given educational goals in the cognitive domain, the student will be able to write behavioral objectives including audience, behavior, condition, and degree (ABCD) at the lowest level of Bloom's taxonomy and a level higher than the lowest level without error.
   h. Student will write two behavioral objectives using ABCD criteria in affective domain without error.

6. *Preassessment Procedures:* Take the pretest. If successful (meet criteria specified by objectives), go on to next module. If not successful, complete the following activities.

7. *Instructional Activities:*
   a. Read "Ten Reasons for Not Using Behavioral Objectives," by Popham.
   b. Work through the programmed instruction packet, "What You've Always Wanted to Know About Performance Objectives but Were Afraid to

Ask," by Tom Kepner and Lanny Sparks for National Special Media Institutes.

c. Read "Writing Worthwhile Behavioral Objectives," by Julie Vargas.
   Optional Activities:
   (1) Work through "Preparing Instructional Objectives," program by Robert Mager.
   (2) Listen to tape, "Writing Behavioral Objectives," adapted from Thorwald Esbensen, and complete worksheet.
   (3) View slide-tape presentation, "Educational Objectives," by James Popham, and complete worksheet.
   (4) Read handout, "Teaching Aimed at Learning Above Mere Recall of Knowledge" by Bloom.
   (5) Work through programmed instruction, "An Introduction to the Taxonomy of Educational Objectives" by Clyde St. Romain.
   (6) Read "Writing Behavioral Objectives" handout, adapted from Thorwald Esbensen.
   (7) Read handout, "Illustrative Verbs," from Norman E. Gronland, *Stating Behavioral Objectives for Classroom Instruction.*
   (8) Study handout, "Behavioral Objectives as Competency Statements."
d. Attend scheduled help session #1.
e. Attend help session #2, optional for student.

8. *Postassessment Procedures:* Take the posttest. If successful, go to next module. If unsuccessful, either recycle the module or see your adviser for an alternative method for meeting the objectives.

UNIVERSITY OF TOLEDO

Elementary Education 312:328

Module 6

1. *Department/Context:* Educational Media and Technology/Educational Technology

2. *Subject/Topic:* Instructional Simulation and Academic Games/Selection, Utilization, Evaluation and Design of Simulations and Games

3. *Title:* Instructional Simulation and Academic Games

4. *Prerequisite(s):* None

5. *Objectives:*
   General Objectives:
   a. To develop an understanding of and familiarity with the use of instructional simulations and academic games in education.
   b. To develop an awareness of effective utilization practices for simulations and games in instruction.
   Behavioral Objectives:
   a. Given a list of alternative instructional objectives to indicate, in writing, which are more and which less appropriate for the use of instructional

simulations or academic games in terms of an affective strategy/media match, with less than 15 percent error.
   (1) Given a list of descriptive examples, to label each as a nonacademic simulation or game, a simulation, academic game, or simulation game such that eight out of ten instances are correct.
   (2) Given a list of terms pertaining to simulations and games and their definitions, to match the term and its definition with 90 percent accuracy.
   (3) Given various defining characteristics related to specific simulations and games, to match the characteristic with the simulation or game that best represents it, with less than 15 percent error.
   (4) Given various alternatives, to select those which are representative of the advantages of simulations and games, with 90 percent accuracy.
   (5) Given various alternatives, to select those which are representative of the limitations of simulations and games, with 90 percent accuracy.
   a. Given various utilization practices for instructional media, to indicate which are more or less appropriate for the effective use of simulations and games, with less than 15 percent error.
      (1) Given a list of various criteria for the selection of simulations and games, to indicate which are more and which less appropriate, with less than 15 percent error.
      (2) Given a list of various preparatory practices for simulation games, to indicate which are more and which less appropriate for success of the medium, with less than 15 percent error.
      (3) Given a list of positive and negative practices for conducting game play, to indicate which are useful for success, with less than 15 percent error.

6. *Preassessment Procedures:* Take pretest for module 6. If successful, proceed to the next module. Should your score fall below minimal acceptable competency, enter into the instructional sequence for this module.

7. *Instructional Activities:*
   a. In large group mode, participate in *Puzzles* exercise.
   b. Read *Games Students Play*, by Clarence Stoll.
   c. Read "It's Not How You Play the Game . . . It's Whether You Talk About it Afterwards," by Clarence Stoll.
   d. Read *A Primer on Games*, by R. Fransecky and J. Trojanski.
   e. Read *Discriminating Among Terminology: Simulations and Games.*
   f. Do exercise, "Sample Simulations and Games for the Elementary School."
   g. Read *Simulations and Games as an Instructional Medium.*
   h. Group discussion on "Simulations and Games in the Schools."
   i. Optional: Listen to audio tape, "Simulation and Gaming in Curriculum Development." Available in UH 206.

8. *Postassessment Procedures:* Take posttest for Module 6. If successful, proceed to next module. If competency is not met, consult the criterion-objectives-means match and recycle the appropriate instructional means and/or consult an adviser as to where the discrepancy might exist.

The Advantages of a Module

Some advantages have already been discussed, e.g., the flexibility of time the student is allowed to complete assignments and the opportunity for alternative materials to help him meet the requirements of the objective. Another advantage is the structural design of the module. Throughout the discussion, frequent reference has been made to the advantage of being able constantly to assess each component in the module in relationship to the other elements. Perhaps the most important advantage is that, using competency-based modules, no prejudgment is made about a student's capability. It is assumed that every student can fulfill the objectives in every module but that the materials, activities, and time required to complete it may vary from student to student. As students move through a program, it may be found that their talents and skills make success questionable. If remediation fails to help, their participation in the program is terminated and counseling is employed to help them enter other instructional programs where success is more probable.

KNOWLEDGE, PERFORMANCE, AND PRODUCT CRITERIA

Knowledge, performance, and product (consequence) criteria, introduced in Chapter 2, have come into the vocabulary of competency-based instruction to distinguish the various kinds of knowledge, skills, and behaviors (teacher and student) an individual needs to possess at the culmination of instruction. These criteria are further important in determining the parameters and evaluating an instructional program. There is not complete agreement as to the definitions of these terms, and some writers suggest a number of subcategories for each term.

It is generally accepted that *knowledge criteria* refer to the intellectual skills and experiences an individual possesses at the end of a course of instruction. Some knowledge criteria are presently unassessed because of a lack of consensus on mastery or of a way to measure learning. Sometimes learning and the knowledge criteria category need not be measured, usually in the case of expressive objectives where the teacher merely wants the students to have been "made aware" of or to have experienced a situation.

Performance criteria refer to the development and assessment of teacher behaviors that facilitate pupil development in the three domains (cognitive, affective, and psychomotor). Behaviors associated with performance criteria would include, for example, positive reinforcement of proper student behavior, asking questions of a higher cognitive level, teaching a specific subject matter concept in a specified way, etc. Determining what skill level or behavior constitutes adequate performance is not a simple matter. Rosenshine and Furst indicate that four areas of research can be examined for "promising variables which could be incorporated into rigorous classroom experience or be developed into performance criteria."[11] These four areas are laboratory studies, subject matter research, experimental classroom studies, and process-product studies (investigations that attempt to relate observed teacher behaviors to student outcome measures). These authors indicate, however, that information from studies in these areas is limited or tentative as it applies to establishing the proper performance criteria for teacher education programs.[12] They further state:

We propose that the evaluation and research components of the teacher education programs . . . be greatly strengthened to conduct research on the *validity* of the performance criteria. Currently, the evaluation proposals in the model programs (U.S.O.E. Elementary Teacher Education Models) focus on how effectively the programs train teachers to behave in ways which have been predetermined in the behavioral specifications. Unfortunately, there are few if any well-developed designs for evaluation in terms of the teacher's classroom behavior and the learning engendered by the teacher in public school students. It is imperative that plans to evaluate these models include not only ways to increase our knowledge of how best to train teachers to perform specific behaviors, but more importantly, ways to increase our knowledge of the relationship between these specific teacher behaviors and measures of pupil achievement.[13]

Thus, developing performance criteria is a primary concern of all those engaged with competency-based programs.

Product criteria refer to the questions educators ask about the results of competency-based programs. What kind of individual growth and learning results from experiences in a competency-based program? How can we determine more about the student's ability to teach by examining the achievement of pupils that he has taught? Has the competency-based program helped learners to realize the diversity of human nature and the need to treat each person as an individual? Has the program developed a reflective and innovative individual, capable of assessing situations and developing a variety of possible instructional solutions to problems? These are the newest, most demanding questions in the area of competency-based education. As the quotation from Rosenshine and Furst indicates, much experimentation is needed before we have complete answers to the problem of developing performance and product criteria.

The basic question to be answered by the development of criteria for individual and program assessment is, "What will be accepted as evidence of successful performance by the teacher candidate?" The idea of making explicit the competencies of educational personnel is a powerful force in improving preservice and inservice teacher education. The all-purpose, all-individual, and all-program answer to the evidence question is complex in that it "derives in part from philosophic considerations about the appropriateness of specific criteria for objectives of the teacher education program, and in part from technical issues bearing on the feasibility of collecting, analyzing and interpreting data pertinent to criteria of individual and program effectiveness."[14] In addition, answers to the criteria question must, to a degree, be situation-specific in terms of the unique needs and factors operating in any particular instructional effort. Because our present knowledge base about knowledge, performance, and product criteria is not complete, there is not at this time a full and satisfactory list of crucial skills and behaviors that teachers must possess in order to perform well in classrooms.

Awareness of the difficulties of establishing adequate individual and program criteria does not mean that the development and use of competency-based education programs and relevant criteria should be curtailed or abandoned. Usual programs of teacher education make little effort to establish appropriate criteria for teacher performance. CBE programs *demand* attention to such criteria. Student and pupil learning are the appropriate criteria for assessing the effectiveness of teacher educators and teacher education programs.

Criterion judgments are now made on an a priori basis, utilizing the results of past teacher behavior research. There is obviously the need to conduct more research in this area and to improve measurement procedures so that better relationships between teacher behavior and pupil learning can be established.

The developers of the Ohio elementary teacher education model and the other USOE model builders have concerned themselves with the question of criteria. The creation of behavioral objectives in all of the model programs were the first comprehensive attempts to establish criteria. The behavioral objectives for each model, by whatever classification scheme used, represented attempts to classify knowledge, performance, and product criteria. Admittedly, the efforts of the model builders resulted in a great preoccupation with knowledge and performance criteria with relatively little or no production of product criteria. For example, the Ohio model program created, in its behavioral objectives for each topic and subject in each context area, an ordering of knowledge and performance criteria for a competency-based teacher education program. These criteria came from our assessments of research on teacher behaviors and considerations of instructional organization, the teaching-learning process, the use of educational technology, the factors in society important to education, and educational research about teacher performance and teacher preparation. But, most important, the Ohio model concerned itself with the difference between preservice (process) and inservice (product) evaluation. The Ohio group realized that there would be no ongoing effort to attack the criteria problem and program effectiveness without the development of a complete system for student and program evaluation.

The Ohio model provided an evaluation design that included information on four types of educational decisions: planning, structuring, implementing, and recycling. This design is being further developed and implemented in our CBE efforts. We said then and still believe that

> Education today is suffering because of a lack of systematic evaluation in teacher education. It is one thing to plan a course of training for teachers, but it is quite another thing to forecast how future teachers will behave once they take the full responsibility for their own classrooms.[15]
>
> There are many innovative features in the specifications for a new teacher education program. Among these none is so important as the evaluative process. For the first time in history a program has been arranged in behavioral terms so that it may not only be evaluated at a given point in time, but also so that it is self-correcting. Provisions for prompt and objective feedback are the most innovative elements and will enable all concerned to discuss the success or failure of the program to prepare educators in meaningful terms. This enables the implementing institutions to enter into a new program with confidence that if the selected specifications are not complete or not relevant they will be supplemented or modified in *the regular course of the program.*[16]

Thus, one of the most promising procedures for pertinent criteria establishment, enumeration, and validation, is in the ongoing evaluation efforts of CBE programs. The research possibilities in these efforts are considerable and promise to add considerably to previous research on teacher behavior. Only in the real world with real teachers, both students and inservice, will effective teacher behaviors be identified, tested, and proven relevant.

Procedures for establishing proper criteria for teaching performance and program development can be aided by considering Turner's levels of criteria.[17] Six different criterion levels are suggested along a continuum from a low (level six) to high (level one) competence. The intention of the levels is to make clear the points at which feedback to teacher education programs can be generated and where performance-based certification can occur. These levels refer to learning in the cognitive, affective, and psychomotor domains and also relate to the three types of criteria (knowledge, performance, and product). Turner summarizes his six criterion levels as follows:

Criterion level six is concerned with the effects of a training program on improvements in teacher knowledges and understandings. *Criterion levels five and four* are concerned with the effects of teacher training on improvement in pedagogic skills under laboratory or simplified training conditions. (Level five differs from level four in that the teacher need not perform before live students; simulation experiences are acceptable; and demonstration of *one* teaching skill is required rather than a broader range of teacher behavior specified for level four.) *Criterion level three* addresses itself to the effects of training on a teacher's behavior under actual classroom conditions. The concept of pupil change as a criterion of teacher effectiveness is introduced at *criterion levels two and one*. *Criterion level two* is concerned with changes in pupil behavior that can be effected in a relatively short time period (one to two weeks) and under actual classroom conditions. *Criterion level one* is concerned with the long range effects of teacher behavior on changes in pupil achievement and well-being.[18]

It is obvious that there are fundamental differences between criterion levels six through three and levels two and one. Criterion levels six through three focus on the impact of training on teacher behavior. Criterion levels two and one are concerned with both the effects on teacher behavior and the effects of teacher behavior on pupil performance. The most appropriate criterion level for accountability in teacher education is three, which is concerned with demonstrations of change in teacher competency under actual classroom conditions. However, the major basis for assessing the validity of competencies comprising a teacher education program is found in criterion levels two and one. The basis for decisions related to the progress of an individual through a teacher training program would seem to be best answered with criteria from levels six through three. The assessment of the teacher training program itself would best be served by using criterion levels two and one. Turner's classification scheme for criteria should be useful in helping students evaluate, regularly and frequently, their performance as prospective teachers as well as helping to provide the evaluation and research function needed to assess the program in which such students participate.

The criteria question concerns all who are involved with competency-based education. Unfortunately, some teacher educators attempt to achieve acceptable CBE standards merely by organizing their old content material and putting it into a behavioral format. Others properly realize that this is not the promise or the process of CBE, although competencies that are easier to describe and to evaluate are likely to dominate first attempts to develop any CBE system. The criterion problem and its solution is evident in all serious CBE projects. A beginning has been made and teacher educators and their students are nearer than ever before in the exposition and attainment of the behaviors explicit in knowledge, performance, and product criteria.

SUMMARY

The exposition so far has explained the CBE strategy. This chapter has identified essential elements in the process—behavioral objectives, criteria, and modules. The discussion must now consider the field-based characteristics of CBE to prescribe conditions in the cooperating public schools that serve as the cooperative laboratory for teacher educators.

Notes

1. See, for example, Instructional Objectives Exchange, P.O. Box 24095, Los Angeles, California 90024.
2. Benjamin Bloom et al., eds., *Taxonomy of Educational Objectives, Handbook I: Cognitive Domain* (New York: David McKay, 1956).
3. Ralph W. Tyler, *Basic Principles of Curriculum and Instruction* (Chicago: University of Chicago Press, 1950), p. 72.

4. David R. Krathwohl et al., eds., *Taxonomy of Educational Objectives, Handbook II: Affective Domain* (New York: David McKay, 1964).

5. Donald W. Oliver and James P. Shaver, *Teaching Public Issues in the High School* (Boston: Houghton Mifflin, 1966).

6. Commission on Reorganization of Secondary Education of the National Education Association, *Cardinal Principles of Secondary Education*, United States Bureau of Education, Bulletin no. 35 (Washington, D. C.: Government Printing Office, 1918).

7. Nolan C. Kearney, *Elementary School Objectives* (New York: Russell Sage Foundation, 1953); Educational Policies Commission, *The Central Purpose of American Education* (Washington, D. C.: National Education Association, 1961).

8. The Committee on Quality Education was made up of members of the Pennsylvania State Board of Education. This committee contracted with the Educational Testing Service to develop goals of American education and how such goals were to be evaluated in Pennsylvania. Experts in the behavioral sciences from all parts of the United States constituted a standing advisory committee for the project. The report produced was in three volumes titled *A Plan for Evaluating the Quality of Education Programs in Pennsylvania*, published by the Educational Testing Service, Princeton, N. J., 1965.

9. *Highlights*, a report from the Educational Testing Service to the State Board of Education of the Commonwealth of Pennsylvania (Princeton, N. J.: Educational Testing Service, June 30, 1965), pp. 10-13.

10. Don Davies, address to the American Association of Colleges for Teacher Education, School for Executives, Ashland, Oregon, August 22, 1968.

11. Barak Rosenshine and Norma Furst, "Research on Teacher Performance Criteria," in *Research in Teacher Education*, a symposium, ed., B. Othanel Smith (Englewood Cliffs, N. J.: Prentice-Hall, 1971). p. 40.

12. Ibid., p. 65.

13. Ibid.

14. Committee on National Program Priorities in Teacher Education, Benjamin Rosner, chairman, *The Power of Competency-Based Teacher Education*, Project no. 1-0475 (Washington, D.C.: National Center for Educational Research and Development, U.S. Office of Education, July 31, 1971), p. 5.

15. George E. Dickson, *Educational Specifications for a Comprehensive Elementary Teacher Education Program*, vol. 1, OE-58023 (Washington, D. C.: Government Printing Office, 1968), p. 209.

16. Ibid., p. 242.

17. Richard L. Turner, "Levels of Criteria," Appendix A, in *The Power of Competency-Based Teacher Education*, op. cit., pp. 34-37.

18. Committee on National Program Priorities in Teacher Education, Benjamin Rosner, chairman, op. cit., p. 5.

Suggested Readings

Arends, Robert L., John A. Masia, Wilford A. Weber. *Handbook for the Development of Instructional Modules in Competency-Based Teacher Education Programs.* Syracuse, New York: Center for the Study of Teaching, Syracuse University, January 1971.

Armstrong, Robert D., Terry D. Cornell, Robert E. Cranner, and E. Wayne Roberson. *The Development and Evaluation of Behavioral Objectives.* Worthington, Ohio: Charles A. Jones Publishing Co., 1970.

Bloom, B. S., J. T. Hastings, and G. F. Madaus. *Handbook on Formative and Summative Evaluation of Student Learning.* New York: McGraw-Hill, 1971.

Elam, Stanley, ed. *Performance-Based Teacher Education, What is the State of the Art?* American Association of Colleges for Teacher Education. Washington, D.C.: 1971.

Flanagan, John C., William M. Shanner, and Robert Mager. *Behavioral Objectives, A Guide for Individualizing Learning, Primary—Intermediate—Secondary* (Language Arts, Social Studies, Mathematics, Science). Palo Alto, California: Westinghouse Learning Press, Westinghouse Learning Corporation, 1971.

Gronlund, N. E. *Stating Behavioral Objectives for Classroom Instruction.* New York: Macmillan, 1970.

Houston, W. Robert et al. *Developing Learning Modules.* Houston, Texas: College of Education, The University of Houston, 1971.

Johnson, C. E., and G. F. Shearron. *Specifying Assumptions, Goals and Objectives for Teacher Education.* Georgia Educational Models, University of Georgia, 1971.

Kibler, R. J., L. L. Barker, and D. T. Miles. *Behavioral Objectives and Instruction.* Boston: Allyn & Bacon, 1970.

Lindvall, C. M., ed. *Defining Educational Objectives.* Pittsburgh: University of Pittsburgh Press, 1964.

McAshan, H. H. *Writing Behavioral Objectives: A New Approach.* New York: Harper & Row, 1970.

Mager, R. R. *Preparing Instructional Objectives.* Palo Alto, California: Fearon Publishers, 1962.

Mills, Belen C., and Ralph A. Mills. *Designing Instructional Strategies for Young Children.* Dubuque, Iowa: William C. Brown Co., 1972.

Popham, W. J., and E. L. Baker. *Establishing Educational Goals.* Englewood Cliffs, New Jersey: Prentice-Hall, 1970.

Rosner, Benjamin, ed., chairman, Committee on National Program Priorities in Teacher Education. *The Power of Competency-Based Teacher Education,* Final Report, Project no. 1-0475, Grant no. OOEG-0-71-2849. Washington, D.C.: U. S. Office of Education, July 31, 1971.

Smith, B. O., ed. *Research in Teacher Education: A Symposium.* Englewood Cliffs, N. J.: Prentice-Hall, 1971.

4/ Organizing Elements: Multiunit Schools and Individually Guided Education

Joan Inglis
William Wiersma, Jr.

Thus far we have focused on the need for educational change and a description of the selected vehicle to accomplish change, competency-based teacher education. However, as we indicated in our discussion of the systems approach, change at the level of teacher education is necessary but not sufficient in the educational hierarchy. The basic level for change is the elementary school. This is the level at which preservice elementary education students will apply their skills and knowledge. This is the level at which present elementary teachers are practicing their profession. Most important, it is at this level that children first participate in the educational process. All the strategies and planning for educational change in the elementary school will be ineffectual if the context and climate are not receptive to change.

What does it take to make the elementary school receptive to change? Certainly, most educators would agree that it takes a combination of things. The complexity of the problem has already been suggested in earlier chapters. In this chapter, we deal with the two primary elements necessary at the elementary level: (1) an instructional organization conducive to change and (2) an instructional programming model designed to meet contemporary educational needs. The instructional organization is the multiunit school (MUS) and the instructional programming model is individually guided education (IGE).

OVERVIEW OF THE MULTIUNIT SCHOOL
AND INDIVIDUALLY GUIDED EDUCATION

The multiunit school is designed to produce an educational environment in which IGE can be applied and refined. The multiunit school is a comprehensive concept, involving the pupils, teaching staff, administrators, and supportive personnel not only of a single school, but of an entire school system. Methodologically, it involves. not only instruction, but also provides the organization for decision making, evaluation, communication and/or dissemination, and supportive research. Providing the proper environment for applying IGE merits special emphasis—indeed, the originators of the multiunit school view it as one of the seven major components of IGE.[1] This is not to give the multiunit organization a secondary position in conceptualizing change, but rather puts it in proper perspective. The multiunit organization is not the end in itself but an essential component among means to improved education. It may be characterized as a comprehensive instructional organization involving team teaching and differentiated staffing that provides the context for IGE.

With this general concept of the multiunit school in mind, let us turn briefly to the concept of individually guided education. There exist any number of systems for individualizing education, but IGE is a defined comprehensive system of education and instruction. It provides for differences among student characteristics, such as rate and style of learning. As a comprehensive system, IGE includes components such as the instructional process, curriculum materials, evaluation, and continuing research. The specific operational elements of these components are sequenced (and recycled as necessary) in the instructional programming model. The IGE model basically consists of "doing." For example, it is not limited to an individual student interacting with a teacher or teaching machine, although it may utilize such instructional arrangements among many others. An instructional model is usually immediately viewed in the context of the classroom or school, but IGE also involves a component of home-school communication designed to reinforce the school's efforts.

We have introduced the MUS and IGE as concepts that when operationalized together can bring about effective educational change; a rationale for this was implied above when the MUS was identified as an essential component of IGE. Developing an instructional organization like the multiunit school without providing for instructional programming is certainly not adequate for educational change—that is, providing the context without the process would yield little action. Conversely, developing the process but having no supportive context in which to apply it would not meet with success. Therefore, we consider MUS and IGE in combination to improve elementary school education.

HISTORICAL DEVELOPMENT OF THE MULTIUNIT SCHOOL

The multiunit school was initially conceived and then developed by the Wisconsin Research and Development Center for Cognitive Learning, through the systematic application of research and development strategies. The forerunner of the multiunit school was the research and instruction (R & I) unit instructional organization. The initial organization of schools under the R & I unit arrangement took place in 1965-66 in selected Wisconsin cities.[2] During the early years, numerous operational changes and adjustments were made as the R & I unit picked up momentum. In 1967, a cooperative project between the University of Toledo and the Toledo Public Schools was initiated that incorporated many of the R & I unit concepts.[3] This project, which involved converting an entire inner-city school to R & I units, included a component for preservice teacher education. Since the initial project school in 1967, the number of schools implementing multiunit organization increased by fall 1972 to twenty-five, and the University of Toledo was awarded a federal contract[4] that resulted in our CBTE model. This model included preparing teachers for R & I unit instruction, later refined to multiunit schools. Elementary teacher education at the University of Toledo was thereafter based on the multiunit organization.

We mention the connection of multiunit schools to teacher

education because of its relevance to CBTE as implemented in our model. However, the R & I unit enjoyed marked expansion in Wisconsin and other states, independent of its association with teacher education in Ohio. As entire schools adopted R & I unit organization, the terminology experienced an evolutionary process. The emphasis on the original and developmental research subsided and the instructional process received increased attention. (It should not be inferred from this that emphasis on research was or will be eliminated, since the research characteristic enhances the ability not only to accommodate change, but to identify necessary change in the first place.) This resulted in a change of terminology to I & R units, and shortly thereafter the term *multiunit* school was adopted to emphasize the organization of the entire school rather than that of a single unit.

The multiunit school is not a flash-in-the-pan educational innovation that defies implementation except in a few isolated instances. Rather, it is an effectualized concept that has evolved through several years of research and development. While the concept originated at the Wisconsin R & D Center, and center personnel were actively involved in its implementation, the MUS was and is being implemented in existing elementary schools. The concept has received national attention, and its wide applicability is demonstrated by multiunit schools in inner-city, suburban, and rural situations in numerous states; small and large schools in cities of varying sizes have adopted multiunit organization. The adaptability of the MUS concept in teacher education programs is an example of its versatility. State departments of education have implemented multiunit schools on a large scale. In summary, the multiunit school developed from a modest beginning approximately seven years ago to nationwide recognition and extensive implementation.

The multiunit school was developed as an alternative to the traditional, self-contained classroom to provide more effective elementary school instruction. It is one thing to set such a goal; it is another matter to attain it. Clearly, it would not have been satisfactory to claim success by ad hoc inspection. What was needed was a program of evaluative research as a component of the developmental research, to gather facts and guide necessary adjustments. Such a program was conducted, and the results conclusively favored multiunit schools.[6]

DESCRIPTION OF MULTIUNIT ORGANIZATION

As multiunit implementation gains momentum there may be a tendency to consider it as a generic concept. To some extent this may be permissible. The MUS is flexible and several variations can be incorporated into its implementation, but there are certain essential characteristics. Not just any ad hoc team teaching arrangement comprises an MUS, nor does an individualized education program necessarily meet the requirements of IGE as applied in a multiunit school. To clarify this point we will consider a prototype organization of the multiunit school and some variations.

The basic elements of the MUS are the instructional units that teach the groups of students, 100 to 150 in each group. Each unit has a unit leader and two to three staff teachers, depending on the number of children in the unit and possibly on the number of noncertified or paraprofessional personnel assigned to the unit. Every unit should have the services of at least a part-time instructional secretary and one full-time teacher aide. For schools involved in teacher education a student teacher or an intern would be included in the unit's staff. In rare instances, two interns might be assigned to a unit and this may reduce the number of staff teachers needed.

The instructional decision-making body for the school is the instructional improvement committee (IIC). The IIC is chaired by the principal and has as members, in addition to the principal, the unit leaders of the several units in the school. If a school system has two or more multiunit schools a systemwide policy committee (SPC) is also established, which consists of various representatives from the multiunit schools and selected members of the central office. An organizational layout of the MUS prototype is presented in Figure 4-1.[7]

The multiunit structure contains three distinct but interrelated levels. The instructional unit, at the classroom level, is basic; it replaces the traditional self-contained classroom. At the building level there is the instructional improvement committee (IIC), and at the system level the system-wide policy committee (SPC). Anything occurring at any one level affects the others. Each level has decision-making roles. In this way the multiunit school is designed to provide for responsible participation in decision making by all the personnel

Figure 4-1. Organizational Chart of a Multiunit School

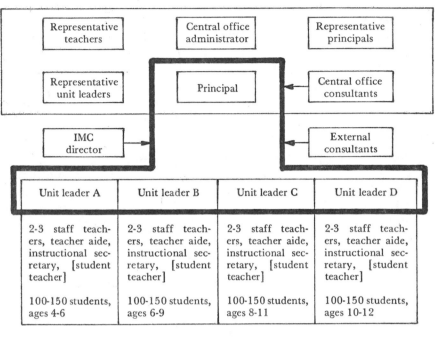

| Unit A | Unit B | Unit C | Unit D |

 Instructional improvement committee (IIC)

Systemwide policy committee (SPC)

of a school system. As we shall see in the discussion of the various roles, the unit and building levels both contain hierarchical structures.

The organizational chart of Figure 4-1 is adequate to identify the components of multiunit schools. However, some descriptive comments about the components are in order. The unit conducts and evaluates the instructional program for its students. Research is also a function of the unit because each unit must continuously engage in applied research to develop and evaluate an appropriate instructional program for each student. The unit teachers engage in staff development and inservice training along with the necessary planning for the unit.

There may be a number of variations at the unit level of the prototype presented. A unit may be involved in preservice activities and may contain one or more (preferably only one) student teacher. Intern programs may not be available to a specific multiunit school and perhaps not all units will have a first-year teacher. The number of certified teachers assigned to a unit depends on the number of the noncertified staff, such as interns or students, in the unit. One constant of unit staffing is the single unit leader—this is a necessary condition. Also, the unit should include paraprofessional supportive personnel such as a teacher aide and instructional secretary. Differentiated staffing is an essential characteristic of the unit.

The instructional improvement committee is the decision-making body for the school and, as such, one of its primary functions is to define educational objectives. The activities of the several units in a school are coordinated through the IIC, including, for example, the arrangement of special facilities that units cannot manage independently. The connection between the units and the IIC is through unit leaders, all of whom are members of the IIC. The IIC is connected to the systemwide policy committee through representative principals (not all principals of multiunit schools in a system are necessarily members of the SPC). The IIC is responsible for implementing systemwide policy as it affects the program of the school. The composition of the IIC is always basically the same. The principal is chairman of the IIC; under no circumstances should this responsibility be abdicated. All unit leaders are members on an equal basis. It may be that central staff personnel or university consultants are occasionally invited to participate in IIC meetings, but only by invitation.

A more permanent membership on the IIC may occur in schools involved in teacher education. The university facilitator or supervisor may be a "permanent" IIC member. This arrangement is suggested, since the IIC is the decision-making body for the school. It is a convenient and effective avenue for channeling schoolwide involvement in teacher education. Because teacher education is a cooperative effort and directly affects the educational program, it is reasonable that the university facilitator have equal status on the IIC with the unit leaders.

The conversion of a school system to MUS organization is a substantial task. The SPC was designed to facilitate and coordinate the necessary transition. The SPC would likely be chaired by the superintendent of schools, or, in a large district, by a central staff member designated by the superintendent. Obviously, the concept of the SPC must be flexible since its composition and functions are directly related to the size of the school system. In a large system a variety of central office staff would probably be on the committee (e.g., consultants, supervisors, researchers). In a small system the central staff representation might be limited to the superintendent and elementary supervisors.

Although the SPC is a policy-making committee it does have some tasks to perform. The SPC is responsible for identifying and arranging the necessary inservice education for the system. The recruitment of personnel for unit schools of the system is a logical function of the SPC. Dissemination of information on multiunit development and operation is a concern of the SPC, not only within the system but throughout the community. It may be that in a given system there are other central office components to assume many of the functions identified above. If so, the SPC can simply assume a more advisory role. In contrast to the IIC, whose function and composition are more fixed, the SPC has considerable flexibility in structure and activity to meet the needs of the specific situation.

ROLES OF PERSONNEL IN MUS ORGANIZATION

If properly implemented, the multiunit school is truly a differentiated staff arrangement. There are numerous professional roles in addition to those found in a self-contained classroom, and the remaining traditional roles are markedly changed. Each role is operationally defined by the tasks performed in the instructional process. Roles are not professionally isolated, but are related to each other in order to enhance the instructional process within the school.

The unit leader, or lead teacher, is the instructional leader of the unit.[8] An important point about this position is that it is instructional and not administrative or supervisory. The unit leader chairs the unit meetings and is responsible for the cooperative (with other unit members) planning and coordination of instruction, including efficient use of materials and resources. The unit leader is a member of the IIC and, through it, contributes to program planning for the entire school. By serving on the IIC the unit leaders are able to coordinate activities among the units, so that the educational program does not become isolated within the units but is in fact a building program.

The unit leader does not teach full time during the instructional day. Klausmeier recommends that the unit leader teach from 50 to 80 percent of the time. The size of the unit, both in staff and students, affects the amount of time the unit leader can teach; the larger the unit, the smaller the percentage of time spent teaching. The unit's involvement in activities such as research and development and teacher education also affects the unit leader's teaching time. As these activities increase, the unit leader requires additional time for planning and coordination.

The role of the staff teacher (sometimes called the regular teacher of the unit) is markedly different from that in the self-contained classroom. In a team situation the teacher participates in unit planning and evaluation as well as in instruction. The pupil-teacher ratio may vary from one-to-one to one teacher for a large group. The unit arrangement also requires the specialization of tasks and areas according to staff capabilities. Thus, the teacher in a unit has the opportunity to specialize to a degree, capitalizing on individual teacher strengths. Specialization is not limited to subject areas. It may include tasks like developing instructional materials, designing evaluation instruments, or counseling certain pupils.

A unit may also include an intern or student teacher. These are staff members who anticipate becoming teachers. Their functions are similar to the teaching tasks of the unit teacher, but they are not likely to specialize or to assume leadership roles. The intern or student teacher's teaching time will also be less than that of a regular teacher, since time for conferences and other activities must be allotted. The intern or student teacher role is an apprenticeship role.

The paraprofessional, supportive personnel of a unit consist of either an aide or an instructional secretary, or both. Aides function much as teacher assistants in routine activities like grading papers and conducting practice exercises with students. The aide may be a parent, paid or volunteer, or a preservice teacher education student not acting in a student teaching capacity. The instructional secretary has a clerical role involving tasks such as the preparation of materials. In some situations, high school students may act as instructional secretaries; this may be a channel for part-time employment for high school students with appropriate clerical background. The number of supportive personnel varies according to unit size and resources. However, all units should have at least one noncertified staff member.

The role of the principal in multiunit schools is different from the traditional role. The unit school principal is the instructional leader of the school. The principal chairs the IIC and, through it, is directly involved in planning the instructional program of the school. The principal works directly with many people. At the unit level he works primarily with the unit leaders. He brings in central staff personnel and consultants as necessary. He may serve on the SPC, which involves working directly with people outside the school. He has the responsibility of utilizing staff and consultants and coordinating activities for effective instruction.

We have alluded to the possible inclusion of consultants, central staff personnel, and teacher education professors in the operation of a multiunit school. Unit organization facilitates the use of supplementary personnel. A research consultant might be used to plan study within a unit or within the entire school. A teacher education professor may work cooperatively with unit staff in training student teachers, possibly offering a methods course at the school for the student teachers. Such supplementary personnel may work directly with one or more units. Their contact might be limited to unit meetings or it might include participation in other unit activities, such as evaluation. They may also work at the building level through the IIC. Although not part of the regular staff, their participation should not be overlooked.

RESEARCH ON THE EFFECTIVENESS OF THE MUS

The MUS in itself would have little merit if it were not operationally feasible or if it did not in fact result in an improved educational program. How do we know the unit is a desirable alternative to the self-contained classroom? Before we were able to answer that question, it was necessary to identify criteria that might be used in evaluative research. Certainly, the selection of the elementary school would merit consideration. Factors such as pupil attitude and job satisfaction of the MUS personnel are also important criteria in conducting evaluative research. Feasibility of operation is, of course, evidenced by the MUS applicability and its ability to function within practical constraints.

Let us consider first the matter of feasibility of operation. The multiunit school has been successfully implemented in a variety of schools: inner-city, suburban, rural. By June 1971 there were 283 units in 99 multiunit schools in Wisconsin. During the five-year period 1966-71, less than 5 percent of the units formed in Wisconsin were discontinued and not a single school with an IIC reverted back to a self-contained organization.[9] In the Toledo area no multiunit schools have reverted to former organizational plans. The multiunit organization was implemented in a variety of school locations with a wide range of different types of school buildings, ranging from small to large, and new to old. Thus, with this type of implementation and growth in a variety of situations, the evidence is conclusive that the MUS is operationally feasible.

One possible approach to research on the multiunit school is to make comparisons with control schools, using measures like student achievement. This approach has an inherent difficulty in that it is generally difficult to locate control schools so that the characteristics are approximately matched. Nevertheless, in a study checking student achievement between a developing unit school and a self-contained classroom control school, it was found that student performance was not adversely affected by the transition.[10] The finding on pupil attitude was inconclusive because the attitude inventory had been constructed specifically for the schools and had not been validated elsewhere. In the context of that limitation, the fifth graders in one of the multiunit schools did show more positive attitudes than those in one of the control schools. Other studies involving the use of control schools are available.[11] In general, pupils in unit organization tend to demonstrate greater gains in achievement than their counterparts in other schools, and also greater gains than might be expected on the basis of past performance in a traditional school.

Over the years, studies in various curriculum areas have been conducted in multiunit schools. The results have demonstrated conclusively that, when properly implemented, the unit organization provides a good environment for innovative practices. Pupils generally tended to perform higher in subject matter and skill areas than would be expected on the basis of previous performance, or when compared with established norm groups.[12]

Marked differences were found between job satisfaction of multiunit teachers and those in control, self-contained classroom, schools.

On a ten-item, job satisfaction scale, seven items showed significant differences, all favoring the teachers in the multiunit school, and three items showed no differences.[13] Multiunit teachers indicated greater satisfaction on factors such as progress towards one's personal goals in present position and seeing positive results from one's efforts, to select just two examples. Thus, the teacher perception of unit organization appears to be favorable, and no serious blocks to implementation are anticipated from teachers.

To summarize the implications of the research results, it has been demonstrated that the multiunit school is operationally feasible in a wide variety of situations. The unit organization is conducive to innovative curriculum practices and it can accommodate change; the MUS is an organization that will not become static and fixed in curriculum procedures. Student performance has generally taken the desired directions, and both pupil and teacher attitudes toward it have been favorable. The desirability and effectiveness of the MUS is based not only on the responses to written tests and inventories, but is also evidenced by the almost one hundred percent of multiunit schools that continue and the acceleration in developing new ones.

COORDINATING STRUCTURES

Implementation of multiunit schools on a large scale can be enhanced through the use of networks or groupings that provide coordination among the participants. At the time of this writing, the use of networks is in its infancy. However, various networks have been proposed and planned as coordinating structures and some have been put into operation.

One useful arrangement is a network of schools associated with a university. The university can develop its competency-based teacher education program to support unit implementation, and the multiunit school provides the necessary field context for teacher training. Supportive activities like curriculum research can also be conducted cooperatively by university and school personnel. An example of this type of network is the Ohio Elementary Teacher Education Model and its connection to multiunit schools.

Another basis for network development is through the state departments of education, which can work directly with schools or through universities. In the latter case the degree of university involvement must be resolved. For example, is the state department going to conduct extensive inservice or will it, by giving financial support, channel inservice through universities? Both approaches have been used effectively. The capabilities and resources of the participants, along with the specific conditions of the situation, dictate the approach.

Thus far in this chapter we have discussed the multiunit school, its components and operation. The unit is an instructional organization; it is not curriculum or subject matter. In order to conceptualize and implement the multiunit school, a compatible instructional programming model is needed. This model is individually guided education.

INDIVIDUALLY GUIDED EDUCATION

The long-range goal of educational change today is to individualize instruction for children and youth in the classroom. The unique quality of the instructional model presented here is that all personnel involved in the educational process are reorganizing in an intense effort to do exactly that: individualize instruction. Competency-based teacher education, with its emphasis on field experience, and the multiunit organizational framework, designed to facilitate IGE, constitute a cooperative support system for meaningful reform. If each system works independently and cooperatively the goal of individualization has for the first time a chance to be implemented.

HISTORICAL DEVELOPMENT OF INDIVIDUALIZATION

Until recently, schools were built and organized to place thirty children of the same age in a self-contained classroom with one teacher. For the most part the curriculum, textbooks, and materials have been assigned to these age-graded classrooms according to some generalized notion of what children should accomplish within a given school year, as if all children whose birthdays occur in the same year necessarily have the same interests, abilities, motivations, experiential backgrounds, and personal styles of learning. The elementary course of study is sequenced and allotted to grade levels in a lockstep fashion. Textbooks, manuals, and workbooks are selected for a school system and parceled out to the classrooms, largely dictating the instructional sequence in the classroom. The children are assigned

to this sequence—some proceeding faster than others and internalizing successfully, some more slowly and struggling, while still others
are simply exposed. Both teachers and children feel responsible to
cover the materials to get ready for the next year and the next
teacher.

Moreover, what has been considered acceptable in the schools is
the average, or grade norm, and, like Procrustes' visitors, pupils suffer
to fit approved grade norm specifications. Such norming has not
been successful mainly because it cannot be done; it works in
opposition to all that is known about the physical, intellectual,
emotional, and social growth of children and youth.

However, this has been the scene since Horace Mann became
enamored of the Prussian graded system early in the nineteenth
century and proceeded to restructure the American system along the
same lines. The first graded school in America, Quincy Grammar
School, opened in 1848. In far too many schools today this basic
structure of age gradedness is still in effect.

This is not to say that there was no concern for individual
differences in children until recently. The fact that individual differences do exist among children of the same chronological age has been
known for many years. Teachers of teachers have taught and preservice teachers have listened to the collected data of decades of
opinion and research about nature and nurture, individual growth
patterns, learning plateaus and spurts, and individual interests. The
question is not of the awareness of differences, but of how the
school deals with differences.

Nor has the concern for individual differences remained only
theoretical. Historically, the practical strategies to attend to individual needs in the classrooms have resulted in two instructional
practices: (1) adjusted instruction and (2) differentiated instruction.[14]

Adjusted Instruction

Much of the attention to individual differences among pupils has
materialized in various forms of adjusted instruction. Administrative
plans to adjust the lockstepped, average-oriented curriculum have
resulted in such arrangements as special classes for slow learners, for
the physically handicapped, and for emotionally disturbed and gifted

pupils. Flexible acceleration and retention policies are included in adjustment practices. The intent is to fill the regular classrooms with normal—i.e., average—students. Average is honored in the school; special is tolerated, but removed from the regular classroom.

Once the obvious deviants have been skimmed off, further attention to individual differences among the regular pupils resulted in various grouping patterns. The intent of most grouping procedures is to reduce the range of pupil differences (primarily academic) to which a single teacher needs to attend.

A common grouping procedure is homogeneous grouping based on general achievement or ability, by which an entire school can be organized. Teacher A has the bright pupils with IQs from 115 to 140, Teacher B works with IQs from 90 to 114, while Teacher C is assigned children at the 70 to 90 level. Popular terms like phasing, tracking, or streaming may be used, but always inherent in such strategies are segregation and teacher expectation according to assignment. Similar programs in specific subject areas—such as the Joplin plan in reading—organize children in much the same way. The high school science programs are rather vivid examples of these structures.

Within classrooms, the three-ability-grouped reading plan has long been a standard practice. Robins, bluebirds, and sparrows, all with their separate basal readers, proceed through the books, manuals, and workbooks at their own group pace. This pace in practice has often been set by the slowest member in any one group. It is possible to restructure the composition of these groups according to the changing progress of its members, but this seldom occurs—in so doing, some pupil might miss a part of the book. How deadly to be a sparrow all through the second grade and persist as a sparrow through the sixth, because the cumulative record says that's where you belong, regardless of changes in programs, methodologies, your personal interest, and motivation!

Some educators have defended these grouping patterns on the premise that reducing the range of differences enables the teacher to reach the individual child more efficiently and effectively. However, past and present research does not support this. In fact, the effect of such organizational arrangements is seriously questioned. Such techniques are for the most part based on false assumptions,[15] among them that

1. Arranging children into homogeneous groups is possible;[16]

2. Intelligence and achievement tests, on which such groupings are made, really measure what they purport to measure;[17]

3. Speed of learning is the most important characteristic of learning;[18]

4. Tests that report gross scores can identify individual needs (at least eight components of reading must be examined in any attempt to group homogeneously—but there is not such a thing as a homogeneous group anyway as individuals are not homogeneous in themselves);[19]

5. Like groups once formed maintain their homogeneity although children within these groups develop in uneven growth patterns;[20]

6. Teachers will individualize instruction to a greater extent when the range of differences is reduced (psychologically the opposite is true, for teachers treat these groups with less individualization because they tend to think of the children as all alike).[21]

When attempts are made to group children homogeneously one sure thing results: heterogeneity.

Extensive evidence reported by Passow and Goldberg should put an end to decades of research on the subject. Narrowing the range of ability or achievement does not in itself improve the achievement of the children so grouped.[22]

Other studies have investigated self-concept, attitudes toward others, and creativity in such grouping plans. Children in low groups often have poor attitudes toward self, while children in high groups often have poor attitudes toward those less capable than they are and overly "snobbish" attitudes toward themselves.[23] Creativity is not necessarily fostered in homogeneously grouped schools or classrooms.[24] Finally, teacher attitudes toward low-grouped children may be tolerant at best and often without expectations for improvement.[25]

Differentiated Instruction

In differentiated instruction the emphasis is placed on accommodating instruction to existing differences.[26] The role of the teacher in planning for a wide range of differences in the classroom is stressed. Individual differences within a given group are more honored than tolerated and methods and techniques are varied to meet these differences. Pupils are encouraged to proceed through materials at their own rate and, when possible, to pace themselves.

The principle that each child should progress at his own rate is certainly compatible with what we know about growth and maturation. Based on this principle, nongraded schools and continuous progress plans have demonstrated acceptance of individual differences in speed of learning.

Early contract plans such as the Winnetka and Dalton programs, which initiated widespread acceptance of workbooks, and the present programmed learning material permit children to proceed at their own rate and to work independently. Intrinsic to such plans, however, is that all children must pass through each small step in orderly sequence before they can go on to the next small chunk of content. This, coupled with the fact that the material is designed so that the slowest learner can achieve, hardly attends to individual differences in learning. As a total program in any subject area, programmed learning is the antithesis of true individualization.

Educators have recently moved toward greater individualism by varying "what" is to be learned as well as "how" and "when" it is to be learned. Not all children are required to cover identical content and material. Diagnosis, once reserved for remediation classes, has become a more recognized usage in the regular classroom. Instruction is more specific to the individual weaknesses and strengths of each child. Individual learning experiences using many texts, resource materials, interest centers, learning carrels, and instructional media centers are appearing in the elementary classrooms.

Individualized Reading Instruction

This trend toward greater individualization is due largely to the proponents of individualized reading, the first area of the curriculum to be individualized and personalized.[27]

The individualized reading approach capitalized on pupil interest and developing positive attitudes toward learning. Self-selection from a wide variety of tradebooks was used as motivation, replacing the use of the graded basal reader for all. The individual conference replaced round robin and group reading. Of greatest importance in the development of individualization was that, on the basis of diagnosis, children with similar identified needs were temporarily brought together for task group teaching, thus eliminating the static three-ability-grouped plans. Workbooks were replaced by open-ended, self-selected language arts activities. In such a program there is no need for all pupils, as a class or in groups, to do the same thing, to begin at the same time, or to finish together.

Individualized reading was heavily researched during the fifties and sixties. A summary of the evidence indicated clearly that children taught in this way did as well as if not better than children taught in the traditional way. In addition, other findings that are difficult to measure, such as positive attitudes toward reading and learning and the amount of children's literature read, favored individualized reading.[28] This program is the final link in the long history of individualization of instruction: from adjustment instruction to differentiated instruction to individualized reading instruction and, lastly, to a more complete individualizing of the total curriculum.

Although the reading experts have attempted to bring about individual instruction, it has not become as widespread as had been hoped. One or several teachers in a building may organize programs to match instruction to pupil need, but for the most part the plan does not spread beyond the language arts. The second grade teacher may have an excellent prototype of individualization, but this need not result in similar articulation throughout the school. Isolated pockets of individualization exist in many schools, but a coordinating system is lacking. It is difficult if not impossible to implement individualized learning without a total support system that combines the efforts of school administrators, the central office, teachers, pupils, parents, and teacher education institutions.

Askov studied individual reading using the Wisconsin Design for Reading Skill Development—the first published curriculum component in IGE—and reported that the lack of system stifles experimentation.

Attitudes of teachers using a system for individualizing reading instruction were more positive toward the philosophy of individualization than were teachers who had no such system. If teachers are provided with objectives and assessment tools they react positively toward diagnosing each student's needs and planning individual instruction programs accordingly. If they have no system to facilitate individualization, their attitudes toward the philosophy are less positive. If one wishes to promote individualization then some systematic means for aiding teachers with the process of individualization should be provided.[29]

Since the establishment of the Wisconsin R & D Center in 1964 the major goal has been to develop an exemplary instructional program for individual students, starting with the organization for instruction and the related administrative arrangements—the IGE system and the multiunit framework. From the outset, the design emphasized the attainment of individual objectives.[30] Finally in 1968 the Wisconsin R & D Center and the Institute for Development of Educational Activities (I/D/E/A), the educational affiliate of the Kettering Foundation, agreed to publish inservice materials and media for implementation of IGE within the MUS.

THE IGE INSTRUCTIONAL MODEL

At this point it is important that the term IGE be clearly understood. IGE is not programmed learning, it is not one-to-one instruction, it is not independent learning by means of learning packages. It does not eliminate teachers, nor reduce them to monitor only in the classroom. IGE does not provide for the teaching of skills to the exclusion of problem solving, discovery, or creativity. "Moderate emphasis is put on skill mastery and the acquisition and recall of factual information; much emphasis is on concept formation, application of skills and concepts, creativity and evaluation of information."[31]

IGE does not predetermine behaviors to the exclusion of incidental learning, pupil interests, or social and human development. IGE is and does none of these things per se. Rather, it is all of them and much more.

IGE is a more comprehensive design than individual instruction when individualized instruction is viewed as a student learning through direct interaction with instructional materials or equipment with little or no assistance from a teacher. Some educational objectives can be attained by some students under certain conditions through the use of computer-assisted instruction, programmed packages and sets of curriculum materials as usually organized in a school setting. However, many younger children who do not read well and have not yet acquired a store of fundamental concepts especially need the personal stimulation and guidance of skillful teachers in most curriculum areas.[32]

There is no one best method for all children and for all subjects. The same set of materials is not suitable for all children nor is the independent learning mode best for all children.

IGE, which appears to be an extension of the individualized reading efforts of the fifties and sixties, is a strategy or system by which teachers can assess, observe, and accept the fact that each child is different not only in the amount that he learns, or the speed with which he learns, but also in the way he learns and what he wants to learn. IGE attempts to recognize, in the classroom setting, more varied degrees and kinds of differences than was previously done by either adjusted or differentiated instruction.

IGE acknowledges that some children learn best in small groups, some in one-to-one instruction, and some in the independent learning modes. IGE accepts that some children learn best by reading, some by listening, some in discussion sessions; some learn best by sight and some by sound. This does not mean that once the observation has been made and recorded that for those children who learn best through discussion in small groups, all instruction will then take place in such a setting. What it *does* mean is that when something is difficult for a child to learn, instruction will be given in his optimal learning style.

The instructional model in IGE demands that specific learning objectives be established for each child based on diagnosis and assessment (both testing and observation). This ensures that students are taught only what they don't know, and have the opportunity to apply independently those skills that they have already acquired.

Moreover, individualization in IGE moves from teacher-directed patterns of instruction to learner-directed modes of learning. The teacher will undoubtedly be involved in providing for adjustment at times, but will go one step further and stress personal goal-setting by the learner to develop self-directive, self-responsible students capable of making their own decisions.

In addition to eliminating the failure-frustration syndrome that has existed in the age-graded classroom, a goal of education should be to teach respect for all persons, each with his different talents and abilities, and thereby develop positive concepts of self and other and a feeling of self-worth. When IGE is properly implemented this concept is reinforced by the instructional process.

A further curriculum emphasis of IGE is the integration of subject matter by which false subject area barriers, for example, between spelling and reading or between reading and the social studies, can be eliminated.

To summarize a description of IGE we might enumerate its major components. These can generally be identified as the following seven major components:

1. An organization for instruction, a related administrative organization at the building level, and another arrangement at the central office level (the multiunit organization outlined in the preceding section of this chapter);

2. A model of instructional programming for the individual student (the IGE learning cycle to be presented);

3. A model for developing measurement tools and evaluation procedures (the "IGE Implementation Guide and Outcomes," published by I/D/E/A, and "Evaluation Procedures for Use with Multiunit Elementary School Personnel," working paper no. 21, published by the Wisconsin R & D Center);

4. Curriculum materials, related statements of instructional objectives, and criterion-referenced test and observation schedules (the Wisconsin Reading Design and Math Program);

5. A program of home-school communications that reinforces the school's efforts by generating the interest and encouragement of parents and other adults whose attitudes influence pupil motivation and learning;

6. Facilitative environments in schools, school systems and central offices, state education agencies, and teacher education institutions (the Ohio and Wisconsin models);

7. Continuing research and development to generate knowledge and to produce tested materials and procedures.[33]

The components can be structured into a programming model that basically provides a systems approach to instruction. This model is provided in Figure 4-2 (note the emphasis on objectives early in the programming).

Basic to implementation of IGE in the classroom is the IGE learning cycle. This cycle provides a framework in which important instructional questions about each child can be answered: (1) What has he already learned? (2) What does he need to learn? (3) What learning activities and materials should be made available to him to meet his needs? (4) What teacher and learning style would be most appropriate? (5) How well has he achieved the objective? An example of this cycle, applied to arithmetic, is presented in Figure 4-3.

If a student does not meet his objective he is recycled. The specificity of the error made should be noted and a new learning program designed with new materials, possibly with a different

Figure 4-2. The IGE Instructional Programming Model[34]

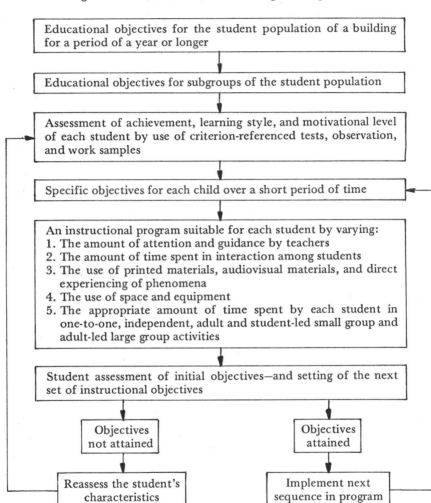

Educational objectives for the student population of a building for a period of a year or longer

Educational objectives for subgroups of the student population

Assessment of achievement, learning style, and motivational level of each student by use of criterion-referenced tests, observation, and work samples

Specific objectives for each child over a short period of time

An instructional program suitable for each student by varying:
1. The amount of attention and guidance by teachers
2. The amount of time spent in interaction among students
3. The use of printed materials, audiovisual materials, and direct experiencing of phenomena
4. The use of space and equipment
5. The appropriate amount of time spent by each student in one-to-one, independent, adult and student-led small group and adult-led large group activities

Student assessment of initial objectives—and setting of the next set of instructional objectives

Objectives not attained

Objectives attained

Reassess the student's characteristics

Implement next sequence in program

teacher and/or a change in learning style for the second time around. However, when a pupil does not achieve his objective under altered circumstances he should not be perpetually recycled, but moved on to a different objective.

The IGE learning cycle is particularly appropriate for use in skill teaching when closed objectives—that is, those that specify a particu-

Figure 4-3. The IGE Learning Cycle Applied to the Addition of Fractions[35]

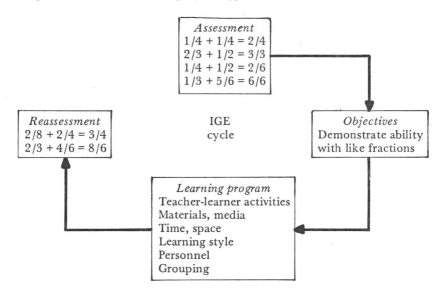

lar outcome—clearly state the behavior expected of the student after instruction. However, much that is important in education can only be stated in open or expressive objectives.

Expressive objectives do not specify the behavior the student is to acquire after having engaged in one or more learning activities. An expressive objective describes an educational encounter: it identifies a situation in which children may work, a problem with which they are to cope, a task they are to engage in—but it does not specify what from that encounter, situation, problem or task they are to learn. An expressive objective presents both the teacher and the student with an invitation to explore, defer or focus on issues that are of peculiar interest or impact to the inquirer. An expressive objective is evocative rather than prescriptive.[36]

The Wisconsin Design for Reading Skill Development, the existing IGE curriculum model, specifically deals with this problem by dividing reading into six components: the skills of (1) word attack, (2) comprehension, (3) study skills, (4) self-direction, and (5) interpretive and (6) creative reading. Closed objectives with the parameters of behavior stated in advance, along with criterion-referenced tests, have been written for the first three areas, but not for the latter areas.

It is virtually impossible, and, we feel, undesirable to specify objectives in the same way for areas IV, V, and VI. They call for open or expressive objectives, if, indeed, they call for objectives at all.[37]

THE TEACHER'S ROLE IN IGE

All teachers teach all subjects in IGE. However, there is a division of labor according to expertise in subject areas. Traditionally, the teacher has been responsible for all subjects, often lacking depth in any one. Passow's research on the ability of teachers to be equally adept in all subjects indicated that teachers achieved better results in one or two subjects than they did in others.

These findings raise some questions about the adequacy of one-teacher classrooms especially for the more able students and suggests that exposing students to several teachers with diverse subject matter competencies would result in higher level learning than results from narrowing the ability level of pupils but retaining one teacher for all instruction.[38]

The IGE teachers on a team are expected to develop considerable competency in one area, and to acquaint themselves with the structure and process involved in a particular discipline, as well as to familiarize themselves with new methods and materials by which to instruct and guide students to greater knowledge and appreciation of what they are studying. In this arrangement not all teachers necessarily do the initial planning in all subjects. For example, the teacher on the team who has a special strength in science may do the early planning of a science unit by developing objectives, collecting books and materials, and organizing science centers, learning options, and evaluation devices. The teaching unit thus developed is then brought to the team meeting for teacher criticism and team modification. After changes are agreed on by teachers, the particular tasks are assigned to each teacher in the unit. The teachers will decide how the teaching unit will be organized and operated, according to the needs of the children and teachers, and the structure and process involved in the content to be studied.

Teachers in this model cannot follow the "cookbook" approach; in a multiunit setting it is impossible to close the door and teach from a manual. The planning within the team and through the IIC cannot help but stimulate ideas. In IGE/MUS the teacher is expected to be a curriculum developer, decision maker, critic, and student of child behavior and learning theory. He is expected to be an instructional experimenter. As the instructional leader, the principal is knowledgeable about the instructional process. As decisions are cooperatively made and the responsibility for implementation shared, the administrator vs. teacher syndrome is weakened.

Teachers in units can no longer be whole class lecturers, nor dispensers of knowledge, nor knowers of all things. A teacher in IGE/MUS functions as a diagnostician, monitor, instructor, planner, and, hopefully with help from a paraprofessional, recordkeeper. The teacher helps youngsters find answers by introducing them to new ways of seeing, doing, and understanding phenomena.

Evaluation of student progress is, of course, still important, but the distasteful job of sorting and grading pupils no longer exists. Children are not classified as satisfactory or unsatisfactory, acceptable or not acceptable, because grade norms are not acceptable in individual education. Each child is acceptable, to be valued for what he is, not for how well or how poorly he compares with someone else.

Changes are taking place in the elementary classrooms, and included in this change is the professional role of the teachers. Unit teachers control their own unit budgets, order their own teaching materials, join professional associations, and seek out professional opinion and research. They develop curriculum and experiment with methods, materials, and principles of learning theory. They free children to challenge and question and to establish self-direction. They also see themselves as teacher educators. Unit teachers accept the principle of greater autonomy for themselves and for the children they teach.

OPERATIONAL STRATEGIES

What is to be taught, *how* it will be taught, and *when* and to *whom* are joint responsibilities of the team members. These decisions are made at the unit meetings, held during the regular school day at least twice a week. Planning is the key to success in IGE. The planning system includes the goal-setting meeting, the design meeting, the grouping and scheduling meeting, and the situational meeting.[39]

The *goal-setting meeting* is used to determine (1) the broad instructional goals, (2) the content to be used to achieve the goals, and (3) which teacher will organize and develop the major teaching design. The *design meeting* provides the team with the opportunity to modify the plan prepared by the assigned teacher. Teacher assignments, a schedule outline, and an assessment plan may be made at this meeting. The *grouping and scheduling meeting* takes place after the initial assessment is accomplished. *Situational meetings,* in which the teaching plan is continually evaluated and adjustments made, take place after the program is in progress. The activities discussed at these meetings are exactly what the names imply.

The following is an example of how a unit might use the IGE planning system. Two goals were chosen in the goal-setting meeting: (1) solving simple and complex problems and (2) self-direction in learning to learn. Science was selected as the subject area, and the teacher with an interest in science selected "classifying" as the process to be learned.

At the design meeting the team agreed on their specific objectives: (1) the students would participate in self-selection of learning activities and (2) answer the question, "Why do scientists classify things?" Figure 4-4 shows the result of further decision making in the planning system. After initial introduction of the settings, students can select a topic and pursue the fixed activities. Or, one or more students may plan other activities in small-group, one-to-one, and independent modes for open days.

COMBINING IGE AND MUS

IGE/MUS is a total support system for reform and renewal of the educational process. Its combined impact is dependent on the strength of each link in the system.

In the Ohio CBTE model, provision is made for the treatment and utilization of four populations: (1) university personnel and program, (2) preservice teachers, (3) inservice teachers, and (4) administrators.

The CBTE program described in Chapter 2 operates on the same principles as does the multiunit school. The teacher education professional sequence employs a similar learning cycle. The basic unit, the instructional model, consists of instructional objectives, assessment to test the student level of achievement prior to instruction,

Figure 4-4. An Example of Instructional Grouping and Scheduling[40]

Topic: Why scientists classify things
Time: Three weeks
Setting: Learning stations: (1) senses, (2) animals, (3) machines, (4) library
Modes: Large, small, one-to-one, and independent
Organization: Both self-selection and fixed activities
Teacher assignment: Self-selection
Evaluation: Observation (Parents' Day discussions)

		Monday	Tuesday	*Fixed activities* Wednesday	Thursday	Friday
Weeks	1	Teacher presentation on machines (Large group)	Classifying by senses (Large group)	Film on classifying animals (Large group)	Library services (Large group)	Touching and tasting games
	2	Field trip to places that classify (museum, library)		Field trip to zoo		Construction of simple machines
	3	Zoo project		Classifying musical sounds	Parents' Day (sharing)	

instructional activities, and postassessment. College faculty members, organized into cross-disciplinary teams, developed the modules and are accountable for their implementation.

The CBTE program provides for earlier and more frequent experiences in the schools, to facilitate achieving the objectives of the modules. These activities have been planned, with the modules as a blueprint, by the college teams jointly with public school personnel in multiunit schools. The preservice teachers will aid the teaching teams in at least some of the schools throughout their professional training and in that way will also become agents of change.

The programs for teacher education and the elementary school are being developed and operated simultaneously. Both the CBTE and the IGE/MUS have as their major goal a more individual, personal, efficient system of education. The gap that often exists between teacher education and teaching is being accounted for. Neither will achieve its potential unless all who are involved experience the same process. Preservice teachers must be prepared to function in multiunit schools and the public schools where the graduates will teach must be ready to benefit from their training.

In addition, the model calls for college faculty to be active in the schools in order to understand the real world of teaching children and to unite the two basic agencies, teacher education institutions and the schools, in their common goal of educating the children they service.

Implementation of both the CBTE and the IGE/MUS requires (1) preservice preparation and (2) an inservice program for teachers and administrators in the schools.

Inservice needs have been served by cooperative school and university efforts in several ways, such as:

1. Initial federal funding and subsequent grant support;
2. Clue-in conferences to acquaint area teachers and administrators with the objectives and operations of IGE/MUS;
3. Unit leader workshops;
4. Advanced unit leader workshops;
5. Graduate classes in curriculum development in IGE /MUS;
6. Graduate classes offered in the schools implementing IGE/MUS;
7. Assignment of college faculty as university facilitators to the multiunit schools to aid in the implementation;
8. Methods classes taught in the multiunit schools;
9. Inservice sessions offered by subject area consultants;
10. On-site visits by area teachers conducted by facilitators;
11. Principals' workshops;
12. Public school personnel, trained by college faculty, conducting inservice sessions.

A schoolwide committee to coordinate program development and educational activities in schools moving from the self-contained setting to multiunit operations can also provide inservice of a kind as well as a communication network.

One of the components of IGE is a strong home-school-community relationship. In this regard the facilitator (the college faculty member assigned to each cooperating multiunit school in the Toledo area), as well as additional faculty members, participated in parent community meetings prior to initial implementation of IGE/MUS and reported progress and changes to PTA meetings. The Toledo planners are aware of the importance of parents and community in the combined support system, which requires continuing interaction to achieve success.

SUMMARY

Two organizing elements that accompany and facilitate CBTE are multiunit schools and individually guided education. Much has been written about these two elements, separately and together. They are combined in our presentation to reinforce the notion of their interrelatedness. We have also attempted to establish the necessary relationships with CBTE of the roles of university personnel offering preservice and inservice work in the schools.

This completes our introduction of key concepts of CBTE. In Chapter 5 we turn to the task of developing the program.

Notes

1. H. J. Klausmeier et al., *The Development and Evaluation of the Multiunit Elementary School, 1966-1970*, technical report no. 158 (Madison: Wisconsin Research and Development Center for Cognitive Learning, 1971), p. 1.

2. The initial four cities were Janesville, Madison, Racine, and West Bend. For a summary of the early activities, see H. J. Klausmeier and D. M. Cook, *Project Models*, working paper no. 5 (Madison: Wisconsin Research and Development Center for Cognitive Learning, May 1967).

3. Toledo Board of Education, *Roosevelt School, Research-Instruction Plan, A Cooperative Project*, Title III ESEA, 1965 (Toledo, Ohio: Toledo Public Schools, June 1967).

4. G. E. Dickson et al., *Educational Specifications for a Comprehensive Elementary Teacher Education Program* (Toledo, Ohio: The University of Toledo, October 1968), vols. 1, 2.

5. See, for example, *The Ohio Multiunit Plan: Planning for a Statewide Network of Multiunit Schools, Competency-Based Teacher Education and Performance-Based Teacher Certification* (Columbus: Ohio Department of Education, 1972).

6. See, for example, H. J. Klausmeier et al., *The Development and Evaluation of the Multiunit Elementary School, 1966-1970*.

7. H. J. Klausmeier et al., *Individually Guided Education and the Multiunit*

Elementary School (Madison: Wisconsin Research and Development Center for Cognitive Learning, 1971), p. 21.

8. Ibid., p. 23.

9. H. J. Klausmeier et al., *Development and Evaluation of the Multiunit Elementary School, 1966-1970.*

10. R. G. Morrow et al., *Student Achievement and Attitudes in I and R Units in Two Elementary Schools in Janesville, Wisconsin, 1967-68,* technical report no. 76 (Madison: Wisconsin Research and Development Center for Cognitive Learning, 1969), p. 23.

11. See, for example, H. J. Klausmeier et al., *Research and Development Activities in R and I Units of Five Elementary Schools of Racine, Wisconsin, 1966-1967,* technical report no. 52 (Madison: Wisconsin Research and Development Center for Cognitive Learning, 1968), p. 43.

12. For a partial summary of representative curriculum studies, see H. J. Klausmeier et al., *Development and Evaluation of the Multiunit Elementary School, 1966-1970,* p. 16.

13. Ibid., p. 12.

14. Virgil M. Howes, "Individualized Instruction: Form and Structure," in *Individualization of Instruction,* ed. Virgil M. Howes (New York: Macmillan Co., 1970), pp. 71-75.

15. Anne Morgenstern, ed., *Grouping in the Elementary School* (New York: Pitnam Publishing Corp., 1966).

16. Fred Wilhelms and Dorothy Westby-Gibson, "Grouping: Research Offers Leads," *Educational Leadership* 18 (April 1961): 410-13.

17. J. Franseth, "Research in Grouping: A Review," *School Life* 45 (1963): 5-6.

18. Ibid.

19. Irving Balow, "Does Homogeneous Grouping Give Homogeneous Groups?" *Elementary School Journal* 63 (May 1962): 31.

20. Anne Morgenstern, *Grouping in the Elementary School,* pp. 71-75.

21. Jim Olson, "Should We Group by Ability?" *Journal of Teacher Education* 18 (summer 1967): 201-205.

22. Harry Passow, M. Goldberg, and J. Justman, *The Effects of Ability Grouping* (New York: Teachers College Press, 1966).

23. Maxine Mann, "What Does Grouping Do to the Self-Concept?" *Childhood Education* 36 (April 1960): 357-60; Abraham and Edith Luchins, "Children's Attitudes toward Homogeneous Grouping," in *Elementary Curriculum,* ed. Robert Chasnoff (New York: Pitman Publishing Corp., 1964), p. 546.

24. Paul E. Torrance, *Rewarding Creative Behavior* (New York: Prentice Hall, 1965), p. 203.

25. Jim Olson, "Should We Group by Ability?" pp. 201-205.

26. Virgil M. Howes, "Individualized Instruction: Form and Structure," p. 75.

27. For further information on individualized reading, see Jeannette Veatch, *Reading in the Elementary School* (New York: Ronald Press, 1966). See also materials written by Helen Fisher Darrow, Alice Keliher, Leland Jacobs, Water Barbe, Sam Duker, Patrick Groff, Sylvia Ashton-Warner, Willard Olson, and Lyman Hunt.

28. Patrick Groff, "Comparisons of Individual and Ability Grouping Approaches as to Reading Achievement," *Elementary English* 40 (March 1963):

258-644; idem, "Comparisons of Individual and Ability Grouping to Teaching Reading," a supplement, *Elementary English* 41 (March 1964): 238-41.

29. Eunice Askov, "Assessment of Teachers' Attitudes toward an Individualized Approach to Reading Instruction" (using the Wisconsin design for reading skill development), a paper presented to AERA (American Educational Research Association), February 1971.

30. H. J. Klausmeier et al., *Individually Guided Education and the Multiunit Elementary School*, p. 3.

31. H. J. Klausmeier et al., "The Multiunit Organization and Elementary Education in the Decade Ahead" (position paper), in G. E. Dickson et al., *Educational Specifications for a Comprehensive Elementary Teacher Education Program* (Toledo, Ohio: The University of Toledo, 1968), vol. 1, p. 31.

32. H. J. Klausmeier et al., *Individually Guided Education and the Multiunit Elementary School*, p. 2.

33. Ibid., pp. 12-14.

34. Ibid., p. 13.

35. *Individually Guided Education* (Dayton, Ohio: Institute of Development of Educational Activities (I/D/E/A) 1970), p. 13.

36. E. W. Eisner, "Instructional and Expressive Educational Objectives: Their Formulation and Use in Curriculum," paper presented at AERA, February 1969, quoted in Wayne Otto and E. Askov, *Wisconsin Design for Reading Skill Development* (Madison: Wisconsin Research and Development Center for Cognitive Learning, 1970), p. 40.

37. Wayne Otto and Eunice Askov, The Wisconsin Design for Reading Skill Development (Madison: Wisconsin Research and Development Center for Cognitive Learning, 1970), p. 40.

38. Harry Passow, M. Goldberg, and J. Justman, *The Effects of Ability Grouping*, p. 162.

39. Kenneth M. Schultz, *Study Guide, IGE Planning System*, I/D/E/A Change Program materials (Dayton, Ohio: I/D/E/A, 1971).

40. _____, *Study Guide, Managing the IGE Learning Program*, Change Program materials (Dayton, Ohio: I/D/E/A, 1971).

Suggested Readings

Beugen, Joan, Ira Kerns, and Norman Graper. *Principals Handbook*. Dayton, Ohio: Institute for Development of Educational Activites (I/D/E/A), 1971.

DiPego, Gerald. *Unit Operations and Roles*. Dayton, Ohio: I/D/E/A, 1970.

Klausmeier, Herbert J., et al. *Individually Guided Education and the Multiunit Elementary School*. Madison: Wisconsin Research and Development Center for Cognitive Learning, 1971.

5/ Institutional Development of CBTE

George E. Dickson
Castelle G. Gentry

CREATING THE OHIO (TOLEDO) MODEL

The task of designing a program of teacher education that is not out-of-date before it is fully implemented has frustrated the best efforts of teacher educators. If we liken such a task to the impossible dream of the man of La Mancha, the existing archaic curricula for teacher education seem so many lances shattered in vain attempts to relate past insights to the flux of the present and future.

For the first time, however, events suggest that a relevant program of teacher education may not have to remain a quixotic notion. In the fall of 1967, the Bureau of Research of the U.S. Office of Education announced the inauguration of a multiphase elementary teacher education project, which would provide designs for outstanding—or model—programs for training elementary teachers, and eventually result in the implementation of the best models produced. The Office of Education's request for proposals provided guidelines for designing and implementing exemplary model programs in teacher education. These programs were to do more than incorporate or adjust to current innovations; they were to provide the structure and impetus for continuing change in teacher education. The request for proposals asked for conceptual models that would result in "educational specifications for a comprehensive undergraduate and inservice teacher education program for elementary teachers."[1]

More than eighty proposals were submitted by universities, colleges, and other research organizations. From these, nine were selected and funded by the Office of Education through an expenditure of approximately 1.5 million dollars. The proposals accepted came from the universities of Florida State, Georgia, Massachusetts, Michigan State, Pittsburgh, Syracuse, Toledo, Columbia University's Teachers College, and the Northwest Regional Educational Laboratory in Portland, Oregon. In the second phase of the project the University of Wisconsin, which had prepared model specifications separately, was added to the original nine, making ten sets of model specifications ultimately available. The results of each institution's research were published in multi-volume reports, which are available from ERIC or from the institutions involved.

These definite specifications, or blueprints, from which model programs of teacher education could be developed were the first generation of a systems approach to teacher education. They provided prototype components of elementary teacher education containing new educational concepts. The model designs were a deliberate, planned effort to provide preservice and inservice education in programs responsive to the changing present and future educational needs of schools, teachers, and children. They were comprehensive documents that contained the best thinking of the designers about teacher education and offered a variety of strategies for elementary teacher training, as well as potential reform in secondary teacher education. The ten teacher education models were distinct: no two took exactly the same approach to designing educational specifications. All accommodated the fundamental components of competency-based teacher education (a term not then in use), but each design emphasized different factors.

Historical Development of the Ohio Model Design and the Design Produced

As was indicated in the discussion of objectives in Chapter 3, the Toledo designers began model development efforts by assuming that existing programs of teacher education were not adequate to prepare teachers for changing conditions. Because of the pervasive impact of change on education, we chose to prepare programs that dealt with *all* groups of educational personnel who were actively involved in the education, induction, and support of new teachers, calling them the major target populations for a changed program in teacher education. They were identified as (1) preservice—preschool and kindergarten teachers, (2) preservice—elementary teachers (grades 1-8), (3) inservice teachers (all levels), (4) college and university personnel (teachers of teachers), (5) administrative personnel (principals and supervisors in elementary schools), and (6) supportive personnel (paraprofessionals and teacher aides).

Since existing plans of teacher education were not to be considered as models or limitations, we agreed that the present structure of elementary teacher education need not be continued and that teacher education traditions need not be maintained. We also assumed that any new and challenging teacher education model program coming from our efforts would result in corresponding changes and innovations in the elementary school setting where the model was to be applied and our new teachers placed. Hence, we abandoned the concept of teacher preparation for the graded, self-contained classroom and incorporated the idea of a multiunit school and team teaching approach developed by the Wisconsin Research and Development Center for Cognitive Learning.

The conceptual design for the project is represented in Figure 5-1. Our efforts involved: (1) defining general goals of teacher education; (2) examining these goals in five contexts (instructional organization, educational technology, contemporary learning-teaching process, societal factors, and research); (3) developing behavioral objectives for the five contexts; (4) creating educational specifications to incorporate the behavioral objectives for each of the six target populations; and finally (5) bringing together these specifications into composites called model programs.

The broad statement of goals (see Chapter 3 for listing) for the program of teacher education was adapted from the report by the Committee on Quality Education of the Pennsylvania State Board of Education.[2] There are doubtless more ideal and rigorous ways to attain the goals of American teacher education, but the Pennsylvania group had applied a most comprehensive and objective process to goal development. We decided to build on their groundwork.

Figure 5-1. Conceptual Design

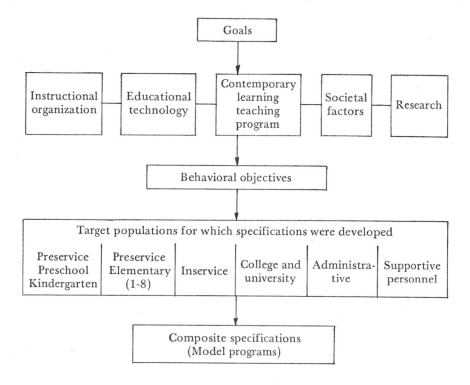

Because the overriding concern was to accommodate the forces of change, the Toledo designers decided to refine the general goals by first considering them from the perspective of the five contexts mentioned above. These contexts represent the more important sources of change in teacher education today. An authority in each context field prepared a position paper on his topic. Other knowledgeable people in each field were provided with the position papers for their respective fields and asked to react to them. These papers and the reactions, which were written analyses of the papers, provided a rich source of data for the preparation of behavioral objectives.

The Toledo designers and their consultants prepared behavioral objectives within the five contexts for the six target populations. This effort generated more than 2,000 behavioral objectives arranged by context, with each context divided into major subjects and further divided into topics. Behavioral objectives were then prepared for each topic. Tables 5-1 through 5-5 provide an overview of the project, revealing something of the scope of the behavioral objectives and the educational specifications that resulted.

Table 5-1. Context: Instructional Organization

Major subject areas	Topics
Necessary training for instruction	1. General education 2. Curriculum development and evaluation 3. Academic disciplines and skills—methodology 4. Evaluation techniques for multi-sized group instruction 5. Curriculum techniques for multi-sized group instruction 6. Administration of individually guided education 7. Internship
Necessary training for research and development	1. Types of research and formulation of problem statement and hypotheses 2. Experimental design and implementation 3. Statistical analysis of experimental data and interpretation of results 4. Testing and development 5. Development-based research
Multiunit organization and individually guided education	1. The context of American public education 2. Organizational structure and functions 3. Roles and responsibilities 4. Combination: organizational structures and functions—roles and responsibilities 5. Basic pattern of the multiunit elementary school 6. Pupil behavior 7. Qualifications of the teacher aide 8. Functions of the teacher aide 9. Role of the parent 10. Organization of the environment

Table 5-2. Context: Educational Technology

Major subject areas	*Topics*
Instructional media and mediated instruction	1. Selection and evaluation of materials 2. Design and construction of materials 3. Utilization of instructional materials 4. Learning resources center
Programmed instruction	1. Sources of instructional programs and program development information 2. Measurable behavioral objectives 3. Advantages and disadvantages 4. Instructional programs and instructional events 5. Principles of programmed instruction 6. Prompting 7. Learning tasks accomplished by programmed instruction 8. Student performance data 9. Teaching machines 10. Instructional program development and adaptation
Computer assisted instruction	1. Elements of a CAI system 2. Applications of a computer to instruction 3. Advantages and limitations of CAI 4. Pupil performance data 5. Development and revision of programs for a CAI system 6. Sources and evaluation of CAI systems and programs 7. Operation of equipment 8. Administration of a CAI system
Instructional simulation and academic games	1. Introduction 2. Selection 3. Utilization in instruction 4. Evaluation 5. Modification and design
Microteaching	1. Uses of microteaching and characteristics 2. Arrangement of the microteaching situation 3. Participation in microteaching
Research in educational technology	1. Preliminary study 2. Basing the system on research

Table 5-3. Context: Contemporary Learning-Teaching Process

Major subject areas	*Topics*
Cognitive domain	1. Theories of concept learning 2. Concept formation 3. Problem solving 4. Creativity
Affective domain	1. Attitudes and values 2. Personality integration
Social learning (including psycho-motor domain)	1. Social skills 2. Psychomotor skills
Basic behavioral operations	1. Reinforcement 2. Extinction 3. Punishment 4. Schedules of reinforcement
Contingency management	1. Premack principles 2. Successive approximations 3. Task and reinforcing event areas 4. Reinforcing event menu 5. Contract apron 6. Techniques for automatic contingency management generation 7. Contingency contracting 8. Progress checks
Self-management	1. Self-contracting 2. Contiguity principle applied to self-management 3. Elimination of undesirable behavior 4. Coverant control

Table 5-4. Context: Societal Factors

Major subject areas	*Topics*
Culture and cultural transmission	1. Enculturation 2. Culture, education, and curriculum 3. The impact of mass media 4. Discontinuity
Social stratification and social mobility	1. Social stratification and its effect on education 2. Social mobility 3. Methods of increasing social mobility

Table 5-4. Context: Societal Factors *(continued)*

Major subject areas	Topics
Demographic forces	1. Population growth 2. Geographic mobility 3. Population distribution
Cultural change	1. Cultural lag problems in the school 2. The expanding role of the school 3. Modification of educational processes by technology 4. Theories of social change 5. Response of education to sociocultural change
Social control	1. Roles within the school 2. Role of community pressure groups in control of education 3. Role of federal, state, and local government in control of education 4. Role of teacher organizations in control of education 5. Effect of religious control on education 6. Role of industry in control of education
Education as a social institution	1. Interactional patterns 2. Bureaucratic hierarchy 3. Career patterns of teachers 4. Differential standards that affect the status of the profession

Table 5-5. Context: Research

Major subject areas	Topics
Research reports	1. Evaluating a research report 2. Implementing the findings of a research report
Research on teacher education practices	1. Function and objectives of teacher education 2. Admission, retention, and recruitment in teacher education 3. Organization and administration of teacher education 4. Curriculum in teacher education

Table 5-5. Context: Research *(continued)*

Major subject areas	Topics
	5. Instruction and field experience in teacher education
	6. Development of the multiunit school
	7. Research on teaching
Research on teacher characteristics	1. Teacher characteristics
	2. Attitudes
	3. Values, interests, and favored activities
	4. Adjustment needs
	5. Personality factors
	6. Cognitive abilities
	7. Cross-cultural and cross-national characteristics
	8. Projective techniques
Research on teacher behaviors	1. Assessment of teacher behavior
	2. Interaction analysis
	3. Evaluation of teacher behavior
Media and innovations in teacher education	1. Providing efficient observation of classroom behavior
	2. Providing more efficient self-instruction and supervised practice experiences
	3. Providing a direct means of presenting teacher education courses
	4. Providing better standards of teacher performance
	5. Conducting basic research into teaching and learning processes

Educational specifications—the forerunners of what are now termed modules—were formulated to implement all behavioral objectives. Each specification consisted of (1) a behavioral objective (or objectives), (2) the treatment or activities to be utilized in accomplishing the objective, (3) the materials needed for the instructional process, and (4) evaluation procedures to determine whether the objectives had been achieved. Because of overlap, 818 specifications were able to accommodate all of the more than 2,000 behavioral objectives.

It is difficult for anyone who has not examined the original Ohio model report to comprehend the hundreds of educational specifications that were produced. A sample specification is provided in Table 5-6, which deals with the context Instructional Organization and the major subject area Necessary Training for Instruction. The topic considered is academic disciplines and skills—reading methodology.

Table 5-6. Sample Specification

Number: 1114

Context: Instructional Organization

Major Subject Area: Necessary Training for Instruction

Topic: Academic disciplines and skills—methodology (reading)

Target population: Preschool, elementary, inservice, college/university

Behavioral objectives: 2
  (1) The student will list the factors to be considered in adjusting instruction in reading to the individual differences in pupils.
  (2) The student will demonstrate that he understands the advantages of reading instruction using the flexible grouping plan and materials written on multiple levels of difficulty.

Treatment:
  The student will read to gain insight into techniques of diagnosing for specific reading strengths and weaknesses, using diagnostic results for differentiated instruction, and organizing the classroom to permit individual and small group teaching.
  The instructor will demonstrate the administration and use of diagnostic tests in reading and the student will practice their administration in identifying specific strength and weaknesses of each pupil.
  The student, in simulated teaching situations, will experiment with a variety of methods of grouping the classroom for differentiated instruction.

Materials:
  Heilman, A., *Principles and Practices of Teaching Reading;* Veatch, J., *Reading in the Elementary School.*
  The Gray Oral Reading Test. The Durrell Diagnostic Test of Reading Difficulties.

Evaluation:
  The student will listen to taped recordings of a child's oral reading and will record his specific difficulties in word attack skills and comprehension abilities. From diagnostic findings the student will indicate the type of instruction necessary for that child and how he will go about organizing such instruction.

The target populations for this specification are preservice preschool and preservice elementary teachers, inservice elementary teachers, and college and university instructors in educational methodology. There are two behavioral objectives, suggested treatment and materials are provided, and an evaluation procedure is suggested. This specification is much like our current instructional module except that the module ultimately included a pretest to see if students could achieve the behavioral objectives prior to instruction. The remaining components of the instructional module—activities, materials, and posttests—are much like the original specifications, which contained treatments, materials, and evaluation. Most of the original specifications were applicable to more than one target population, although some applied to only one population. The statements on treatment, materials, and evaluation were illustrative and were not intended to be the only techniques or sources that could meet the behavioral objective(s).

It was necessary to process the 818 specifications in some way to permit selection, ordering, and reordering according to the target population to be served. This was accomplished with a coding process, which condensed the major parts of each specification into an information form that could be contained on IBM cards and made possible the use of a computer to identify quickly desired specifications, as well as to provide summaries of information about them. Specifications pertaining to a particular target population, a context, a subject area, topic, treatment, type of evaluation or material could be collected rapidly. There was no prescribed way of ordering the specifications; they could be ordered by progressive difficulty of content, ease of administration, the use of a teaching method, or some other technique. It was and is possible to state general goals and specific objectives for particular instructional efforts, to determine the specifications that relate to these objectives, and to reorder or resequence them on the basis of whatever criterion the user wishes to apply.

The process of evaluation finally selected for the Ohio design was basically one of obtaining and providing information for continuous and systematic decision making. The evaluation design was comprehensive and versatile, offering a systematic context evaluation and ad hoc process and product evaluations. It has not been totally implemented and is still being modified.

All the model design effort took place within one year of receiving the original request for proposals. The model design finally produced was an attempt to bring the University of Toledo, the schools, and the community into numerous coalitions that would function cooperatively in a teacher training program. The university would have primary responsibility for the preservice training of potential teachers and paraprofessionals, and for the inservice training of its own faculty. The schools would have joint responsibility with the university for the inservice education of its teachers and administrators. All target populations in the model would be involved in extensive field work both in the schools and in the community, with the basic goal of relating all educational systems to the larger social system.

Certain basic assumptions are implicit in the Ohio model:

—Five conditions of life and education (i.e., contexts) are of major importance to teacher education.

—Modern teacher education must prepare teachers for the schools of the future, which we define as those employing a differentiated staff, team teaching elementary school organization. Students must receive their training under this type of school organization and practice.

—All elements or target populations in the educational system must be given appropriate and adequate training and retraining to the best degree possible in each situation, or there will be only limited, negligible change in teacher education curricula and elementary education programs.

—New and retrained teachers must receive intelligent and sympathetic support in the schools where they are placed to minimize risks of teacher failure and general educational unresponsiveness to change.

—The new program requires the development and utilization of individually guided education.

—Elementary teachers shall be prepared to specialize in one field (social studies, reading and language arts, mathematics, or science) and to generalize in the other three. Preschool teachers shall receive general preparation in the subject matter of elementary education.

—Teachers shall be instructed by, and taught to use, the most recent technological and media innovations.

—The new program shall apply behavioral modification as well as appropriate practices dictated by developmental psychology.

—The new program requires an awareness of the differences existing in society today.

—Teachers who complete the new program will know how to assess and modify their own teaching behavior and style.

—The new program will incorporate various levels of experience (e.g., simulation, games, role playing) in order to approximate more ideally the realities of teaching.

—The public schools are a vital part of the teacher education program.

—The university must be changed in ways conducive to the needs of the new program, and these changes shall precede all other activities.

—Teacher preparation is continuous. The time required for any candidate to complete the training program will depend only on satisfying the performance criteria.

Finally, the teacher education model must be self-renewing and constantly improving by the use of prompt, objective program feedback. Teacher education thus becomes a changing instead of a static process.

DETERMINING MODEL FEASIBILITY

The second USOE Bureau of Research request for proposals (RFP) was received in November 1968. It called for a feasibility study to determine whether or not the model designed in the Phase I effort could be implemented, and made two major requirements: (1) the proposals were to be addressed to estimating the resources, plans, and strategies necessary to carry out the major program of development of the Phase I program specifications selected; (2) projects were to provide estimates of the resources, plans, and strategies necessary for the implementation and sustained operation of the model design selected.

The major charge of the RFP was contained in the following statement:

It is imperative, then, that sufficient cost data be available to those institutions wishing to implement one of the programs or parts thereof, developed at the model institutions. These data should be available in the form which makes possible the rational consideration of alternative decisions, dependent upon alternate amounts of funds available. . . . The proposal [should] describe the procedures which might be used to produce such data, on development as well as implementation costs, with attention to those variables which might provide alternate cost estimates.[3]

The data were required for a five-year period of development to be associated with implementation.

The staff of the Ohio model project prepared a proposal and the University of Toledo was one of eight institutions that received a feasibility study grant. The other institutions receiving feasibility grants were Florida State University, Michigan State University, Syracuse University, the University of Georgia, the University of Massachusetts, the University of Wisconsin, and the Teacher Research Division of the Oregon State System of Higher Education, which assumed the feasibility efforts for the Oregon model design.

The Toledo feasibility project effort used a planned program budgeting systems approach (PPBS) and ascertained that a simulation of the Toledo model on a computer would best determine costs and time estimates. Procedures to estimate and relate the appropriate costs to each of the program components, and to allocate such costs to program development, program implementation, and sustained operation were clearly required. Also needed were procedures to establish costs on some particular basis, e.g., cost per student or costs per program unit, so that other institutions would be able to estimate the cost of operating the program. Finally, procedures to relate the actual cost of the program components to program effectiveness were considered.

The simulation process was given the following inputs:

1. Information on the amount of student time necessary to complete any portion of the Ohio model;

2. The cost of materials for that model;

3. The cost of faculty and other types of paid personnel necessary to carry out the instruction for the model;

4. Scheduling the model within a reasonable period of student time.

Phase II feasibility efforts were divided into four activity categories:

1. Preliminary procedures prior to specification analysis;

2. Specification analysis, simulated development, and cost of analysis considerations;

3. Specification eliminations, optimal program development, and simulation run;

4. Organizing and reporting simulation results.

The first activity of the project staff was to consider the ideas and elements of the other nine teacher education models (the University of Wisconsin model was not yet available), to determine which ideas or portions of them could be incorporated into the Ohio model. An extensive review of the original 818 specifications of the Ohio model was also undertaken. This resulted in deleting fifteen of the original specifications and writing sixty-three additional ones. The Ohio model finally was composed of 876 specifications.

The Ohio model had originally been developed as a consortium project consisting of the twelve state universities of Ohio. This consortium continued during the feasibility study and the members agreed to provide data about their particular institutions, including a university profile, information on public schools cooperating with the institution, facts about the region and community served by the university, existing programs of teacher education, and the facilities and equipment available for teacher education. Members of the consortium were further asked to provide personnel and cost data for the teacher education program at each institution; this information was needed so that cost analysis considerations developed for the feasibility study would reflect the situations for all Ohio institutions rather than for the University of Toledo alone. The final cost figures represented a hypothetical, "average" Ohio university and not any particular institution, although the data for all twelve could be supplied.

Procedures for Analysis

The analysis of specifications, development of the simulator, and cost analysis operations were expensive and time consuming. The first step was to develop procedures for specification analysis and costing, the principal purpose being to secure the necessary information for the computer to provide an adequately accurate estimation of cost and time for specific program options. To accomplish this task each specification was considered as a cost center and the necessary information was gathered specification by specification. Special forms recorded the many items of information for each specification. This effort was handled by the project staff and consultants and all 876 specifications were fully analyzed for input into the simulator.

Simulation

The New York Institute of Technology was at the same time developing a simulator that would receive and massage (i.e., process) the input data from the specification analysis. A simulator is simply a mathematical model of a limited aspect of a specified environment; as such, its outputs are only as valid as the theoretical design, the operating data, and the constraints on which it is based. Simulation provides the means by which numerous factors of a complex model can be assimilated into possible implementation (or other) patterns, and these patterns can in turn then be evaluated. The Ohio model lent itself uniquely to simulation because the specifications were by context, subjects, topics, etc., affording a well-defined basis for manipulation.

Computer-based simulation methods enabled the staff to consider and evaluate a wide range of possible patterns of implementation and operation, produced realistic cost estimates for these alternative patterns, and also provided the opportunity to tailor particular patterns to specified time, cost, and educational requirements.

Cost analysis considerations were also factors in specification analysis because the method and rationale had to be determined to estimate current and projected costs of Ohio institutions for overhead, plan, equipment, and personnel. Costs for equipment and how much was to be prorated over various specifications had to be determined. Various materials had to be costed and similarly prorated. The cost of personnel, faculty, and other paid personnel aiding faculty had to be determined and applied to each specification. Finally, a method for allocating plant and overhead costs per specification was devised. All of the above required careful attention to detail to obtain reasonable, accurate time and cost estimates

When all information was available and placed in the simulator, the decision had to be made as to which particular educational programs would be simulated. It was decided to simulate all the specifications applying to each of the six original target populations. These six operations were called the *optimal* instructional programs.

Simulation of each of the optimal programs yielded the maximum cost and time estimates when all specifications attached to the instruction of any particular target population were used. It was obvious that a number of *option* programs must be developed for each target population so that varying projections of time and cost requirements could be provided. The method used to develop option programs did not select certain specifications but rather took the entire body of specifications (for any particular population) and then eliminated specifications to reach programs that were less than optimal—essentially a process of eliminating specifications to reach various program options.

Elimination of Specifications

The procedure for specification elimination was based in part on empirical evidence and in part on a priori considerations, i.e., an empirical-judgment process of two steps. First, the topics in a context were rated in terms of priorities, which were used to eliminate specifications for that topic. Second, specifications within the topics were eliminated based on the priority ratings, cost, and time requirements. This process is represented in Figure 5-2. A panel for each of the five contexts was created, consisting of five well-known authorities identified with a particular context. The basic qualifications for a panel member were that (1) he must have knowledge of and understand the assumptions on which the model was based, (2) he must be familiar with the specifications, (3) he must be familiar with the position paper of the context in which the topics were to be rated. The panel members were provided with forms, and rated the topics in each context on the basis of explicit instructions on the mean of the ratings, the procedure, etc. A qualitative percentage of elimination with an upper limit was suggested for each rating. Copies of all forms and instructions and the names of the raters appear in the final report of the feasibility project.[4]

The ratings from the panel were returned to the project staff, who determined medians for each topic. Specifications under each topic were taken from the computer. At this point the staff attempted to eliminate specifications by considering the rating of the topic in which the specification occurred, the content of the specification, and its cost and time data. The priority ratings were primarily used to decide how many, rather than which, specifications to eliminate. There were certain constraints in this process; some specifications were prerequisites for others, and this influenced their elimination or retention. It was further determined that the process would only be

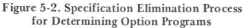

**Figure 5-2. Specification Elimination Process
for Determining Option Programs**

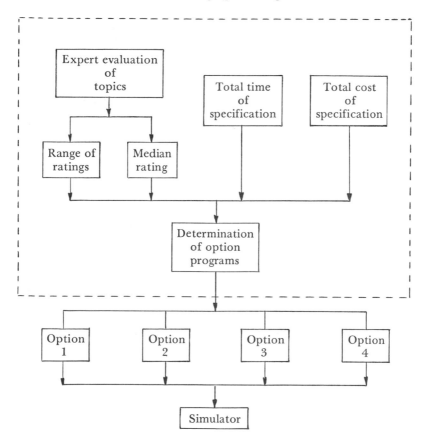

worth the effort if at least four option programs for each target population were created. Each option program was produced by reducing the number of specifications in the preceding option until finally a basic, *option four,* program was established for each population. The option four program was called the minimal program and included only those specifications absolutely necessary for any reasonable, constructive teacher education program.

The option two and option three programs were suboptimal but were, of course, supraminimal; the optimal programs—option one—

contained the most specifications and the minimal programs—option four—contained the fewest. Additional orientation programs for three inservice populations (college personnel, inservice teachers, and school administrators) were also developed and simulated in basically the same manner. The orientation programs were to provide a beginning point for all institutions implementing the Ohio model. From such programs institutions could branch out to meet their unique needs with special purpose efforts. The orientation represented a common programs base from which universities, within limits, could chart their own courses for teacher program development and implementation.

Feasibility of the Ohio Model

The basic question was whether the Ohio model was feasible in terms of time and cost restraints for the various target populations considered. It was found to be feasible in all respects, based on a potential five-year cost consideration for any Ohio university and assuming a population of 200 preservice full-time equivalent students. The average annual budget for any Ohio institution implementing the option four program was estimated at approximately $500,000 (in 1969 dollars), or $2,500,000 over five years. These figures assumed programs for the two preservice populations only. Program costs for supportive personnel plus more than one special purpose instructional program for inservice personnel would total approximately $1,682,000 over five years and would be recoverable from the special programs provided. The cost for developing and implementing an evaluation model to provide a management information system and evaluation process was estimated at $1,750,000, and this sum would have to be provided through securing outside development funds.

It is important to emphasize that the above sums apply to *all* costs (direct and indirect, and including development and implementation) for training or retraining all six target populations in the Ohio model. At the time these cost estimates were made, in terms of all applicable costs over a five-year period, approximately $1,300,000 was being budgeted for the baccalaureate education of 200 FTE preservice elementary education students at the University of Toledo. The Ohio model called for an additional fifth year internship; the additional year of enrollment, at the master's degree level, would increase Ohio university program contributions for 200 FTEs by approximately $720,000, making slightly more than $2,000,000 available. Obviously, in 1969 dollars, the cost of implementing and operating the Ohio model in terms of preservice training was feasible. Student and instructional staff time factors were also found to be feasible. The results of the feasibility study have been partially borne out in present efforts to implement and operate the program at the University of Toledo. Actual costs have been running below feasibility estimates.

The feasibility study demonstrated that it was possible to begin, in terms of cost, time, and personnel, a CBTE implementation project using the Ohio model at the University of Toledo. The feasibility process was completed on January 1, 1970. We were now ready for model implementation and organization efforts.

BEGINNING MODEL IMPLEMENTATION

The closing activity of the feasibility project was a conference attended by members of the national project steering committee, representatives from the twelve universities in the Ohio consortium, and school personnel from northwest Ohio schools where future model implementation efforts would in all likelihood occur. The conference discussed basic ideas for future model implementation with considerable outside funding possible from the U.S. Office of Education and other potential funding sources. On completion of the conference in February 1970, one of the conferees, Dr. Daniel U. Levine, director of the Center for the Study of Metropolitan Problems in Education at the University of Missouri-Kansas City, wrote the project director:

What struck me most forcefully at the meeting was the way in which the project now is so perfect an illustration-in-miniature of the problems facing society as a whole. More specifically, one of the major challenges for an industrial society is to master and utilize technology for desirable human purposes. But as industrial society becomes more complex, more and more structures of knowledge and organization pile one atop the other to form an artificial edifice that seems increasingly inauthentic and fake to large numbers of people. As this happens, technology is renounced as inhumane by larger numbers of people.

In a similar way, the technology of the model (i.e., the three volumes) gives us some hope of systematic improvement in teacher training but the plan itself becomes so large and imposing as to generate resistance and lack of understanding on these grounds alone. As was suggested at the conference, more "selling" may help some, but I think that the possibilities along this line are decidedly limited. If the technology is to take hold, it will have to have a demonstration of success—particularly in order to demonstrate that the purposes and results reflect not inhumaneness but its opposite.

Perhaps this is what bothered me most greatly about discussions concerning the utilization of parts of the model. Although I can see the appropriateness of a few efforts of this sort, at this point I feel that in general such fragmentation will lead to discrediting rather than to proving the model. The parts most likely to be picked up are those on instructional organization; here I fear that the quantifiers and/or the verbalizers will run away with the ball game during a decade when the schools are in danger of collapse under the weight of inappropriate purposes and curricula. Conversely, some others may focus primarily on social context or on contemporary learning process, but without the instructional organization and technology their efforts will tend to perpetuate a history of good intentions and ineffectual outcomes.

Therefore, it seems to me extremely important that the model as a whole (including the data and evaluation components) be given a fair test.

Dr. Levine had clearly indicated the awesome but fascinating task ahead of us. A fair test of the model dictated a full implementation effort.

The University of Toledo is a state-supported, urban university with approximately 15,000 students. Its four-year teacher education program culminates in a bachelor of education degree. The College of Education is the largest collegiate unit in the university, with about 4,000 undergraduate and graduate students. Its full-time faculty of 104 persons is the second largest college faculty in the university. The college has close working relationships with public schools in the area. The college Center for Educational Research and Services (CERS) is the principal unit through which college and public and private school district cooperative working relationships function. The college faculty comprises a young and vigorous group of professionals, many of whom have been involved in the developmental activities in establishing multiunit schools and designing the Ohio teacher education program.

The Ohio model provided the components and potential operation of a systems-oriented, competency-based teacher education effort. However, the model design did not offer a blueprint on how to implement such a model teacher education program; it provided the specifications but did not inform anyone as to how, exactly, to utilize them. The problem was basically twofold. First, the specifications (which would become the basis for instructional modules) were available for all aspects of a model teacher education program, but a great deal of effort would be needed to put these specifications into an educational organization pattern and teachable operation over a period of time. Secondly, it was clear that until the users of the model specifications had internalized them through personal experiences with further model development, all that had been written on "how to do it" with suggested procedures, rationales, etc., was likely to remain just that. The persistent problems plaguing those who would try to change teacher education were not eliminated by a model design process. If model implementation was to succeed, means would have to be found for potential users of new processes to become actually involved with them.

It shortly became apparent that the massive outside funding once contemplated for USOE models' implementation would not be forthcoming, that any real implementation effort would have to be locally supported and sustained. The Ohio model feasibility study had clearly indicated that Ohio model operation costs, once the implementation process was completed, should be within or only slightly more than funds then available for the operation of the traditional teacher education program at the University of Toledo. Having come this far, the faculty and administration of the College of Education at the University of Toledo decided to implement their CBTE model. The implementation effort would be piecemeal, in that the first "course" of the new model program would be introduced to teacher education students in September 1971. Further development would continue over a three-year period until the entire program was serving all elementary education students in the university.

Anyone attempting to initiate and implement a competency-based teacher education curriculum should be reminded of an old educational adage: "Telling isn't teaching." Nor is telling implementing. There is very limited personnel activity in the implementation of a model elementary teacher education program if one is only told about it. College personnel, school teachers and administrators, even college students, all have the ability to sabotage a program they don't believe in, and especially one that they fail to understand by only hearing and not doing anything about it. The initial faculty developmental-implementation efforts with the Ohio elementary model ran into this difficulty.

Our first effort in so-called implementation was actually

dissemination of the program concept. Through a series of faculty retreats and meetings, college administration and the model developers told faculty members, school personnel, and others about the model's rationale, content, and organization. They were told how important the project was to their institution and how the institution had a great opportunity to adopt or adapt the model. The "tellers" in this case forgot that educational personnel at all levels have had a long history of "doing their own thing"; they have been accustomed to deciding things for themselves, although sometimes this autonomy has resulted in duplication of course content, serious omissions in the instructional program, inadequate utilization of teaching methodology, and so on. We learned all over again that a logical, telling approach to the Ohio model program was a clear invitation to inaction. Time was wasted but we better understood something about poor and good educational strategy.

The strategy that emerged was based on the premise that people in general and educators in particular will help to support innovation or change if they believe they are in some way responsible for the change. Although a number of faculty members had been involved in the design of the new teacher education model, some were still skeptical and not fully committed to all the assumptions on which the model was based. The strategy then became one of getting all faculty members (as well as students) who were interested in teacher education change to organize and conduct the necessary effort to implement the Ohio elementary model at the University of Toledo.

A series of meetings was organized for interested faculty members and others on the problem of developing a system to organize needed implementation efforts. A member of the curriculum and teaching department wrote a position paper on implementation, clearly pointing out the need to develop a process system for organizing and operating implementation efforts. On the basis of this input and three two-hour meetings, a process system for implementation was created and presented to the faculty. The process system produced is graphically presented in Figure 5-3 as a flow chart, which represents the implied general flow of model implementation activities and communication. One might ask, "Is that a system?" Fundamentally, a system is nothing more than a way by which input is processed to develop output. In this case *input* consisted of information, concerns, factors, components—anything needed in the process of developing and implementing the model program. *Process* was really a series of processes, in appropriate sequence, to achieve the desired output; it was the means by which educational thinking, organization, development, and implementation were conceived, elaborated on, and put into final form for action and use. *Output* was the product, or the accomplishment of process.

**Figure 5-3. A Process Model for Program Development
and Implementation**

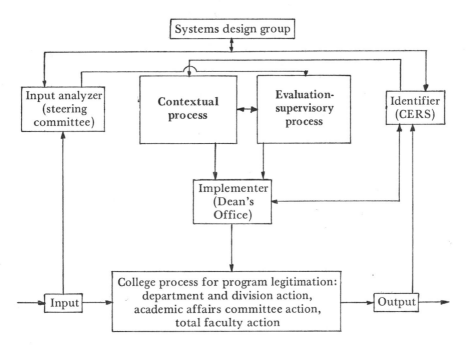

The flow chart in Figure 5-3 is an elaboration of the basic process system used by the University of Toledo to achieve continued model development and implementation. This system emphasized the task description of each of various groups of individuals utilized in the various system positions or components. The arrows indicate the major channels of communication and system movement from component to component. These components will be described and analyzed.

When one looks at the heart of the system—the process portions—there are really two fundamental processes that were considered in the development-implementation effort: the contextual process and the evaluation-supervisory process. All activities of the system were first divided into these two parts.

What was the contextual process? The word *contextual* came from the Ohio model design, which consisted of five instructional contexts: (1) instructional organization, (2) educational technology, (3) learning-teaching process, (4) societal factors, and (5) research. Each context consisted of major subjects, subdivided into topics around which were created educational specifications (beginning modules) of instruction to achieve the desired behavioral objectives for the respective topics and subjects. Thus the contextual process became one of further developing, modifying, or eliminating existing educational specifications in the Ohio model and creating new modules that would become the instructional packages for each context. The modules so created needed sequencing, yearly placement, and general conversion into instructional packages that consisted of course content, delivery systems, plus the application of student credit hours, which could all be coordinated into a total program. The contextual process allowed faculty members and students to work with the specifications in the original design, to change and modify them, to create new specifications when necessary, and then to organize them into usable instructional units. They had full opportunity to become completely immersed in adopting, adapting, amending, or creating workable modules of instruction for a potential five-year teacher education program.

To enable an efficient allocation of faculty and student resources and time, a rough matrix was organized that contained the twenty-six subject areas, or cells, in the five contexts over the five years of program time. This matrix produced 130 cells, with some cells blank because not all subject areas dealt with every year of instruction. Faculty and students selected the particular cell (or cells) in the matrix where they most wished to participate, and were then provided with the existing educational specifications allocated to that cell on the basis of previous model design research effort conducted during the feasibility study. The task of each faculty or student member or faculty-student group in a cell was to develop, from the specifications provided and other identified needs, a program component or complete program package of instructional modules for a particular topic and subject for a particular year (or years) in the total program.

Continuity of program organization was attempted through informing cell members of what other cell groups were achieving at a particular topic and subject level. Continuity was also enhanced when individuals worked in more than one cell within the overall matrix. Cell workers were provided with a set of guidelines (a list of tentative assumptions similar to those mentioned in Chapter 3) about the program, which further aided the coordination and continuity effort believed necessary to achieve programmatic development. Thus, faculty members and students were involved for the first time in the development of the instructional program through the context process effort.

The *evaluation-supervisory process* was not as clearly defined as was the context process. The reason for this was that the Ohio elementary model contained a theoretical construct of an evaluation-management-information (EMI) system that needed much additional development to become operational. Also, the original model specifications were limited to suggested general evaluation procedures for instructional activities. Faculty members who had given time and effort to designing the evaluation-management-information (EMI) model were asked to continue their work in terms of creating a usable EMI system for the overall program. This effort was thought complementary to the contextual process in terms of providing the specific evaluation techniques and tools necessary to determine if instructional and programmatic objectives were achieved as well as providing all feedback necessary for such achievement.

The component labeled *input analyzer* became what some referred to as a steering committee, a group of selected faculty members and students who had the task of searching out all information provided to the system in terms of input and transmitting this information to the proper process group or groups. They acted as an external sensor for the entire system. As well as initially screening any input for the system, they found what was available for it, such as potential teaching materials, student characteristics, etc. They developed system guidelines. Any matter needing consideration by the entire system was of concern to the input analyzers. In summary, they determined what was available, what was needed, and where in the system essential information should be input for further consideration.

The original *identifier* of the system was the college Center for Educational Research and Services (CERS), and was concerned mainly with the internal state of the system and the output coming from the process components. Thus, the identifier had the major function of keeping the process teams, the input analyzers, and the implementer aware of and knowledgeable about the internal condition and performance of the system. Awareness of performance in time came to involve a comparison of actual system output with expected output; the results were transmitted by the identifier back to the proper process personnel teams for further consideration or sent to the implementer for action.

The *implementer* of the system utilized the information or products coming from the process groups and/or identifier and initiated the actual process of legitimizing and implementing the changes recommended or decisions made. The implementer further aided the system by having all conditions available and ready for the implementation of any change that was finally desired by the system. At Toledo, the implementer was the Office of the Dean, which had the responsibility of operating and supervising the total teacher education program.

Systems design had the function of keeping aware of the condition of the complete system and each subsystem through contact with the identifier and input analyzer. The systems design group was composed of two faculty members familiar with systems theory and program planning. Their task was to adjust or change the system to compensate for systems stress, tension, inadequacy, or changed conditions to keep the system operating satisfactorily.

MODIFYING INSTITUTIONAL ORGANIZATION AND OPERATIONS FOR MODEL IMPLEMENTATION

The process system for Ohio model implementation was put into operation in the fall quarter, 1970. For the first few months all went reasonably well and according to plan. However, problems of one type and another arose that ultimately resulted in a modification of the process for moving college personnel toward model implementation and operation. Again, the lesson was clear that no system is fixed or complete in its conception and operation. It must remain constantly modifiable and adaptable to external conditions, inner concerns, and feedback.

The Evaluation-Supervisory Process Committee began its work by obtaining further information on faculty perceptions of competency-based teacher education and the roles faculty members were to play in the implementation of programs. Questionnaires and interviews were employed, with the following results:

—A limited number of faculty members had a total, complete view and conception of all of the components of the Ohio model elementary teacher education design. Most faculty members had partial knowledge of the program. It was evident that there would be difficulty in the integration of all aspects of the program on which faculty were working, especially when it became necessary for a faculty member to go outside his own field of interest and expertise.

—Faculty members were concerned about decision-making processes in program development and implementation. Confusion was developing on faculty roles and responsibilities. It was not clear that faculty members enrolled in a particular development-implementation phase of the program would also be enrolled in the further operation of that program phase. Faculty opportunity for contributions to the decision-making process concerning each element within the system was not clear.

—There were expressions of a lack of confidence in ability to participate and work effectively with a new program design, especially when it differed so greatly from the program then in operation.

—Sufficient up-to-date information and feedback were not being consistently provided to all faculty members involved. Some concerns went unanswered, increasing fear of program change.

—The faculty realized that they were assuming the task not only of helping to develop and implement a new program, but that they were doing this in addition to their normal work responsibilities. In effect, the faculty would be developing and implementing the program on their own time.

—It was apparent that the faculty was still willing to expend the additional effort required to establish a competency-based program, even under the above circumstances.

The Ohio model design was originally based on the assumption that initial implementation would likely be aided by funding outside the regular annual college budget. This would have made it possible to free key faculty for instructional development and implementation, and to hire additional faculty where special areas of expertise were indicated. As 1971 progressed, it became apparent that additional funds would be quite limited or not available. This made necessary some modifications in the implementation process.

The input analyzer committee contributed useful information to the implementation process, and two of its contributions were of great importance in terms of system modification.

First, the committee adopted a position paper on revisable systems. This paper stated that, given existing college resources and the enormity of the program development task, the process system generated for program development was not ideal; the work being done was valuable but there was danger of good faculty effort being lost because of the absence of an objective-means-criterion connection to help prevent such loss. The context process groups were concentrating their energies more on the treatment or means of accomplishing various program objectives and less on further refining the behavioral objectives and developing criteria for determining how and when to accomplish the objectives. If valid criterion items for the objectives could be developed, it would then be possible to make an objective-means-criterion connection, which should (1) provide each faculty member with the necessary information for revising those modules of instruction that he was responsible for and (2) ensure that such improvements would not be lost to the system when a faculty member finished his assigned task and left it.

The basic recommendation was that individual faculty efforts be concentrated more on the refinement of behavioral objectives and the development of assessment criteria than on the "means" for accomplishing objectives, which could just as easily be left to individual professors at some later date. The paper further stated that a major characteristic of a systems approach was that a system should always lend itself readily to revision. If it were to function adequately, the process system must be revisable and open to change.

The second major contribution of the input analyzer committee was its belief that the new teacher education program would probably have difficulty in expanding rapidly to a five-year effort. Instead, all professional education should continue within a four-year time span, with the bulk of the professional education modules confined to the final two years of the program. The first two years would be concerned only with student decisions on teacher education careers, and a student would not be formally admitted to the teacher education program until the beginning of the third year. A fifth year was still considered but principally as a field experience internship with the hope that this program extension could develop over time.

The emphasis on program change and implementation of a model elementary teacher education program soon confronted the faculty with a major responsibility for secondary teacher education. Accordingly, the secondary teacher education faculty, under the leadership of the chairman of the Department of Secondary Education, announced that they too wished to develop a competency-based approach to teacher education. They were organized into various process groups, first to develop and then to implement their own model of competency-based teacher education, which would of necessity incorporate many aspects of the elementary model design. This decision in effect doubled the task of development.

Faculty members early agreed that although the original Ohio model design specifications were a good beginning, they were imperfect in several respects: (1) some of the specification objectives were not stated behaviorally, (2) means for accomplishing the objectives were not always adequate, (3) assessment means in terms of pre and posttests were completely absent, and (4) the relationship among objectives was not always clear in terms of their scope and sequence, and finally, (5) the specifications were not in the proper module form (see Chapter 3), which is necessary for implementing a competency-based program.

Problems of logistics and continuity came up early in the attempted implementation of the program. While individuals in small groups accepted responsibilities, their regular duties made it difficult to coordinate their efforts with others. It was not always possible for committees to meet as often as needed, and the lack of frequent contact meant that when groups *did* reconvene time was lost reorienting the members. Inevitably, there were misunderstandings regarding previous agreements. Also, because of the lack of communication, individuals and groups unknowingly duplicated each others' efforts.

As frustration grew, it was increasingly clear that the structure of the implementation system needed modification to provide the related functions of coordination and communication in a more personal and compact way. The context process groups working on module development were independent of each other and somewhat isolated; they received directives but not personal, supportive direction from the input analyzers, the identifier, and the systems design personnel.

As the academic year of 1970-71 came to a close, it was generally recognized that the implementation effort was not functioning properly. Progress was being made in module development for the five contextual areas and a first course called "career decisions"—to help college students objectively determine whether they wished to become teachers—was taking shape. However, faculty working in contextual process groups did not relate the various parts of the model to the whole enterprise and to the ways in which the results of their work would affect their own classrooms and student outcomes.

The implementers of the process system held meetings with various personnel in the process groups, as well as with the input analyzers and identifier. Decisions were made to modify the process system and to make personnel changes in certain groups.

The process system originally called for a direct, close relationship between individuals assigned to the contextual process and those in the evaluation-supervisory process. However, the two groups had in effect become one, with attention totally directed toward program-course-module implementation. Evaluation could not be separated from the instructional process, and became part of it. To solve this problem, personnel from the evaluation-supervisory process group joined reorganized context process committees. The development of an overall evaluation-management-information system was temporarily put aside, until instructional program concerns could be met. The first concern of evaluation became those efforts (pre and post-tests or other procedures) connected with the building of instructional modules.

Personnel changes in the process system consisted of replacing the two members of the systems design group with the chairman of the Department of Educational Technology and Media. This person was to assume major leadership in model implementation. He and the chairmen of the departments of elementary and secondary education became an ad hoc committee for context-evaluation process coordination and communication; they took over the leadership and supporting roles needed for the activities of the various process groups, and were called systems process coordinators. They reorganized the subsystems (process groups) within the larger implementation system into two basic units—elementary and secondary program developmental-implementation efforts. Their goal was to begin actual program implementation with a CBTE course on career decisions for freshmen and sophomores in the fall quarter, 1971; to have all juniors in a competency-based program starting in September 1972; and to achieve full program implementation for all undergraduate students with the opening of the 1973-74 academic year.

It was also decided to replace the original process system identifier (Center for Educational Research and Services) with a curriculum committee consisting of the directors of the four instructional divisions of the college and the college dean. The task of the identifier would remain the same as originally defined but with more emphasis on the review of process group output. It was clear that the division directors had a greater relationship to new program implementation than the original identifier. The process system input analyzer committee was retained and asked to relate closely to the new system coordinators.

Some time had been lost, but we had not abandoned our schedule in terms of program outcomes or the expected dates of actual program operations.

The new coordinators very early adopted the role of facilitators rather than directors, interpreted as incorporating the following functions:

1. To provide information to individuals and groups working on the model;

2. To develop and maintain a sequence of tasks required to accomplish the model implementation;

3. To develop alternative strategies for accomplishing the different tasks;

4. To anticipate problems in the model's implementation and to develop solutions (trouble-shooting); and

5. To resolve conflicts between groups responsible for implementation by bringing the conflicting parties together with appropriate decision makers.

These functions proved appropriate for the coordinators. They also proved extremely difficult to carry out. Consider, as an example, the function of providing information. The coordinators initially decided that it was important to provide all faculty with all the information about the program's development and implementation. However, they soon discovered two limiting factors. First, the only way other faculty members could become as cognizant of the model's many ramifications as were the coordinators, was for the faculty to spend a comparable amount of time on the model. And second, even less information proved to be an overload for some of the faculty, who were already inundated with data from their regular responsibilities and personal interests. The effect was to discourage the individual faculty member. The flood of information, without sufficient time for analysis, gave faculty members an impression that the college had taken on an impossible task. At this point the coordinators modified their information-dispensing function and decided to provide only that information the coordinators deemed necessary for completion of the tasks assumed by the individuals and groups working on the model.

As an important strategic corollary to curtailing the complete dissemination of information, the coordinators agreed to provide any and all model information on request. Carrying out this function was most difficult. Many errors of judgment were made by the coordinators in selecting appropriate information for the groups, and continual mending of fences was required throughout development and implementation of the model. However, the willingness of the coordinators to provide additional information when queried *did* prove valuable in maintaining faculty confidence in the role played by the coordinators.

Another structural change in the implementation model—necessitated by lack of funding, time, and personnel—resulted from the decision to retain the new college organizational structure for the implementation phase: the offices of dean, division director, and department chairman became key components in future model operations. It seemed both unreasonable and impractical to assign new units when it would not be possible to provide them with either the authority or the control of resources necessary to carry out their function. The deans and the division directors serve the dual functions of advising the coordinators and, with faculty division, committee, or meeting approval, of legitimizing coordinator and faculty decisions. In the initial stages of model implementation, the department chairmen were the most helpful of the groups; they controlled the faculty's time in their departments, and their understanding and cooperation were essential. The coordinators met with chairmen regularly during the 1971-72 academic year. Developmental tasks were worked out in this group, with each of the chairmen accepting selected tasks to be completed by their respective departments.

The major modification was more philosophical than structural, although it had important structural implications. Our limited resources must obviously affect the quality and the quantity of program development and implementation, and it was clearly impossible for our faculty to carry out the development, implementation, and assessment that were ideally required. In fact, even the *minimal* requirements for a valid competency-based program could not be accomplished in any reasonable time prior to implementation. Given our resources and personnel limitations, the program's development and implementation would have required several years, if we adhered to the system's rules for developing an instructional program. Such a period of time with our piecemeal production capability, and the usual attrition of faculty, was sure to create continuity and morale problems.

Our studied consensus was that it was not possible to come up with a tested, systematically developed program prior to full implementation. And yet we were convinced that, if we were to move beyond orthodoxy, it would be necessary to have a system whose effects were measurable, and which was revisable on the basis of objective data. This meant that there must be a clear match between behavioral objectives, the means for accomplishing those objectives, and the criteria for determining if the objectives had been met. Also, the program objectives must be placed in logical sequence so that the effects of prerequisite and successor modules could be studied. In short, a mechanism that would assure continuous assessment and revision was needed. While there currently exist many theoretical schemes and paper models for the development and implementation of instruction, they have either not been put to the test, or have been used in instructional microcosms where neither the number of variables nor the intensity of concern associated with implementation were dealt with.

We resolved our dilemma by formulating a system whose elements, in the main, were not original, but whose synthesis we believe to be unique: a *system of successive approximations*. After clearly delineating the functions and outcomes of the desired program, we would accept imperfect alternatives that approximated the ideal, with the condition that such approximations would be subject to continuous revision towards the ideal. For example, it would have been most desirable to have our program objectives stated operationally, sequentially, and hierarchically, and matched with appropriate learning and taxonomic categories. But our system permitted us to settle, initially, for objectives that included only the Magarian criteria[5] for performance statement, i.e., conditions under which objectives will be met and means of assessment. However, we then developed a schedule to bring these objectives to the ideal state by "successive approximations."

Our first revision, following the first cycle of modules, would be to discriminate between terminal and enabling objectives. After the second cycle the objectives would be matched with taxonomic categories[6] (Bloom et al.) and, where objectives for important taxonomic categories had been omitted, new objectives would be written and incorporated into the program. After the third cycle the objectives would be matched with appropriate learning conditions as stated by Gagné.[7] This process would continue cycle after cycle, until the objectives to carry out all the elements of the program were in the best possible state. This necessitated a philosophical value change for many of our faculty.

The traditional teaching-learning system in which most of us learn and work is predicated on the concept of "closure." That is, once a student or faculty member has finished a segment of instruction, and grades have been given and received, there is a silent agreement that follow-up is unnecessary. The tendency toward closure has resulted in compartmentalized, isolated learning that educators and students alike have long deplored, but have had little or no success in changing. A major reason for this unhappy state of affairs was the lack of, and the inability to develop, adequate assessment instruments to measure learning effects of a particular instruction. In essence, an agreement was implied between teacher and student that the teacher would evaluate on the basis of his superior intuition, resulting from his accumulated experiences in combination with some normative, referenced grading technique. Of course, little else was possible as long as an operational match between objectives, means, and criteria was lacking. But, if (1) teachers and students had clear statements of the objectives of the instruction for which they were responsible, (2) the objectives were individually tied to a specific means for teaching the objective, and (3) objective and means were matched with criterion items for determining how adequately the student had learned the desired instruction, then "closure" could be replaced with meaningful follow-up, remediation, and program revision.

To begin to look at program elements and to see the learning derived from those elements as being "never finished," requiring continual revision and reintegration within the learner, is a necessary outcome of a systematically developed, competency-based program. A number of techniques were and are being instituted to break the habit of closure, including the continuous feedback of assessment data to both students and faculty. Matching objectives, means, and criteria does much to make the instructional and learning process visible and provides direction for learner remediation and program revision.

Our system of successive approximations was clearly dependent on the maintenance of an objective assessment system, on adequate feedback mechanisms, and on continuous revision procedures. Much work has already been done toward formation of these components. In their present state, these components also represented "successive approximations." We finally came to recognize that not only was the original implementation structure a successive approximation, but in all likelihood the revision of our current, modified implementation structure will only be an approximation of the ideal state. Few absolutes should be recognized in education. We now understand that the accelerated change that affects all our institutions will continue to affect our implementation structures as well.

PROGRAM ELEMENTS TO BE IMPLEMENTED

Three major clusters of modules have been developed for the Ohio model CBTE program and either have been or are being implemented.

The first cluster of modules, the Career Decisions Program, resulted from the long-time observation of teacher educators, reflected in the original Ohio model specifications, that education students do not have sufficient information to make an objective decision about becoming a teacher until very late in their studies. Many enter a teaching program because of some idealized or misinformed image of teaching, and may not discover until just before graduation that they do not really want to teach. Despite this discovery, many of the disillusioned remain in teaching, to their own detriment as well as that of their students. By graduation the commitment to the idea of being a teacher, and the investment of time and money, make it difficult to begin again in another field.

The Career Decisions Program (CDP), which all freshmen or sopho-mores interested in becoming teachers must take, is designed to aid the teacher-candidate in making an objective determination about whether to choose teaching as a career. The CDP provides the student with observation and decision-making skills to (1) determine if he wants to become a teacher; (2) select an area of interest from among the many teaching fields; (3) look in some depth at the field of his interest. This field-centered program went through one full cycle—an academic year—before implementation of the other teaching program module clusters.

The second module cluster contained the objectives for preparing elementary teachers. Many of these modules were derived from the specifications originally developed in the Ohio Model Elementary Teaching Program. The original context areas were instructional organization, educational technology, societal factors, contemporary learning-teaching processes, and educational research. While these areas retained their importance, they were no longer regarded as separate entities, but were integrated within a systematic framework.

To a lesser degree, the module cluster designed to prepare secondary teachers originated in the original elementary model specifications. However, to a greater extent than the elementary modules, a larger proportion of them were developed independently of these specifications.

Partly as a means of maintaining the flexibility of the program, and partly to protect academic freedom, the faculty ruled that 65 to 70 percent of the objectives taught within a cluster of modules would remain constant. The other 30 to 35 percent of the objectives in the cluster could be determined by the individual professors and students. The faculty believed that if 70 percent of the instruction (called core objectives) was kept constant, this would be sufficient to ensure continuity and the prerequisite behaviors would be taught. The other 30 percent allows the instructor and his students sufficient time to deal with unique and different interests. It is expected that many of the objectives developed within the independent 30 percent could replace some of the core objectives in the constant 70 percent, if the faculty perceived them as more valuable.

The Effect of External Resources

Previously in this chapter we noted that funds were not available to finance development and implementation of the optimal (ideal) proposed competency-based program. Adoption of the system of successive approximations has made it possible to move toward complete implementation. With a few exceptions, this has been done with little other than the budget allocated to continue the old program. These exceptions, which consisted of a grant from the Sears Foundation ($10,000) and two grants from the U.S. Office of Education ($15,000 and $25,000), were important to our program's continued development and implementation.

The Sears funds were used primarily to set up conditions for faculty members to work together on program problems. USOE funds were also used for this as well as to plan the operation of teacher centers and other developmental activities. As noted earlier, the coordinators saw a principal task to be facilitation of communication among task groups. While much of the needed communication was managed by written memos and personal meetings between the coordinators and faculty, it did not provide the critical mass of information or concentrated involvement needed to reach consensus on complicated issues. Nor were communication efforts of the coordinators, or the brief small group meetings on campus, sufficient to provide the esprit that would give the affective sense of belonging to an important effort to change education. The constant interruptions and requirements of regular responsibilities made each meeting on campus difficult, and as a result work was often transitory. The Sears Foundation and USOE funds made it possible for groups to leave campus to deal with specific tasks. The length of these "retreats" varied from a half-day to three days, and group size varied from four or five persons to the entire faculty.

The first full faculty retreat was about inservice retraining of faculty, a critical affective component in our change process. Our goals and objectives made it necessary that we, as a faculty, reorganize our formal and informal interpersonal communications processes. We were suffering the traditional separation imposed by a departmental structure. The communication between departments and disciplines was minimal. There was evidence that this lack of cross-discipline communication resulted in such problems as similarities in course content, contradictory data provided to students on psychology of learning and the appropriateness of teaching strategies, and competition for resources among departments. Departmental isolation and its resultant duplication of efforts was not only wasteful of monetary resources but it also limited essential intellectual interchange.

The purpose of the first retreat was to seek agreement about (1) the goals of a new teacher education program; (2) the organizational structure of the faculty for achieving the goals; (3) the decision-making process to be used in the planning and implementation stages of the new program; and (4) due dates for completion of tasks. In addition, it was intended that the retreat should serve the social function of maximizing faculty interpersonal interaction. While satisfactory headway was made in getting faculty agreement on the concerns listed above, the more important result of our task orientation was the *process* of interacting. Faculty members expressed the feeling that working together as a unit, rather than in departmental or contact groupings, was a more desirable and useful way of proceeding. For some this was the first time that they had worked with colleagues from units other than their own, and many commented that their perceptions of others had been erroneous and evinced a desire to continue working in a team relationship.

An open atmosphere and a common commitment not apparent before was created by the first retreat. There was not complete agreement on all matters, but there was an agreement *openly* to disagree, to confront each other publicly, and to settle differences through discussion. The faculty also agreed to engage in interdisciplinary teaching, individualized instruction, and to provide competency-based instruction for students.

The other two full-faculty retreats were equally useful. Among the tasks carried out at these retreats were the writing of modules, construction of criterion instruments, consideration of the implementation program's relation to the public schools, selection of schools for field components of our modules, and the movement from developmental to instructional teams. The shorter retreats served a variety of purposes, but primarily the continued production and refinement of modules. Any group seeking to develop and implement a similar program would find it most profitable to get personnel away from campus responsibilities for a time.

Student Adjustment to the Model

Because of limited resources, the college could not support parallel programs, that is, we had neither the personnel nor the resources to run two programs at the same time. Therefore, rather than phasing in gradually, we decided to drop the old program and replace it with the new program, with the exception of student teaching, beginning in fall 1972. A few of the old courses were continued temporarily for students nearing graduation and to satisfy commitments to part-time students, but for the majority of our students the new program completely replaced the old.

The literature about change repeatedly reminds us that attempted change in established procedure will almost always generate some resistance. Although students, like faculty, criticize the old system of preparing teachers, it is after all a system in which they have known some success. They have found ways to cope with or to beat the system. We reasoned that resistance to the new program could be reduced if anxiety and dissonance created by the unfamiliar could be reduced through reorientation. During spring quarter 1972, a comprehensive preregistration meeting with all elementary and secondary teacher candidates was held in which professors met in large and small groups to answer student questions and to allay fears. Students who were not able to attend the preregistration meeting had to make appointments to meet with a faculty member individually to get the needed information.

Program planners anticipated that more difficult problems would arise after students entered the program. A competency-based instructional program has certain built-in controls that prevent students and faculty alike from practicing habits considered undesirable by learning specialists. For example, a student in a competency-based program cannot proceed until he has met the criteria for the behaviors in the module he is currently working on. This makes explicit the need for recycling parts of a module, and the need for alternative strategies for accomplishing behaviors. It also points up the difficulty of mass instruction when the instruction is competency-based. While the first exposure to instruction might carry students along at a common pace, after the first criterion instrument is taken obvious differences in competency become apparent. Most of the students will have met the minimal requirements for all the competencies in a module, others may lack competency in one or two of the module's behaviors, while a few students may fall below the level of mastery on several behaviors. The time required for students to correct their deficiencies will vary, and in the meantime those who were successful will have gone on to other modules. With competency as a requirement mass instruction becomes more and more difficult and individualized instruction becomes increasingly more important.

Individualized, personalized instruction was of course the ideal for our system of successive approximations, but our first approximation necessarily fell far short of that ideal. Our closest approximation during the first year was through a self-instructional laboratory. An increasing number of modules and parts of modules were being put in a self-instructional mode, but during the first cycle the majority of the modules were taught in a conventional classroom setting. Because of the relatively short length of the modules and the frequency of assessment, coupled with rapid feedback of information to student and faculty, it was anticipated that the need to recycle students would be reduced considerably. Nevertheless, in the conventional setting it was still a major problem.

Such cognitive and logistical problems in turn caused affective problems. For both psychological and pragmatic reasons it was important that the student view the new program favorably. A number of plans were in operation to maintain a high student affect. The major plan involved a close relationship between the student and a faculty adviser, who was one of the team members responsible for teaching the modules. This meant that he was familiar with all aspects of the modules. While this fact made his advice more valuable, the effect was considerably increased by the assessment feedback system, which told him almost daily how well his advisee was doing. He received such information as what module the student was currently working on, what modules he had to repeat, what objectives he was having difficulty with, the amount of student time spent on modules, and with what professor and on what team he was working at a given moment. This enabled the adviser to act before problems accumulated to overwhelm the student.

For the first cycle it was the responsibility of the individual advisers to set up conditions of remediation. This did not necessarily imply that the adviser would have to instruct the student in objectives he had failed to master, although he could do so. When the module was in a self-instructional mode, he could advise the student to repeat the portions of the module concerned with the behaviors the student did not master. In cases where the student was taught by a professor, the adviser might get recommendations from him as to an alternative strategy to help the student master the remaining objectives, or the adviser and the student could work out their own alternative.

Equally important were that the adviser congratulate the student on completing a module successfully, and that he deal with students who, although successfully mastering the behaviors of the instruction, were still displeased with the competency-based program. For example, our competency-based program had built in the requirement that students increasingly make decisions rather than be given answers by teachers. Any professor who has attempted to incorporate inquiry into his instructional strategy is familiar with the student complaint that "if he wanted to learn by himself he would have stayed home." He has paid to hear what the knowledgeable expert has to say. Often, many hours were required to bring the student to the point where he could objectively evaluate such a decision-making mode. We think it was well worth it, not only for the continued favorable attitude it engendered, but for the benefit to our advisee's future students—public school pupils—as well.

Visible Instructional Process

We were depending on the visibility of the implementation process and on the accountability resulting from publicizing the expected specific program outcomes to enhance student acceptance. In fact, we were hopeful that such exposure would provide our students with exciting insights to the instructional process that were impossible under the old program. We also relied a great deal on the effect of practicing educational strategies rather than telling about them.

Testing

Testing, with all its associations, represented another possible source of negative affect. Students in the new program did have an advantage over students in more traditional programs, in that they were not in an "all or nothing" situation when they took a test. Because mastery of the behaviors being tested was the issue, those students still lacking competency retook the test or its equivalent to prove mastery. For the sake of efficiency we would have been pleased to restrict ourselves to objective testing instruments, but, given the present state of the art, we recognized the need to include response modes of the constructed test (essay), as well as checklist types. However, we attempted to reduce the subjectivity of the latter two as much as possible, by requiring that objectively stated criteria be specified before the student was given either a constructed response test or a performance test. The faculty saw no reason why these criteria should not be available to the student; so, while the system placed more and more responsibility on the student for his learning, it also provided him more information, when he needed it, for his decision making. For example, when a student went into the self-instruction laboratory to take an objective test, he received (1) immediate feedback on which items he missed, (2) to which objectives and means the test items related, and (3) what alternative materials were available to help him reach the objectives he was having difficulty with. Because of the time-consuming nature of scoring most constructed response or performance tests, feedback to the student was slower, but the feedback told him precisely which criteria he did not meet, so that he had a good chance of correcting the deficiency before continuing.

Problems Searching for Solution

There is a great need for students to be more involved with the decisions in implementation. We were able to involve them to some degree on instructional development teams, but, for reasons of priority and lack of a strategy, we have not been able to get data from students on their ideas for implementation and its attendant structures. We felt some concern, since the students were clearly affected as much as or more than faculty. We have made provisions for gaining feedback, both cognitive and affective, from students in the program, but this after-the-fact information is always biased by exposure to the predetermined structure. We recommend that others attempting program development make provision for including students in the planning process of any program implementation.

A similar argument can be advanced for involving the public schools. The schools necessarily have been involved in the mechanics of implementation where it directly affected them; the extensive field component in our modules made their participation essential, but they have had less to do with determining what would be taught or how it would be taught. This is a communications gap familiar to more traditional programs, and no doubt is a major cause of the common criticism that there is little relationship between what happened to the student in his college classes and his field experiences. Often, survival concerns have forced him to disregard his college learning and model his behavior after his cooperating teacher in the public school where he is doing his field work.

Long conversations with our public school colleagues have convinced us that it is not that they disagree particularly with what we are attempting to do, but simply that they have not been made aware in any specific and detailed way about what needs to happen to student teachers. The continued activities of multiunit school groups (combining team teaching and individually guided instruction) and the close relationships being developed by our instructional team members with specific schools should significantly reduce this gap. We suspect that greater involvement with and more feedback from public school educators would have improved our model considerably.

Closely related to the problem of testing is that of grading. Although few of us wish to defend the normative, referenced grading system, we are caught up in it, and feel secure with it. However, grading students on the basis of how they compare to other students is antithetical to competency-based instruction. If a student has mastered a behavior to the point where he is able to deal with succeeding objectives, that is a sufficient condition for a competency-based program; whether he has met an A or B standard is unimportant. But it *is* still important to universities that have not adopted a pass-no pass grading option. It is the concern of honors programs, and it is still the concern of some faculty and students who perceive academic competition among students as important. We decided to retain the traditional letter grade system during the initial implementation of our program and are using a contract method to determine where students fit on an A, B, C, D, F continuum: a student who wishes an A may be required to complete more modules than a student who contracts for a B. In other cases, different difficulty levels for meeting objectives have been set, and a student's grade will depend on the level of objectives he has completed. Other ideas are being studied. At this point no clear solution is in sight.

Despite the plethora of problems we have dealt with, and have yet to deal with, and despite stopgap measures that our situation often forces on us, we think that the clear specification of where we want to go, and the use of the process of continuous revision through successive approximations, have enabled us to develop an effective CBTE program that is far superior to our former program. As someone once said, "It is far better to have an inexact solution to an exact problem, than to have an exact solution to an inexact problem."

SUMMARY

This chapter has been primarily concerned with developmental activities centered around the university. In Chapter 6 we establish the importance of field-based elements of the program (multiunit schools and individually guided education) to the success of CBTE.

Notes

1. United States Office of Education, *Request for Proposals and Proposal Number OE-68-4* (Washington, D.C., Government Printing Office, October 16, 1967), p. 1.
2. The Committee on Quality Education was made up of members of the Pennsylvania State Board of Education who contracted the project to the Educational Testing Service in Princeton, New Jersey. Experts in the behavioral sciences from all over the country constituted a standing advisory committee for

the project. A three-volume report, *A Plan for Evaluating the Quality of Educational Programs in Pennsylvania* (Princeton, N.J.: Educational Testing Service, 1965), describes the goals and how they were developed and evaluated.

3. *Information for Institutions Preparing Proposals for Phase II of the Bureau of Research Elementary Teacher Education Project* (Washington, D.C.: Department of Health, Education and Welfare, Office of Education, October 31, 1968), p. 10.

4. George E. Dickson et al., *The Feasibility of Educational Specifications for the Ohio Comprehensive Elementary Teacher Education Program* (Toledo, Ohio: Research Foundation of the University of Toledo, 1969).

5. See Robert F. Mager, *Preparing Instructional Objectives* (Palo Alto, California: Fearon Publishers, 1962).

6. See Benjamin S. Bloom et al., *Taxonomy of Educational Objectives, Handbook I: Cognitive Domain* (New York: David McKay, 1956).

7. See Robert M. Gagné, *The Conditions of Learning* (New York: Holt, Rinehart & Winston, 1967).

Suggested Readings

Feyereisen, Kathryn V., A. John Fiorino, and Arlene T. Nowak. *Supervision and Curriculum Renewal: A Systems Approach.* New York: Appleton-Century-Crofts, 1970.

Jung, Charles C. "Competencies for Team Leaders in Facilitating Change." In *Perspectives on the Role of the Teacher Corps Team Leader.* Edited by Richard Saxe. Toledo, Ohio: Team Leadership Development Project, 1971.

Nylen, Donald, J. Robert Mitchell, and Anthony Stout. *Handbook of Staff Development and Human Relations Training: Materials Developed for Use in Africa*, rev'd. Washington, D.C.: National Training Institute for Applied Behavioral Science, 1967.

6/ Development of IGE and MUS

Edward J. Nussel
John F. Ahern
Leo D. Leonard

The school administrator has numerous organizational arrangements at his disposal as he makes decisions on how to commit faculty to implement an instructional program. Since individually guided education is a method for grouping children, it can theoretically be carried out under any organizational plan. It is possible for one teacher in a self-contained classroom to implement IGE. However, the demands of implementing IGE in such a situation would tax the talents of most teachers, and probably only a small percentage of gifted individuals could cope with the variety of tasks involved. Many critics of American education feel that the schools have failed to teach children through conventional plans of organization with traditional curriculums. The multiunit school, which utilizes a type of team teaching, differentiated staff, is an alternative well suited to implement IGE.

The multiunit school does not promise instant success for IGE. It is possible to organize a multiunit school and not implement IGE, just as it is possible to organize an IGE curriculum program without having a multiunit school. But wisdom requires the ability to incorporate both components into the arrangement of people and content. Much has been learned about this aspect of the change process during five years of multiunit development.

Following the recommendations of the Wisconsin R & D Center, it was originally believed that the school would have to be completely changed from a self-contained organization into a multiunit plan. In Wisconsin and Colorado the state departments of education took the lead in reorganizing schools. In Ohio, the University of Toledo has done so. All teachers in a school were expected to function within a unit with a unit leader and to work cooperatively with the instructional improvement committee, which coordinates curriculum and personal development for all staff members.

However, the importance of teacher readiness must not be overlooked. People are culturally creatures of habit and departures from accustomed modes of behavior are threatening to them. Many teachers who have spent their careers in self-contained classrooms are fearful of other kinds of arrangements. Coupling the organizational change with IGE, with its emphasis on specifically stated instructional objectives, creates additional concern. Some fear that this degree of specificity makes for a mechanistic, dehumanized education. Then, of course, there are those who simply are not interested in changing the instructional program because they feel they are already meeting the needs of the children they teach. Even the best inservice program will seldom lead all teachers into enthusiastic support for the innovative model. Conceivably, a school principal or superintendent can direct that all teachers become part of a unit, but he runs the risk of formal and informal teacher resistance, which can defeat the entire plan. It has been demonstrated that this problem can be eliminated if the principle of readiness is observed. This means that, following an initial inservice effort, those teachers who are willing to work in a unit and to develop IGE are given additional inservice support. Necessary materials are also supplied to support the new program.

Further support can be given by providing participating teachers with additional personnel, who may be students from the local university, volunteers, or individuals who have been trained in paraprofessional programs. One advantage of the multiunit school is its ability to accommodate numerous people in a teaching team.

One or two successfully functioning units in a building can become a catalyst for change. In one developing multiunit school, two teachers teamed in sixth grade science. They were assisted by a university professor and were given a student teacher and a clerical aide. They let their colleagues know that they were most pleased with what happened in class. The following year, four teachers formed an upper elementary unit, and three years later the entire school was organized into units. A few individuals who were opposed to the transition transferred to other schools and new teachers sympathetic with a team arrangement took their places. The administration applied no pressure. Multiunit development continued, coupled with IGE, and today the school is a successfully functioning multiunit, IGE school.

Teacher commitment to the multiunit school is required if the transition is to succeed, but support is not always easily obtained. Teachers need information, and this is best obtained through a carefully organized inservice program that offers the professional staff solid grounding in intergroup relations in order for the team to operate effectively. A good orientation to the basic components of the IGE learning system is also necessary. Unless this is done, and unless administrators are prepared to reinforce those teachers who demonstrate a willingness to work with the project, resistance will grow and the project is not likely to succeed. There are always those teachers who can "go through the motions," which benefits no one, particularly the children. As Stinchcombe said:

The process of inventing new roles, the determination of their mutual relations and of structuring the fields of rewards and sanctions so as to get maximum performance, have high costs in time, worry conflict, and temporary inefficiency.[1]

By building multiunit development on teacher readiness and teacher advocacy, the developer stands a better chance of introducing the new development with a minimum of opposition and maximum effectiveness.

Although revision of school organization is preferred, this does not preclude the possibility of implementing IGE programs in more traditional (probably self-contained) classrooms. A developer often must work with school districts that may not be interested in developing multiunit schools, as is the case with one school district in northwest Ohio. Due to the pressing need for curriculum reform, priority was given to the development of a competency-based, IGE program. Since this program is still developing, it is only speculative to predict that as the new curriculum unfolds the teachers will need to work more cooperatively in some kind of team teaching arrangement—it is hoped, the multiunit school.

Shaplin maintains that there is a "deep discontent with the standard organization of the school on the basis of the self-contained teacher and self-contained classroom."[2] He noted that teachers are anxious to work in areas where they are more interested, talented, or specialized and that they want greater flexibility in grouping children.

In developing multiunit schools the danger exists that the teachers will create a traditional, departmentalized elementary school, with each member of the team specializing in his or her own particular area (e.g., social studies, math, science, reading). When this happens, one teacher generally works in a particular area instead of the entire team working cooperatively with a group of children. This is why planning has been called the heart of the IGE program. When the teachers understand the process they should be willing to work together even though one teacher might be somewhat more qualified in a given area than the others. Members of the team may help a weaker member and in this way inservice training becomes part of the team planning procedure. The issue of subject matter areas becomes somewhat academic as members of the team become more sophisticated in developing their IGE learning packages. For example, in a unit on ecology, can agreement be reached on what really constitutes "reading," "science," or "social studies" as isolated subject areas? Does it matter?

NEW ROLES AND RELATIONSHIPS

The principles of readiness and cooperation cannot be overemphasized in developing multiunit, IGE schools. The period of change between the self-contained classroom and the multiunit school is an organizational no-man's-land. It takes time for new roles to be defined and for relationships between faculty, pupils, and administration to become functional in new ways. At this point readiness and commitment are crucial to the entire project; otherwise, problems may grow to the extent that the entire effort would have to be abandoned.

Four principal roles can be identified in a multiunit school: (1) the team leader, (2) the principal, (3) the teacher, and (4) the paraprofessional.

Team (Unit) Leaders

The role of team leader has the greatest potential for conflict because this individual is sociologically a "marginal man." He is given status by the organizational structure, but this status seldom includes more money. Although he is classified as a teacher, he must also be able to mobilize the instruction team so that the IGE program will function effectively. He must be talented in interpersonal relationships. The role is further complicated by the fact that the team leader must also maintain good relationships with the school administration. He must work with the principal and other team leaders in instructional improvement committee meetings, where he may be called on to present a case to the other members of the committee on behalf of his team. He must constantly maintain a delicate balance between being something more than a teacher and something less than a principal.

Principals

The role of the principal has undergone a dramatic change. It seems paradoxical that support and encouragement by the principal are crucial for the success of a multiunit, IGE school, while at the same time his leadership position is changed considerably. For example, he chairs the instructional improvement committee, but has only one vote. (Decisions rendered by an IIC are generally not by vote but by consensus, so "vote" is actually a figure of speech.) Debate can be generated over the dictum: "The principal is the instructional leader in the school." Certainly, if a unit were to plan an activity that ran counter to board of education policy, the principal, with or without the IIC, would undoubtedly assert his authority as firmly as necessary. But for the most part instructional decision making resides within the unit and the principal is likely to find himself in a position of expediter of a team decision rather than director. The principal relates directly to team leaders in a multiunit school, while in a self-contained school he relates directly to each teacher.

In a multiunit organization the principal should find more time available to carry out the important public relations functions that have always been attached to his role. The importance of this activity cannot be overestimated. Most parents will not understand what is going on unless the principal can clearly interpret the changes that are taking place in the school. Since many multiunit schools have working relationships with either the state department or a university, the principal is also responsible for coordination with the personnel from those organizations.

Teachers

The most important change for the teaching staff is the need to establish cooperative working relationships with their peers. No longer can an individual work behind the closed door of a self-contained classroom. A multiunit school enhances the opportunity for professional relationships, channeling teachers into these relationships through the instructional components of the school. Teachers then function not unlike the doctor who performs a team operation in full view of medical students or the team of lawyers that works on the defense of an accused person. Their mistakes are obvious, but so are their successes. The classroom teacher in a multiunit school can more narrowly define his activity in terms of the skills and processes and content areas for which he is responsible. The conditions for appropriate division of labor are actualized in a multiunit school.

Paraprofessionals

In this context, paraprofessionals are defined as all individuals working in a unit who are not professionally trained, contracted teachers. In this group we might find high school seniors, undergraduate students from the university, student teachers, trained paraprofessionals, or volunteers (sometimes referred to as parent aides). These individuals work as adjuncts to the professional members of the team and take direction from the unit leader; their tasks vary in complexity depending on their skills.

Interns

An intern is an individual who cannot really be defined as a paraprofessional yet is not necessarily a full-time professional. An intern works within the unit, is a contracted teacher, but is not usually employed on a full-time basis. He works at the school part of the day and pursues graduate studies at the university during the remainder of the day. In some cases interns perform all functions of the regular teachers.

With such a differentiated staff it can be seen why multiunit school organizations are able to provide for more closely directed individually guided education. No longer need there be concern about the pupil-teacher ratio; what is important is the adult-pupil ratio.

Involvement of College and University Personnel

The present level of involvement of the faculty at the University of Toledo in developing multiunit schools can best be appreciated by reviewing our past activities in effecting change. To many teachers it appeared that we had but one change strategy: lecturing. At teacher's institutes we extolled the virtues of education. At inservice faculty meetings we condemned poor practice and urged innovations. In graduate classes we gladly gave advice and counsel. Our exhortations were frequent, sometimes illustrated, often amusing, but they have appeared to have little impact. For faculties of colleges of education to affect teacher behavior, professors must *communicate:* teachers need to do more initiating and professors need to do more listening.

One of the reasons communication infrequently occurs at educational meetings and inservice sessions is that the professor's relationship with his audience is brief and impersonal. He is a visitor. We need to eliminate the distance—physical and social—between the university and the public school. One way is for a professor to become a member of a school community; this level of involvement is the basic component of the University of Toledo's strategy to implement multiunit schools.

The methods instructors were the first group to create an intensive and personal involvement with a school faculty. Each professor chose a particular school with which to identify, so that each cooperating school had one facilitator. This facilitator was (and is) accountable for the activities of undergraduates in the school and for creating and implementing inservice programs that would result in implementing the multiunit organizational structure in the school.

Although each professor had his own method of fulfilling these responsibilities, a certain commonality in operations emerged. For example, methods professors who were interested in involvement with the public schools also had strong feelings about the need for concentrated and early involvement of undergraduates in field experiences. Consequently, facilitators taught their undergraduate methods courses in the elementary school to which they were assigned. The undergraduates in courses taught by facilitators were more likely to spend their class period teaching small groups of children under the joint supervision of the professor and teachers, rather than listening to lectures. Although the proportion of time spent in the field varied with each professor, in methods courses taught by facilitators, the undergraduates spent on the average about half the course hours tutoring or instructing children. The professor used these experiences of the undergraduates as the basis for his instruction. His knowledge of the school and of the individual children allowed him to give a meaningful analysis of the undergraduate's performance.

In fulfilling his university instructional responsibilities within one elementary school, the professor had many opportunities to confer with the staff. He began to know the teachers as individuals—their strengths and their needs. This contact with the teachers provided the facilitator with the information needed to create meaningful inservice experiences. Often, the facilitator was able to arrange for his former students to be placed in his school as student teachers.

In planning inservice activities, the professor-as-a-facilitator was able to utilize his knowledge of individual teacher competencies in many ways. Most facilitators taught an off-campus graduate class to the teachers in the building. Many became members of the instructional improvement committee. Since the IIC is responsible for initiating curriculum change in the building, membership provides a unique opportunity for a university person to affect the school's instructional program. As a graduate academic adviser of the teachers, the facilitator was able to suggest university courses to help a unit or an individual solve a curriculum or an instructional problem. Other opportunities for communication occurred informally. For example, teachers, like other professionals, tend to talk shop at social functions. At these occasions, the professor could describe possible changes in school practices but, more importantly, he had another opportunity to gain the trust and acceptance of the faculty.

Establishing rapport with the public schools was a difficult but rewarding process. Certain lessons were learned from the experience, for not all individuals were successful. Should another university wish to create a similar relationship, the following suggestions might be helpful:

—*Recruit service-oriented faculty members.* One way of identifying such people is to ascertain their interest in supervising student teachers. Individuals who indicate that they have reservations about accepting this type of responsibility probably lack the competence or commitment needed to be accepted by teachers as change agents. If a professor is not enthusiastic about serving as a facilitator, his ability to gain the approval of a faculty is doubtful. A man or woman who communicates to a faculty that he is eager to work with them is more likely to gain acceptance. As one might suspect, research shows that the trust of the client is greater when the client—in this case the teacher—is in general agreement with the change agent.

—*Suggest to a particular school faculty that they recruit a facilitator from the existing university faculty.* This is based on the assumption that many senior faculty members have a reputation, whether favorable or unfavorable, among teachers in the area. By asking the teachers to choose a facilitator, the program will begin with a decided advantage, for the staff has an investment in the success of the facilitator. Research indicates that the change agent's identification with the client is greater when the client initiates the relationship. This process might also influence a professor's decision to become a facilitator; few professors would not be tempted by a request for their help originated by teachers.

—*Initiate the program by offering a course on individually guided education to be taught in the elementary school building.* Restrict the enrollment to that faculty. The teachers will probably respond favorably to the convenience of attending a university course taught in their building. There also is an appeal to a course taught by an instructor with whom they will be having frequent informal contact. Teaching an on-site course will probably have a double impact: first, it gives the facilitator an opportunity to provide the school faculty with the information needed to become an IGE/MUS school; and secondly, and more important, it communicates to the faculty that a special relationship will exist between the faculty and their professor.

—*Reward the professors who serve as facilitators.* Although an individual may be involved in the schools because of his commitment to public school reform, his activities will be even more satisfying if he receives the reinforcement that can be provided by his university. The number of professors who volunteer to become facilitators may increase as other faculty members note the promotions, raises, and reduced load (more apparent than real) that accrue to individuals who become active in field programs. It is probably true that one cannot become an effective facilitator if one is primarily motivated by the prospect of external rewards. However, individuals make career decisions after considering many factors, and certainly for university instructors those factors include promotions and increases in salary. At the University of Toledo there has been a significant rise in interest in becoming facilitators. This may be explained in part by the fact that the original facilitators received appropriate and substantial institutional recognition. Moreover, their activity was not peripheral to the overall college program—it was the major thrust.

COORDINATION OF PERSONNEL AND STRUCTURE

Despite considerable talk and voluminous writing about the problems of American education, educational change has been inadequate or at best haphazard. Ideas are bandied about but little happens to change the day-by-day operation of the school. Why is this so? Why can't useful ideas discussed in college seminars or found in dissertations be actualized in school practice? The fact is that ideas are only as good as the enabling structures that permit them to be actualized. Michael Katz examined the historical development of school bureaucracy and concluded:

Critics of schools have continued to lament their rigid and formalistic features, their negative influence on the personalities of teachers and students, their inability to accommodate highly individualistic styles of conduct. But an organizational alternative to overcome these deficiencies is still to be formulated; despite nearly a century of criticism, American education still lacks a real alternative model to hierarchical bureaucracy.[3]

It is not unusual to hear talk about a fundamental restructuring, but the truth is that few educational critics are able to offer alternative kinds of organization that facilitate the learning of children. There appears to be a conflict between a latent dislike of bureaucratic organization and the desire to make the schools more effective.

IGE/MUS attempts to philosophically accommodate more permissive open-ended school structures with the more rigid hierarchical systems that currently exist. IGE promotes the concept of matching instruction to the learning style of children. In so doing, the educational program is personalized and individualized. At the same time the multiunit school recognizes that organizational expedients are necessary for a school to function efficiently. The multiunit school bridges the gap between rigidity and laissez faire, while IGE bridges the gap between traditional curriculum and more open-ended, child-centered approaches to teaching and learning.

There cannot be an effective learning environment without a structure that utilizes teacher effectiveness optimally. Allen and Hawkes remind us that

We have been content to treat teachers like interchangeable parts. For instance, suppose we have three third grade teachers who we assign "Russian roulette" style, pretending that all kids will get an equally well-taught third grade. You and I know this simply is not the case. Teachers are not interchangeable parts.[4]

Multiunit schools offer a variation of differentiated staffing based on more appropriate utilization of teacher talent. Teachers are placed together in teams and given the opportunity to function in accordance with their abilities and interests. This departure from self-contained classrooms more closely approximates the division of labor described by Durkheim in 1893; in his classic work *Division of Labor,* he maintained that this kind of organization developed naturally as part of human association and that, "far from being hemmed in by his task [the worker] does not lose sight of his collaborators, that he acts upon them and reacts to them. He is, then, not a machine who repeats his movements without knowing their meaning."[5]

One might not agree that a division of labor takes place in a self-contained classroom or that a division of labor functionally depicts current high school organization. However, Durkheim was not referring to people working in isolation as in those organizational models. He believed that a division of labor produces community and cohesiveness and that each member of society learns to depend more and more on his neighbor. The labor of one cooperates with the labor of the other and thus a cohesive community is produced. "Men cannot live together . . . without acknowledging their need for one another, and this need of course increases with a developing division of labor."[6] The multiunit school represents a kind of organization that more closely approximates the effective division of labor Durkheim proposed.

The reorganization of local schools and the instruction of teachers to help them understand the division of labor are early steps in developing a large scale IGE/MUS system. A research and services bureau within a college is a useful vehicle in more extensive development efforts. Such an organization can become an important coordinator of personnel in assisting a group of school districts to work cooperatively for change. Its activities might include: (1) assistance in proposal writing for special funding, (2) research and evaluation services after a project is funded, (3) specialized workshops for teachers, (4) special off-campus credit courses, (5) short-term seminars, and (6) a variety of consultant services. A center can also serve as a college liaison with other organizations, such as educational associations, the state department of education, or private agencies.

The intrasystem model can be actualized within the college and become operationalized through the center. In the Toledo area, for example, a metropolitan league of multiunit schools has been formed by a USOE Title III grant. (See Chapter 4.) Six school districts have pooled their resources and a project center has been located in a neighborhood school. The University of Toledo, Center for Research and Services (CERS), acted as coordinating agent to assemble school district representatives for proposal writing and continues to serve on a board of directors in the capacity of an adviser. At the same time, CERS helps coordinate consulting or professional services drawn from the college. A director and another individual charged with developing curriculum resources operate the league center. An important feature of the league is the provision of teacher-to-teacher inservice, which is coordinated by the director: teachers who have experience in multiunit development help those teachers who are less experienced or who need help in developing particular skills. Such a league is in keeping with the I/D/E/A concept of IGE dissemination. It would appear that the center concept within a college structure is imperative in development activity, and a center should be given wide latitude in developing coalitions with other organizations.

If the IGE/MUS process is to spread beyond a local school district, cooperation is necessary, but school districts are unlikely to cooperate with one another in such joint efforts unless an impartial coordinating agent—the college center—provides the impetus to bring local representatives together.

Dissemination of IGE/MUS beyond the local or regional level can be accomplished through one of two procedures:

(1) The state department of education, which has school district ties throughout the state, can be an invaluable aid in IGE/MUS dissemination. State department personnel can sponsor meetings anywhere in the state to emphasize IGE/MUS. They can help local school districts find funds for their own inservice efforts. These funds can come from the state itself or the state can serve as an intermediary to obtain grants from the federal government, which can then be disseminated to school districts which write proposals for IGE/MUS.

(2) Colleges and universities can provide useful assistance in IGE/MUS development to individual school districts or to leagues of school districts. Furthermore, they can work cooperatively together if the state department of education is willing to work in coalition with them. However, many college and university personnel themselves have not been trained in the basic development of IGE/MUS; when this is so it might be necessary for leagues of colleges and universities to work cooperatively in inservice efforts so that the faculties will be trained to work effectively within their respective spheres of influence.

The development of coalitions among colleges, universities, research service bureaus, local school districts, groups of school districts, county school districts, and state departments of education is imperative if IGE/MUS developments are to take place. Financial support from the federal government and a commitment for change from the U.S. Office of Education are certainly helpful, if not necessary.

OVERVIEW OF A CASE STUDY

Although the University of Toledo is actively involved in four operating multiunit schools, and currently (1972-73) twenty-one professors are working with twenty-one other schools in seven school districts, the program began with but one school. In September 1969, two professors were assigned to Martin Luther King Jr. School in Toledo, Ohio. They were called facilitators and were responsible for helping in the conversion of the school from self-contained classrooms into a multiunit school. They were also expected to establish lines of communication between the school and the College of Education. The instructions were specific: "Listen to the teachers. Find out what they need and give it to them." Although what the professors heard was familiar, their involvement in the school made it possible for them to do something about what they heard.

The teachers at King School expressed many concerns about teacher education, universities, and change agents. They felt that professors—whether in graduate courses or at inservice workshops—tended to avoid the realities that confront classroom teachers. University personnel were accused of describing an ideal environment without explaining how that environment could be achieved. Teachers indicated that they wanted the "nitty-gritty" to achieve the goals identified by the experts. In a sense, they were asking universities to become competency based. They wanted to know, in behavioral terms, what do you *do* if you have a program that is individualized, personalized, and promotes inquiry? Their observations evidenced skepticism about the relevance of education programs. The practitioners seemed to be saying that schools are where the children are, and, if universities want to have an impact on education, that is where professors and undergraduates ought to be. They were arguing that teacher education and teacher educators should be field based. Fortunately, their concerns reflected the concerns of the faculty of the college.

It also became apparent that some members of the public school staff were anxious about an association with the university because they had experienced frustration as students. Some suspected universities of racism; some perceived universities as closed institutions: bureaucracies concerned more with forms and records than with people. Others felt that the professors expended energy on evaluation that should have been spent improving student performance. As a result of these discussions, it became clear that the inservice program would have to deal with both cognitive and affective goals. Based on the observations made by the staff, the role of the facilitator began to take shape. Four specific activities were identified:

1. *Encouraging teachers to pursue graduate training.* Teachers receive additional compensation for having a master's degree. However, for some, seeking a master's degree is often postponed out of fear of

failure and of the unknown. The facilitators had blank application forms and college catalogs delivered to the school, and before faculty members were encouraged to apply to graduate school, the facilitators determined the probable disposition of the applications. They also offered assistance in completing forms, to let their names be used as recommendations, and to serve as advisers. Their help probably accounts for the fact that every member of the faculty became involved in a graduate program.

As advisers, the facilitators informed their advisees which courses dealt with the basics of educational change and suggested that members of one unit enroll together in the same course. When this was possible, the facilitator asked the instructor to allow the teachers to work as a team on the course assignment.

2. *Teaching graduate courses off-campus.* During the first two years three graduate courses were taught at the school by the facilitators: Revising the Curriculum, Utilizing Student Teachers, and Creating Individualized Learning Activities. These courses were addressed to a particular problem at King School. The courses were structured so as to ensure that the teachers experienced new practices. For example, in one course the teachers were required to employ interest grouping in a social studies unit; to have residents of the neighborhood come in as guest speakers; and to try out classroom seating plans other than the traditional six chairs in a row, five rows across the front.

3. *Providing student teachers.* Another strategy to promote change was the systematic assignment of student teachers to units. Each quarter, each multiunit team was assigned one or more student teachers, who not only provided the manpower for small group instruction, but also had a positive impact on the educational climate of the school. Their enthusiasm for teaching was contagious, and with it they brought a familiarity with new techniques. In the team planning sessions, the student teachers suggested new approaches to the curriculum, and they informed the teachers in the unit about new strategies. In this way they acted as important change agents.

4. *Personalizing inservice.* Except for the graduate courses, all formal inservice was done in small groups. The facilitators used the planning time that was provided to each unit during the regular school day to explain new programs and techniques. Because each unit contained only three to five people, it was possible to respond

to individual concerns about possible changes. These sessions appeared to be most effective when the professors cooperatively planned curriculum units with the teachers in a team. Curriculum units included practices which the facilitators hoped the teaching unit would adopt. Growth occurred because professors and teachers together planned a unit in which both were responsible for implementation. The professor gained credibility, and the teachers were provided with a model for future planning sessions.

We offer the following suggestions to professors involved in implementing competency-based teacher education in a multiunit school:

—Establish credibility with the teachers by volunteering to work with individual teams that are planning and implementing instructional units.

—Ask the teachers for suggestions about the teacher preparation program. Teachers can provide fresh insights from a different perspective.

—Protect and promote the school's reputation. Change occurs slowly; when it does, reinforce the staff: let them know you are aware of their accomplishments. Defend the school when it is criticized by individuals who are not members of the school staff.

—Provide the staff with professional recognition. Invite teachers from the public school with which you are associated to speak to university classes and to professional groups Units frequently implement learning activities that deserve description in local and regional professional publications. When this happens, help them draft a press release or article.

ANOTHER CASE STUDY

Competency-Based Education and Multiunit Schools in the Catholic Diocese of Toledo

The Catholic Diocese of Toledo approached the College of Education in 1970 for help in developing new curriculum guides for all subject areas in its elementary schools. The diocese recognized the advantage of the IGE/MUS schools for individualizing instruction and developing alternative learning programs, but rather than commit themselves to the existing multiunit school network, diocesan officials suggested that multiunit schools might be the logical answer to staffing and curricular needs after a competency-based curriculum had been developed.

The diocese had not had a major curriculum revision in fifty years. Most of the schools had self-contained classrooms; several had degrees of individualized instruction, with students assigned to task or ability groups. Others used various forms of team teaching in subject matter areas. Outside of the assistance offered by the instruction supervisors, there was little guarantee of consistency of instruction.

The initial task of the university coordinator was to work with diocesan supervisors to develop target dates for both the experimental and final editions of the curriculum guides. For this it was necessary to prepare a planned feedback system for the collection, analysis, and organization of data into a curricular format.

An initial task group composed of diocesan teachers, supervisors, and administrators was organized and given inservice training in competency-based education by university personnel. At the conclusion of this course, the diocese was ready to develop competency-based curriculum guides. These guides would sequence concepts for grades 1-8. Diocesan supervisors for each subject area developed guides for their specific subjects. Wherever possible, the guides were developed so that certain concepts could be simultaneously taught in several subject matter areas. For example, units on ecology and drugs could be taught across subject matters. As the program developed, every attempt was made to integrate art and music with language arts and social studies.

Once the decision for competency-based materials was made, a planned process feedback system was developed (see Figure 6-1). Diocesan supervisors and teacher volunteers began collecting data on the school, students, community, and curricular needs. Data was processed by the task group, categorized by subject, and translated into concepts and instructional objectives. As these objectives were developed, a number of appropriate activities and methods were selected. The entire program was put into modular format and field tested during the 1972-73 school year.

During the field testing, the task group was concerned with the internal sequence of the module, the appropriateness of each component in the module, the time it took students to complete assignments, and the setting of proper levels of mastery for each objective. The curriculum guides typically listed only one or two methods of instruction for each objective. During the field testing, teachers were

Figure 6-1. A Planned Process Feedback System for
Performance-Based Curriculum Development

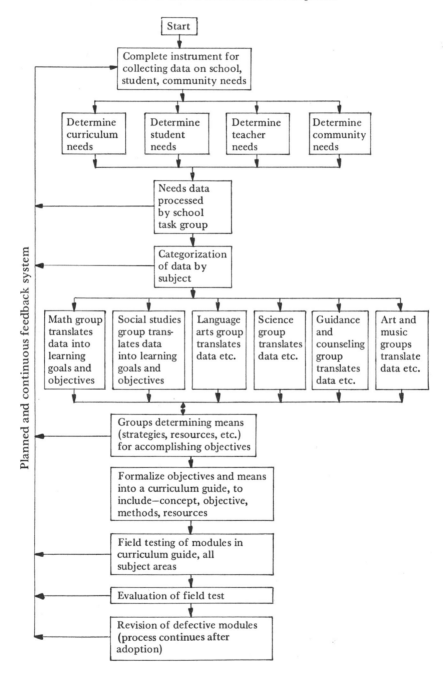

asked to suggest other more efficient instructional activities. It was particularly important to obtain more self-instructional activities for teachers in the self-contained classroom.

One of the assumptions of competency-based education is that team teaching is more efficient. If a team arrangement is not possible, the use of self-instructional modules provides a helpful alternative. Self-instructional modules free the teacher to act as a resource agent or to deal with individual problems. The teacher in the self-contained classroom must be free to handle acceleration and remediation needs. The field test attempted to find how teachers in the self-contained classroom individualized their instruction by using modules.

After the field test, the diocese made two decisions. The first was to eliminate defective modules—modules that were judged inappropriate by the established criteria. The second decision concerned the staffing arrangement—self-contained, multiunit, or other structure—judged most efficient in implementing a competency-based curriculum. The final decision on staffing has not yet been made, but the diocese has published curriculum recommendations for review in all parish schools.

The Planned Feedback System

Figure 6-1 shows the system developed by the Diocese of Toledo. This structure allowed for continuous assessment of data and problems. Working groups could react to problems by making changes where necessary. For example, if it was found during the field test that a particular module was inappropriate, the field test report form would alert the task group so they could correct its deficiencies.

Because this is a continuous feedback system, task groups may receive feedback at any time from any teacher in any school. Although published curriculum guides will be available in 1973, they will continue to be under constant reassessment.

Triumphs, Mistakes, and Suggestions

The Catholic Diocese of Toledo is one of the first school districts to attempt to move to an entirely competency-based education system. Everything from physical education to guidance and counseling has been included in their curriculum revision. By setting up a sophisticated report and evaluation system, the diocese should be able to assess continually the success and weaknesses of the program.

Perhaps the greatest success has been the recognition by university and diocesan personnel that teachers can and should be the primary decision makers and creators of curriculum. The new curriculum was developed entirely by volunteer teachers who donated their time to receive training in competency-based instruction. These teachers reviewed research and curriculum programs and selected materials most appropriate for use in the guides. Working in subject matter groups at the district level, they listened to suggestions from the community and students as to what should be included in the new curriculum program. Here was an excellent example of the creativity and dedication of teachers.

Another plus was the perceptive decision to revise the curriculum *before* making any new staffing or schedule changes. This allowed curriculum and student needs to dictate policy decisions, and in the long run may prove to be the most efficient way of making broad changes within a school district. The diocese used a systems approach for this program development.

The diocese quickly realized that volunteers who had not been trained in competency-based instruction should not be involved in program change. The diocese used its own trained staff for inservice training, and the best results were obtained when this training was formal. Developing competency-based modules is a sophisticated endeavor and requires constant cooperation among all members of a subject matter team. Providing inservice training, while attempting to develop the program, put a heavy strain on the diocesan supervisory personnel.

The program's implementation has been limited to schools and staff who have received inservice training in CBE. An adequate model for inservice training of all faculty in all schools over a relatively short period of time has not yet been devised. The final success of the program awaits a solution to this problem. Schools contemplating a competency-based program should develop a means of inservicing all school system faculty before implementing the competency-based program. It would also be helpful to develop a report form at the outset to provide information on all phases of the curriculum's successes and failures in the classroom.

MAXIMIZING CHANGE

The activities described in the two case studies did not happen by accident. They were a product of coordination between various agencies whose efforts were designed to promote change. A useful change model to apply in this kind of purposeful effort is characterized by Chin[7] as an intersystem. Basically, an intersystem is a synthesis between a more structured systems model and evolutionary developmental models. An intersystem model is characterized by six postulates:

1. *Change is controlled and induced.* In IGE/MUS development the change agent deliberately attempts to reorganize elementary schools, encouraging teachers to depart from self-contained organization while teaching them skills needed to function in a team setting. Teachers are also taught to build instructional modules that will lead to a competency-based curriculum.

2. *Change is induced by a change agent.* University of Toledo College of Education personnel have played important roles as change agents. At the school level, college personnel working as facilitators in elementary schools have become change agents. One project exchanged teachers in multiunit schools with teachers in non-multiunit schools, forming a teacher-to-teacher inservice change effort. An organization within an organization, such as the Center for Educational Research and Services at the University of Toledo, is an example of an organization that can supply personnel who understand the processes to be utilized in multiunit or competency-based programs. These personnel are used as consultants, called on when necessary, and have effectively served as change agents.

Administrative personnel within a school district may also act as change agents. This particular approach is a difficult one unless the administrator—particularly the principal—has a good working relationship with his teachers. Principals themselves are sometimes reluctant to become involved in an activity for which the payoff might not be commensurate with the effort required. Outside consultants can function more objectively and will be better accepted by teachers, who should be given wide opportunity to make decisions on organizational and curriculum change.

3. *Goals are established through a collaborative process.* It might

be said that the entire IGE/MUS or CBE effort has been a product of cooperation from a variety of several state and local institutions as well as private corporations and private school systems. A school can hardly do it alone. A school system might do it alone, but for the most part the development effort noted here has been characterized by interaction among a variety of educational organizations. Once a school has decided to make a change, the collaborative effort does not terminate. Assistance and support from parents and children become prerequisites for success. Impartial outside observers such as facilitators or consultants are invaluable in helping the school note its own shortcomings and assisting the staff in defining immediate needs.

4. *Intervention is determined by perceived needs.* Again, the readiness principle is applicable. If the staff does not determine that there is a need for changing the school, it will do little good for outside resources to apply pressure.

5. *Improvement is the goal of intervention.* If the staff is convinced that the IGE/MUS and/or CBE program will offer a greater opportunity to ply their professional skills and that children will experience significant learning and behavioral changes, the new program has a chance for success.

6. *The change agent is active now.* If the five points above are understood, there is little need to wait. The time for change is *now.* This is easy to say, but only the educative process itself can make clear to the professional and to the community that IGE/MUS and/or CBE provide such a useful vehicle for change.

SUMMARY

This chapter was written by three facilitators—active change agents combining efforts of the university and private and public schools. Problems of helping people assume new roles received much attention. University facilitators must do this on site to gain the necessary confidence and to earn the necessary trust to fulfill their own new roles. Two case studies were presented to suggest the variety of new situations facing all concerned with changing the educational system. Finally, we offered a list of important principles that have directed our efforts as a general guide to others involved in similar enterprises. The next chapter continues to describe the development and initiation of a new cooperative program.

Notes

1. A. L. Stinchcombe, "Social Structure and Organization," in *Handbook of Organizations,* ed. James March (Chicago: Rand McNally, 1965), p. 148.
2. J. T. Shaplin, "Cooperative Teaching: Definitions and Organizational Analysis," *The National Elementary School Principal* 44 (January 1965): 14-21.
3. Michael B. Katz, *Class, Bureaucracy and Schools* (New York: Praeger Publishers, 1971), p. 104.
4. Dwight W. Allen and Glen W. Hawkes, "Reconstruction of Teacher Education and Professional Growth Programs," *Phi Delta Kappan* 52 (September 1970): 4-13.
5. Emile Durkheim, "Division of Labor," in *Varieties of Classic Social Theory,* ed. H. M. Ruitenbeek (New York: E. P. Dutton, 1963), p. 552.
6. Robert Bierstead, *Emile Durkheim* (New York: Dell Publishing Co., 1966), p. 4.
7. Robert Chin, "The Utility of System Models and Development Models for Practitioners," in *The Planning of Change,* 2d ed., ed. Warren G. Bennis, Kenneth D. Benne, and Robert Chin (New York: Holt, Rinehart and Winston, 1969), pp. 297-312.

Suggested Readings

Havelock, Ronald G. *Planning for Innovation through Dissemination and Utilization of Knowledge.* Ann Arbor, Mich.: Center for Research and Utilization of Scientific Knowledge, 1971.
Inglis, Joan D., ed. *Field-Based Teacher Education: Emerging Relationships, Educational Comment, 1972.* Toledo, Ohio: The University of Toledo, 1972.

7/ Combining the Unifying Theme Organizing Elements for Educational Renewal

Joan Inglis
Richard Ishler

RELATIONSHIP AMONG ELEMENTS OF CBTE AND IGE/MUS

Educational change cannot take place unless the two basic institutions that educate the young do so concurrently. The old chicken-and-egg controversy is not worth debating. In the past colleges of education have had minimal impact on the "real" world of the classroom.[1] It does little good to educate preservice teachers under one philosophy, one set of principles and practices, if there is no market for their achievements once they leave the university; nor is there much chance that what is learned in college will be perpetuated if educators in the elementary and secondary schools do not endorse or practice the same philosophy and practices.

Innovative teachers who sense a need for change can provide only isolated pockets of excellence and experimentation. The large majority of classrooms will maintain the status quo unless the colleges graduate teachers who are enthusiastic about educational change and who are equipped to employ new practices and strategies. In addition, public school teachers and administrators need the support of college personnel for retraining and inservice activities. The schools cannot change if the colleges prepare their students for the status quo.

To survive and serve in the future, both institutions must change. The success of one program is intimately tied to the success of the other. The need for change has been stated by both colleges and elementary and secondary schools; a most promising trend is the recognition that efforts must be unified and coordinated. This realization that they are partners in an enterprise is long overdue.

Where working relationships between institutions involved in CBTE and in IGE/MUS schools have been established, they have found their needs strikingly similar, their concepts of education much alike, their goals almost identical, and their strategies parallel.

Concept Similarities

A major goal of education today is individualized instruction. Most educators now feel that it is more important to educate than to grade, sort, and select. The basic concept that each learner—child or youth—is an individual who learns in his own unique way, is a long-accepted psychological principle. The problem is not to persuade that such individuality exists, but to provide structures and situations that accommodate and encourage individuality.

Both CBTE and IGE/MUS use a similar, if not identical, learning cycle of five elements: (1) general objectives, (2) assessment, (3) individual objectives, (4) treatment, and (5) postassessment.

Instructional objectives are basic to both CBTE and IGE/MUS. It is possible to establish *general objectives* by making decisions about what the learner should be able to do after instruction: what competencies are needed by teachers, and what competencies children and youth should have when they leave the schools. Professors and teachers are expected to help make and carry out these educational decisions, and whenever possible to state desired competencies in behavioral terms.

An important premise in both CBTE and IGE/MUS is that each individual brings his own experience and degree of expertise to the learning situation. It would be a waste of time to expect all students, in college or lower schools, to have identical learning experiences and to finish these experiences in unison. The learner can find little stimulation in listening to a teacher present what he already knows. Hence, the second step in the learning cycle is *assessment*. The purpose of assessment is not to grade or mark but to identify just what the student does not know and then to match instruction to identified need. This element is common to both college CBTE and multiunit school IGE programs.

In both CBTE and IGE/MUS, when a student demonstrates competency in a particular objective he need not receive instruction in that objective. Rather, he pursues independent areas of interest or, in CBTE, he may accelerate in the program.

Inherent in assessment is that each student is aware of his own learning objectives. Until recently the student in both settings was kept in the dark about what he was specifically expected to learn. Instead, a body of content was presented and the student was tested on it. To let him in on what he had to learn and do was seen as "giving away the answer."

When instruction is needed to meet an objective a *learning program* is planned—including time, space, materials, teacher, and activity. Learning options are provided whenever possible, as self-directed learning is considered of value. Because not all students learn in the same way or at the same speed, judgment about the degree of competency demonstrated by the student is made by means of postassessment. Postassessment is done both by paper-and-pencil tests and by observation of learner behavior.

CBTE and IGE/MUS are performance based; when a learner does not demonstrate competency he is recycled. In most cases, especially in elementary classrooms, the learning program is changed, offering a different set of activities and materials, and possibly a different teacher. The basic principles and practices of instructional programming in CBTE are like those in IGE/MUS. In both programs the individual learner is a unifying theme.

Organizational Similarities

As well as similar concepts about individualization and instructional programming, CBTE and IGE/MUS have like organizational structures: team teaching and differentiated staffing.

In a multiunit elementary school teams of students, teachers, and paraprofessionals are referred to as units. At the college level the teams are composed of five or six professors, who represent the professional academic areas of curriculum, instructional methodology, societal factors, educational psychology, early childhood education, and educational media. One member of the college team assumes additional responsibility to operate as a field representative, or liaison, between the college and the school serving as a center for teacher education field experiences. Graduate assistants also serve on the college teams, while student teachers serve on the multiunit teams. Leadership is provided in the school by the unit leader and at the college level by the team leader. Each is primarily responsible for coordinating the functions of his team, chairing the weekly planning meetings, and preparing the agenda for these meetings. Neither is an administrator and should not be viewed as such by his colleagues.

In the schools the unit leaders meet weekly in the instructional improvement committee to coordinate the work of the various units, while the college team leaders and field representatives meet the college coordinator of field experiences to assure a smoothly functioning operation in the schools. A subject matter specialist on each team assumes the major responsibility for designing and planning modules of instruction. In the school units, this element of the IGE/MUS structure encourages each member of the team to develop expertise in a particular body of content.

At both levels the team structure has brought about awareness of the problems and benefits of team teaching. The credibility gap between college professors and classroom teachers diminishes when those in higher education demonstrate their involvement in teacher-learning activities in cooperative efforts. Moreover, the advantages of teaming—for example, joint planning and sharing of ideas—are experienced at all levels. As faculty members in cross-disciplinary teams share ideas—some for the first time—from their subject areas and discover new applications and relationships, they find that subject area barriers become less rigid than before. Skill in group processes and willingness to function as team members are essential to the success of CBTE and IGE/MUS.

Change Strategy Similarities

Educational change cannot take place by edict from the top. The most effective change strategy is one in which participants are involved in the change process itself. Successful implementation depends largely on the degree to which those who are expected to change, design the process of change. This principle is apparent in both the development and implementation of CBTE and IGE/MUS.

In the Ohio CBTE model, college and school personnel have been simultaneously involved in the grass roots process of change. The goal was not instant revolutionary change, but progressive evolution over time. Deep commitments have resulted from this process of personal involvement.

Members of the college faculty helped generate hundreds of behavioral objectives and instructional specifications for these objectives in each of the five subject areas: instructional organization, educational media, contemporary learning-teaching process, societal factors, and research. Following this initial stage of development, objectives and specifications writers became cost and time analyzers and the feasibility of the program was determined. The specifications selected as feasible were put into modular form and additional modules were developed. Countless hours of work, in which modules were sequenced and combined, were followed by still more hours of planning and working in teams to begin implementation procedures. Criterion-referenced assessment, record keeping, grouping students, and recycling plans became serious concerns for the college faculty. As a result of this extraordinary effort, a high degree of excitement and personal commitment characterized our implementation efforts.

Elementary school faculties were concurrently participating in the same process, although several schools began to implement IGE/MUS before implementing CBTE. These schools were highly involved in the process of change, designing objectives, developing learning programs, and struggling with similar problems of assessment, record keeping, and recycling. School and college faculties found common ground in the elementary school classroom, where the college students in CBTE also participated in field-based teacher education.

The entire process has resulted in a massive inservice program for both faculties. The college faculty has inserviced itself and helped in the inservice programs for IGE/MUS in the schools. The school faculty has inserviced the professors about the problems and needs of the real world of the elementary classroom, and has participated in field testing curriculum innovation.

School-University-Community Relationships

The school operates within the social context of the home community it serves. No child really comes to school alone; in a sense he brings with him his family and all his preschool life experiences. A good relationship between home and school is vital to the child's success and well-being, because parents and other significant adults influence the child's motivation, learning ability, and attitudes toward school. They also influence the quality of education by their financial support, or lack of it, of the school. The community creates the environment in which teachers work. All concerned need a positive environment, one in which there is support and understanding for the school and its educational program. In the IGE/MUS school the home-school relationship is not incidental but is a basic component of the program. The parent community needs to be involved in (1) understanding the goals of the program through group meetings and visits, (2) participating in the program as aides, substitutes, resource persons, and friends of the school, and (3) evaluating the program through questionnaires, interviews, and observations.

The schools, especially during a period of innovation, look to the university to help explain and support their program in the community. College personnel take this component of the IGE/MUS system seriously and find themselves joining with principals, unit leaders, and teachers to present the goals and procedures of IGE/MUS at PTA, mothers clubs, and other parent-participating school meetings.

A college of education's primary function is to prepare teachers for service in the classroom and in the larger community. The college cannot educate the community's future teachers without the extensive field experience of early and frequent work with children. In CBTE, the elementary school and the community are the learning laboratory. Classroom teachers become teacher educators along with college professors. In the past there has been little articulation between what colleges teach their students and what the teachers teach their pupils. The period of student teaching has done little to unite the two institutions in the total community enterprise. An important goal of IGE/MUS and CBTE is to involve all concerned with the education of children in designing learning experiences for students in college programs and children in the schools. Such experiences extend beyond each institution and its particular community (the school and the parent community, the college and the school community) to the larger society. It has been said that a city is only as good as its schools. A general respect for the educational process and educators is important to the health and welfare of the larger communities—neighborhood, city, and state.

Similarities in Evaluation and Feedback

In competency-based education, student evaluation is much the same in both college and school programs. Instructional objectives, closed (those that can be measured by paper-and-pencil tests) and open (those that are primarily encounters during which student behavior is formally and informally observed), exist in both programs. At the college level a student must demonstrate competency in one instructional task before going on to another module. His completion of the sequence of modules depends on his achieving competencies judged to be necessary for successful teaching.

The elementary school is also concerned with mastery of basic skills rather than presentation of content. Objectives are stated and the acquisition of skills is determined. However, more attention is given at the elementary level to the uneven developmental stages of childhood. No child is expected to do anything he is incapable of doing at a given time.

At any level of instruction, program evaluation is continuous during the process of change. Ongoing experimentation and measurement are inherent in CBE and IGE/MUS plans.

Elementary schools have employed several evaluation strategies:

(1) Pupil growth rate as measured by traditional standardized tests;

(2) Individual pupil growth as determined by mastery of specific objectives;

(3) Student attitude toward IGE/MUS as determined by student questionnaires;

(4) Teacher attitudes toward CBE and IGE/MUS as determined by questionnaires;

(5) Student teacher opinions as determined by questionnaires and interviews;

(6) Parent opinions and attitudes as determined by questionnaires and interviews.

The college teams have evaluated the teacher education program by level of student mastery attained in modules attempted. A total program evaluation is currently being designed by research and evaluation experts.

In the future teacher education will be dependent on developers of educational materials and programs in colleges, universities, and schools working together in new, responsible, cooperative, and mutually beneficial ways. Responsibility for the education of teachers must be shared by colleges, schools, and the broad educational community.

BLENDING PROFESSIONAL RELATIONSHIPS

Historically, colleges and universities have assumed major responsibility for the preservice education of teachers. To a limited degree this duty has been shared with public schools, especially in professional laboratory experiences. Control and responsibility, however, have largely remained with the colleges or universities. By the same token, public schools have been unwilling to assume operational responsibility for the education of teachers, except to make classrooms available and to provide teachers to supervise student teaching. They have not made a serious commitment, intellectually or financially, to the preservice or inservice training of teachers.

Thus educators have staked out certain professional boundaries: colleges and universities have viewed teacher education as their responsibility and public schools have viewed the education of children as theirs. Factors of tradition, professional status, and salary levels make the existing educational boundaries understandable—but not acceptable. It is necessary to build cooperative relationships among all members of the educational community. One possible way of achieving this goal is to establish teacher education centers that recognize the principle of shared sovereignty. More than a physical place, a teacher education center is a concept. It involves colleges and universities, public schools, industry, and the total education community in continuous teacher education. Further, the center recognizes the concept of parity in the allocation of responsibility for educating teachers.

Competency-based, field-centered teacher education programs taking place in teacher education centers will require professional relationships that cross existing institutional territories. What follows is an attempt to clarify how this might occur in a united effort to prepare teachers for tomorrow's classrooms.

The need for cooperation between public schools and universities in preparing teachers has never been greater. Society demands better teachers, and teacher educators must provide relevant courses and earlier, more frequent, and more meaningful laboratory and field experiences for future teachers.

The concept that universities produce and the public schools consume teachers is no longer operationally feasible. Both institutions must perceive themselves as preparing teachers, with the public schools having much to gain by sharing the responsibility for teacher education. In developing such cooperative arrangements there will be a linkage of certain roles. Certainly, new roles and functions will be created.

Cooperating Teachers

Teacher education programs in general lack articulation between what the preservice teacher learns during his training program and what he actually does on completion of his training. Application of the knowledge base acquired in college courses is frequently delayed until student teaching, and too often the supervising teacher is unfamiliar with or may even be opposed to some aspects of the prior training of the student teacher. This presents a conflicting situation not uncommon in traditional teacher education programs. The basic problem in preparing preservice teachers is how to provide continuing opportunities for the trainee to translate knowledge into practice effectively.

The literature on student teaching clearly demonstrates the importance of the cooperating teacher (the public school teacher with whom a student teacher is placed) in shaping the future teaching behaviors of preservice teachers. Teacher education programs should take full advantage of this influence by systematically involving the cooperating teacher. Such involvement requires superior teachers who have the skills and qualities to successfully integrate teacher education with teaching. Both must be synchronized within the same system to realize the common goal of improved teaching, and the apprentice teacher is also spared the dilemma of university *or* public school standards: he knows that both are working together and have similar expectations of him.

As a teacher educator, the classroom teacher provides a laboratory in which the prospective teacher can develop and practice under the skilled eye of a master teacher. The teacher educator facilitates the preservice teacher's understanding of the relationship between theory and practice and, most important, he focuses strongly on the prospective teacher's ability to teach. His responsibilities should be clearly defined: he should not have to assume full responsibility for the laboratory phases of teacher education, nor should his responsibility be undermined by a college professor who visits the classroom a few times to "supervise" the preservice teacher.

The teacher educator is, of course, not alone. He complements university personnel and his fellow teachers who also work with preservice teachers. Because of his exceptional teaching and leadership qualities, he acts as a liaison between university and public school personnel.

The classroom teacher who serves as a teacher educator has many roles to perform. Three of the most important are:

(1) *Supervisor.* He supervises preservice teachers at all stages of the training program that require experiences in a laboratory setting.

(2) *Diagnostician.* He helps diagnose specific needs of preservice teachers as they progress through the laboratory experiences in their training program. When specific needs are diagnosed, the teacher educator works with the university professors in selecting appropriate experiences.

(3) *Evaluator.* He helps preservice teachers evaluate their competencies in developing teaching behaviors, and reports the progress to the appropriate university personnel.

Teacher educators must be carefully selected and then trained to perform their roles. In addition to being master teachers, they must demonstrate their skill in performing the functions described above. They themselves must be students of teaching and should participate in the continuous education program provided by the cooperating teacher education institution.

Principals

Cooperative teacher education programs with public schools as local teacher education centers demand new functions of principals. The principals of teacher education center schools must be educational leaders who are committed to the cooperative center concept.

They must be amenable to experimentation and receptive to change, for educational change will not occur in their schools unless the principals enthusiastically initiate and support it. The principal's ideas about what constitutes a good school determine the quality of experiences available to preservice teachers.

The principal of a teacher education center must do more than assign preservice teachers to cooperating teachers for their laboratory experiences. He must be directly involved in the teacher educator functions of his classroom teachers. The following are some of the primary roles the principal must perform:

—He must involve the community in planning the teacher education center. In so doing he must be aware of the merits to be derived for the children and must be able to communicate these to the parents.

—He plays an important part in selecting classroom teachers to be teacher educators and in making the proper training available to them.

—He provides for inservice teacher training in the school and impresses on the entire faculty the importance of the school's task in the professional preparation of teachers.

—As a member of the instructional improvement committee of the multiunit school, the principal is an integral part of all decision making, but does not act unilaterally.

—The principal provides opportunities for both preservice teachers and teacher educators to become more knowledgeable and competent by arranging for demonstration teaching, workshops, institutes, and visitations to master teachers' classrooms.

—The principal conducts meetings or seminars with the preservice teachers to discuss routine school matters, the school's philosophy toward education, and its role in the teacher education program.

—The principal visits preservice teachers and aids them in developing teaching strategies and skills.

Relating Roles of College and University Personnel

Educational change comes about slowly, and is usually motivated when outside forces become irresistible. We seem to live from one crisis in education to another, with little impetus for planned change generated in between.

The task of teacher educators at all levels is to prepare personnel who will have the special role of guiding the young into a future about which we can only speculate.[2] But we must hypothesize about the future so that we can prepare tomorrow's teachers and students to cope with it. Traditional teacher education programs will not suffice for this important responsibility; while competency-based teacher education programs are not a panacea, they will enable us to prepare for, and possibly avert, the next crisis.

To effect needed change in teacher education a considerable reeducation effort is in order for current teacher educators. Prerequisite to this is a significant change in the attitudes of college and university personnel toward the changing society and the kind of teachers needed in the future. Competency-based and field-centered teacher education programs will bring about changed attitudes in college and university personnel and provide motivation for their reeducation.

To implement CBTE, existing roles of college and university personnel will have to be reorganized and new roles created for preservice and inservice teacher education. CBTE requires role changes by:

—Replacing the typical course structure of traditional teacher education programs with instructional modules designed so that when successfully completed they provide the preservice teacher with specific skills and competencies, which he must demonstrate;

—Being field-centered, calling for many modules to be carried out in a laboratory setting with children;

—Employing an interdisciplinary instructional approach in which teams of instructors from several academic areas work together to bring about the desired outcomes;

—Requiring cooperative relationships with the schools that serve as local teacher education centers where the laboratory phase of the program is carried out;

—Eliminating the distinction between preservice and inservice training, viewing it as a continuing, developmental process.

Competency-based teacher education programs require public schools to serve as more than student teaching centers. CBTE utilizes classroom teachers in teacher educator roles, and emphasizes laboratory experiences that require college and university teacher educators to work closely with school-based teacher educators. In some cases, public school personnel will take over roles previously performed by college and university teacher educators. New roles and responsibilities will be assumed by the college- or university-based teacher educator. In general terms, some of these changes are:

College and university teacher educators will become more specialized and will use their specialties as members of a faculty team. The generalist college professor will be replaced by specialists working together whose collective skills will provide a more meaningful teacher education program.

The primary function of college and university personnel will shift from transmitting information to demonstrating, modeling, and managing. If future teachers are to be effective, the teacher education faculty must themselves be able to demonstrate or model the principles of team teaching, they must be good learning managers, and they must individualize instruction.

College and university teacher educators will be more accountable for the professional quality of their graduates. Competency-based programs provide extensive assessment and feedback on the performance of preservice and inservice teachers, supplying empirical data on which to base program changes and adjustments. College-based teacher educators will take the initiative—but in cooperation with school-based teacher educators—for continued program improvement and development. Thus, teacher educators' competencies will be measured by varying forms of personnel and program accountability.

In competency-based programs college and university personnel spend a great deal of time working in the schools with school-based teacher educators. Some of their specific tasks in this setting are to:

—Conduct orientation sessions to acquaint new school-based teacher educators with the program, policies, and procedures for laboratory experiences;

—Plan continuing education programs for school-based teacher educators;

—Conduct inservice training to upgrade the supervisory skills of school-based teacher educators;

—Help school-based teacher educators plan meaningful graduate programs that will assist them in their roles or prepare them for new functions;

—Identify new schools that are interested in becoming local teacher education centers and select qualified classroom teachers to become teacher educators;

—Assist school-based teacher educators with problems that arise as a result of preservice teachers receiving much of their teacher training experiences in schools.

College and university teacher educators can perform these and other activities as cooperative arrangements are established for competency-based teacher education programs. This promises to strengthen teacher education at both the preservice and inservice levels—and obviously also implies a major task of faculty reeducation. The future of quality teacher education programs depends greatly on how readily and how effectively teacher educators can meet the challenge.

Involvement of Paraprofessionals in Teacher Education

In addition to professional teacher educators, numerous nonprofessional individuals and groups will play an important part in competency-based teacher education programs. The future "classroom" for teacher education will not be on a college campus, but will be wherever the resources are available to make a particular contribution to the education of teachers. Educators will at times be nonprofessionals from the community who have specific skills that can be used as part of the teacher training program. Paraprofessionals of all types will augment the professional teacher educator teams, utilized in activities such as record keeping, development of materials, maintenance of equipment, etc.

Personnel from education industries will sometimes be called on to serve as collaborators with the teacher education teams. Many of the instructional materials necessary to maximize the effectiveness of competency-based teacher education programs do not now exist and therefore must be produced. The education industry has the technical competence to produce the materials, but must do so in collaboration with teacher educators.

Competency-based teacher education programs will provide the "consumers," or students, with opportunities for making decisions about their own training. Systems will be established so that input and feedback from preservice teachers (students) can be taken into consideration when programs are being developed or altered.

Future teacher education will be in and of the local community: not only will preservice teachers study the school in the context of the community, but people in the community will contribute to the teacher education program. Preservice teachers will be expected to participate fully in the life of the community. This firsthand knowledge of the community and its resources will add immeasurably to the training of preservice teachers.

All groups and individuals who will participate in competency-based teacher education programs in the future have not yet been identified. Participants will vary with changing conditions and according to situational needs. Professional teacher educators will continue to have primary responsibility for teacher education, but nonprofessionals will have new roles. Collaboration and cooperation of all who have a stake in the training of effective teachers can only be viewed as a step in the right direction.

NEW ROLES AND NEW ACTIVITIES FOR ALL PERSONNEL

Competency-based teacher education programs call for redesigning many of the existing roles in college and university and public school teaching and administrative functions, as well as the creation of various new roles for all persons involved in teacher education. If these programs are to succeed, both schools and colleges must face certain major changes.

One needed change is the application of technology and media to improve instruction. Used properly, technology can improve learning by making instruction in fast-changing areas of knowledge more valid, freeing educators for other more vital functions. This needed change has implications for all teacher educators.

Another change that must be forthcoming is the introduction of process learning at all educational levels into the curriculum. Such processes as identifying needs, analyzing constraints, communicating feelings, planning and developing improvement strategies, making educational decisions, and evaluating one's own personal growth must be included in the curriculum of tomorrow's schools.

Schools in the future must be dynamic organizations. To think and act functionally in relation to objectives, teachers need instruction in particular knowledge and skills. Currently schools at all levels tend to function statically in terms of roles and traditions. If the potential for improvements like team teaching, IGE/MUS, and CBTE is to be realized, new skills in organizational functioning are clearly needed. The past has shown that most structural changes in organizational functioning are only disruptive unless they are preceded by adequate training to provide the teachers with the competencies required to function in the new structure.

Another needed change is the development of evaluation systems to verify learning in terms of established goals. Whatever program goals are devised, teachers, students, and parents must be involved, and there must be effective ways to determine whether the goals have been achieved.

Change or reform in education cannot be piecemeal. Edelfelt describes the magnitude of the problem:

Not only does . . . reform require an examination of the purpose and content of education, it also requires reviewing what teaching is and how one learns to teach. Not only does it involve a basic reassessment of how teachers are prepared, it also prompts thinking about changing the whole character of the profession. Not only does it require specifying clear and valid goals for education and teacher education, it also calls for laying out process and strategy for achieving reform.[3]

According to Edelfelt, the persuasion for such reform in education is based on the following assumptions:

1. Schools and teaching need radical reform.
2. All segments of the teaching profession must be involved in planning, carrying out, and evaluating reform in education and teacher education.
3. Instruction and teacher education must be closely related.
4. Teacher education should be a career-long enterprise.
5. Teaching must have a career pattern.
6. Parents and students must be involved in the reform of education.[4]

College and university teacher educators no longer have exclusive dominion over teacher education, nor do they have the option of continuing to function in traditional, obsolete ways. A sample of what is in store for teacher education and teacher educators can be seen in the action taken by the state of Texas. The Texas state legislature has passed a law which in effect: (1) requires all teacher education programs to be competency based by 1977, (2) requires any new program for certification of teachers to be performance based immediately, and (3) mandates that there be evidence that planning for new teacher education programs is cooperatively done by colleges and universities, schools, students, teachers' organizations, and the community. Several other states have taken similar steps or are in the process of legislating cooperation in the development of competency-based programs. Since state governments have ultimate responsibility for education, they have the means to bring about the needed changes in teacher education and to establish responsibility for such changes with the entire educational community.

In creating new roles for teacher educators, institutions will have to consider that some roles will require more training than others, some will be more difficult to perform than others, and some should be rewarded more than others. Colleges which prepare teachers cannot deal with role differences in isolation from schools. Assessment procedures must be established to discover the level of complexity of various roles. Testing the difficulty of various new roles will require considerable conceptualization and research.

CBTE programs must focus on the retraining and continuing development of current and future teacher educators and school personnel. Accordingly, higher education institutions must continue to serve as sources of information, as stimulators of new ideas, and as leaders in the educational process.

Some have stated that competency-based teacher education is ahead of its time, but as the action taken in Texas indicates, its time is coming—ready or not. The same can be said about IGE and MUS. While not panaceas that will overcome all our educational ills, these are significant developments of great potential.

SUMMARY

In this chapter we have shown the basic similarities between the changes occurring in the CBTE components in college and university and those occurring in cooperating IGE/MUS elementary schools. We maintain that artificial boundaries must be removed or made permeable to permit free and open entry on *both* sides of the old school/university chasm. Colleagues in both types of institutions are repeatedly urged to retrain and support persons moving into changed or new roles and responsibilities. Chapter 8 describes the manner in which the CBTE program deals with the traditional basic subject areas of the curriculum.

Notes

1. See for example B. Othanel Smith et al., *Teachers for the Real World* (Washington, D.C.: American Association of Colleges for Teacher Education, 1969).

2. See for example Walter Hack et al., *Educational Futurism 1985* (Berkeley, California: McCutchan Publishing Corp., 1971); and Edgar L. Morphet and David L. Jesser, eds., *Designing Education for the Future no. 4: Cooperative Planning for Education in 1980* (New York: Citation Press, 1968).

3. Roy Edelfelt, "The Reform of Education and Teacher Education: A Complex Task," *The Journal of Teacher Education* 23 (summer 1972), p. 117.

4. Ibid.

Suggested Readings

English, Fenwick W., and Donald K. Sharpes, eds. *Strategies for Differentiated Staffing.* Berkeley, California: McCutchan Publishing Corp., 1972.

Joyce, Bruce, and Marsha Weil. *Models of Teaching.* Englewood Cliffs, N.J.: Prentice-Hall, 1972.

Pharis, William, et al. *Decision-Making and Schools for the 70's.* Washington, D.C.: National Education Association, 1970.

Smith, B. Othanel. *Teachers for the Real World.* Washington, D.C.: American Association of Colleges for Teacher Education, 1969.

Trusty, Francis M., ed. *Administering Human Resources.* Berkeley, California: McCutchan Publishing Corp., 1971.

8/ CBTE and the Basic School Subjects

Joan D. Inglis
Thomas C. Gibney
John F. Ahern
John Schaff

Because our focus in this book is on the education of teachers and specific practices designed for that end, we have not attempted an extensive treatment of changes in the elementary school curricula. Clearly, an adequate consideration of elementary school curricula is beyond the scope of this volume, or of any one volume. However, to suggest our model's readiness for and development of change in school content and the compatibility of probable curricular changes to CBTE, CBE, and IGE/MUS, we discuss briefly here trends in elementary language arts, mathematics, social studies, and science. Our comments are necessarily restricted to the role of the college in preparing future teachers to teach their respective subject fields.

LANGUAGE ARTS

For too long the language arts curriculum has been dictated by the basal texts in reading, spelling, phonics, and English grammar and usage. The time-honored ability-grouped reading structure reduced reading to skill learning as prescribed by these materials. Instruction was provided when it came next in the basal manual. Ceilings were placed on able readers and pressures were put on the slower members of each group to catch up to average, again as determined by the materials. Within this constricting environment teachers tried to develop affection for reading by creating enthusiasm for the prescribed stories in the reading series.

If five children in a language class of thirty could not write a sentence, instruction was given to all thirty although twenty-five children did not need it and were wasting their time. Today, the five can be task grouped and taught by a teacher, or they can use prepared materials while others work in areas appropriate to their needs.

To individualize reading and the language arts involved not only a change in procedures and organization but a supporting philosophy as well. Although sight vocabulary, word attack, and comprehension are necessary in learning to read, these skills are not ends in themselves, but means to an end. Careful sequential teaching of reading and language skills does not serve the real purpose of the school; the acquisition of skills is only a means to read what the learner needs and wants to read. The final evaluation is not whether the child *can* read but whether he *does* read. The language arts area of the elementary curriculum accepts skill teaching as its responsibility, but also focuses very strongly on enthusiasm and facility in all the communication arts, both oral and written.

It stresses:

1. *Imagination*, the area of extending feeling and thinking;
2. *Power*, the ability to use language for a purpose—the power of words, the power of language as a medium;
3. *Understanding*, the ability to relate (what is read or heard) to your own experience.[1]

Previous attempts to individualize reading and the language arts have fallen short of their potential. Although well-prepared classroom management designs have been available,[2] the elementary schools have adhered doggedly to the prescribed programs of the basal materials in which the individual is simply expected to keep pace. Tovey reported that, in fact, matching instruction to individual need was largely fictitious.[3] Diagnosis to determine specific need has not typically been a practice in the usual elementary classroom.

Reading of anything other than the assigned materials generally takes place only after all other work is finished. No wonder children like Friday free reading period best, for only then are they permitted to read what they want, for a longer period of time, without the interruptive questioning of the manual. It is then that they *can* read.

Individually guided education (IGE), with its emphasis on the components of diagnosis not only of specific skills and abilities, but also of learning styles, motivational patterns, interests and self-directive and creative skills, has given encouragement and support to the implementation of individual reading programs. A real commitment on the part of the college, the state department of education, and public schools has resulted in increased preservice and inservice instruction in individual reading. The components of individualized reading and language arts are being implemented under an approach that involves the total elementary curriculum. Fewer basal readers are being used exclusively, and more books of literature are being used in instruction. Many schools have changed their schedules to include a language arts block rather than separate, isolated time slots for spelling, writing, and reading. Self-selection of books and of independent language activities is encouraged. The number of learning centers is increasing. Traditional ability-grouped (three groups) reading, which included both skill teaching and appreciation for story content, is being replaced by task group teaching for skill acquisition and the individual reading conference for sharing the delights of children's literature. Table 8-1 compares the traditional reading program with a program organized for individuals.

The Wisconsin Design for Reading Skill Development (WDRSD) has been developed as a model of instructional programming in IGE. The important elements in this diagnostic inventory of skill acquisition are that (1) specific weaknesses can be identified, (2) a system of record keeping is presented, and (3) no total score, grade point equivalent, or reading level can be computed. It is therefore impossible to assign pupils to reading groups on the basis of some generalized data. Rather, children with similar identified weaknesses are grouped together for precision skill teaching. These groups are not static over time, but exist only as long as the need exists.

It must be said, however, that there is a danger, not necessarily inherent in the inventory itself but in teacher misconception of the design. The WDRSD is not to be viewed as the total reading program.

Table 8-1. Comparison of Traditional and Individualized Reading Programs

Traditional	Individualized
Vocabulary controlled	Child's own language used for initial reading (language experience approach); vocabulary is not controlled from the outside
Materials selected for the child	Self-selection from a variety of sources
Children are grouped according to generalized ability as determined	Diagnosis Task grouping
Directed reading lesson —Motivation —Directed silent reading —Directed oral reading —Word work	Motivation is self selection USSR (uninterrupted sustained silent reading) Teacher-pupil individual conference Centers Sharing
Often a specific time for reading, another time for writing, spelling, and oral language	Unified language arts block
Independent activities (seatwork) —Workbooks —Teacher-made dittos	Open-ended independent activities—no need for all to do the same activities, to start at the same time and finish in unison, not always a right answer
Material centered	Child centered

This is made explicit in the *Rationale and Guidelines* that accompany the material, but not everyone reads with care. The WDRSD functions only as the diagnostic tool and task grouping monitoring system in a total program.

Otto describes reading as having six components: (1) word attack, (2) comprehension, (3) study skills, (4) interpretive reading, (5) self-directed reading, and (6) creative reading.[4] The IGE instructional programming model, which includes assessment, instructional objectives, and reassessment, is most appropriately used with the first three components. In both word attack and study skills, predetermined learner behaviors can be stated and pupil mastery assessed against these objectives. The assessment, monitoring, and record keeping materials have been developed, published, and field tested, and are available at this time through the National Computer Systems.

The comprehension skills component, which includes only the skills involved in literal comprehension, will not be available for another year.

The last three components—interpretive, self-directed, and creative reading—do not lend themselves to the IGE programming model to the degree that predetermined behaviors within closed objectives can be stated. In these areas of the design Otto has employed open or expressive objectives. Objectives so stated are best described as learning encounters for children.

Otto claims that the WDRSD is compatible with any reading program—basal, langage experience, and individual reading. However, when coupled with the philosophy of IGE, it appears most suitable to a full-scale individualized reading program.

A typical module for the language arts instruction in the CBTE program is shown in Table 8-2.

Table 8-2. Sample Module for CBTE Language Arts Instruction

Department/context: Instructional Organization

Subject/topic: Necessary Training for Instruction, Elementary Language Arts

Title: Diagnosing Reading Strengths and Weaknesses

Prerequisite: The reading process and children's literature modules concurrently

Behavioral objectives:
(1) The student will demonstrate a knowledge of the definition and scope of the reading act by administering a reading diagnostic instrument and analyzing the data collected with 60 percent accuracy.
(2) The student will designate a teaching strategy in reading that is consistent with the data collected in (1) above and will defend the selection in terms of diagnostic findings.

Preassessment: None for preservice teachers.

Instructional activities:
(1) The instructor will demonstrate the use and administration of a diagnostic instrument.
(2) The student will listen to an audio/video tape of a child reading orally and identify specific strengths and weaknesses using a diagnostic instrument.
(3) The instructor will discuss the following teacher strategies as possible options to be employed in light of the diagnostic findings:
    (a) Language-experiences.
    (b) Word attack techniques.
    (c) Comprehension strategies.
    (d) Independent, self-selected reading.

Table 8-2. Sample Module for CBTE Language Arts Instruction *(continued)*

Materials:
Goodman and Burke, *Reading Miscue Inventory Manual: Procedure for Diagnosis and Evaluation* (New York: MacMillan, 1972).

Goodman and Burke, "Do They Read What They Speak?" *Grade Teacher* (March 1969).

Postassessment:
The student will (1) administer a diagnostic instrument to an individual child; (2) analyze the data; (3) evaluate strengths and weaknesses; and (4) prescribe an appropriate teaching strategy and materials for this child.

Criteria:
For (1) above, complete the diagnostic testing.

For (2) above, analyze the data with 60 percent accuracy.

For (3) and (4), the instructor will judge consistency between data and recommendations.

MATHEMATICS EDUCATION

The preparation of preservice elementary teachers in mathematics education has changed rapidly within the past decade. Many of the changes reflect the findings of federally funded experimental projects such as the School Mathematics Study Group (SMSG) and the University of Illinois Committee on School Mathematics (UICSM). The SMSG materials have been particularly significant in bringing about content changes in the elementary mathematics program, while the UICSM materials have been similarly employed at the secondary level.

A relatively new mathematics program for elementary students, Developing Mathematical Processes (DMP), is currently under development by the Analysis of Mathematics Instruction project of the Wisconsin Research and Development Center for Cognitive Learning. The DMP is a research-based, elementary mathematics program. As the mathematics component of the Wisconsin center program of IGE, DMP will provide a complete mathematics program for the elementary school, including the usual topics in arithmetic and also an informal, intuitive introduction to major ideas of geometry, probability, and statistics. The DMP program is based on the assumption that children learn best in an active environment where they can seek answers to problems of personal interest. This active environment stems from the development of arithmetic through a measurement approach, with the elementary children generating and working with numbers and their relationships. Another aspect of the DMP program is its emphasis on individually guided education. The program emphasizes assessment and evaluation of each child's progress and needs. A pupil's instructional program is designed around a variety of learning situations. For example, materials can be used for independent study, or they can be used with small groups so that pupils learn from each other and from the materials.

Table 8-3 lists some of the differences that exist between the traditional mathematics program and an individually guided mathematics program.

Table 8-3. Comparison of Traditional and Individualized
Mathematics Programs

Traditional	*Individualized*
Instructional groups are formed by homeroom assignments for each year.	Instructional groups are formed by preassessment for each topic or skill.
The adopted textbook is the content.	Teachers decide what a student is expected to learn by defining instructional objectives.
The instructional needs of each student are met within the two covers of the textbook, with all students expected to complete the same assignments.	Based on the specific objectives stated for each mathematical topic or skill, the following questions are answered before a student begins instruction: (1) How much of what is to be learned is already known? (2) Does the student have the necessary capabilities for the instruction to be prescribed? (3) What instructional activities should be prescribed for each student?
Manipulatives do not comprise an integral part of the mathematics program and are seldom used by all students.	Manipulatives are required and purchased as a part of the individualized program; all students use the manipulatives and are capable of demonstrating mathematics principles with them.

Table 8-3. Comparison of Traditional and Individualized
Mathematics Programs *(continued)*

Traditional	*Individualized*
Instruction is sometimes facilitated by ability grouping within a classroom or by departmentalization. Once these groups are formed, they usually remain as groups for a year with students moving when they are unable to fit into a group.	Students constantly interact with each other in discussing, explaining, and sharing mathematical ideas. Individualized instruction permits students to work alone but does not preclude small and large group instruction. Groups are formed by tasks, interests, abilities, etc.; if a student does not fit into a group the instruction is changed to meet his needs.
All elementary students are placed in the textbook that corresponds to their grade level in schools. Weekly and unit tests are used to measure the progress of all students.	All elementary students are given a placement test and then placed at their achievement level in each mathematical topic. After the level of achievement is established, topic tests are used to determine the knowledge each student has of specific operations and skills before and after instruction.
Evaluation is measured only at the end of a unit or a grading period. The grade on the report card is the evaluation.	Continuous evaluation and remediation provides each student with feedback of his errors, which enables him to identify his mistakes and correct them. A record-keeping system is jointly kept by the student and his teacher. Instruction is continually offered at an appropriate level for each student.
Evaluation of the students is done by the teacher and the answer key of the textbook.	Self-evaluations help the students validate their progress for the teacher and then plan with the teacher for subsequent instruction.

Like the reading program, an individually guided mathematics program should be based on the psychological principle that students learn best in an active environment where they can seek out answers to problems of personal interest. Teachers must plan instruction jointly to prevent mistakes, allow various grouping patterns, and promote varying techniques of instruction. If a problem exists, a team of teachers planning together can immediately change a grouping pattern and adjust instruction to solve the problem. Too often in departmentalization or ability grouping, we do just the opposite and change the student rather than the grouping or the instruction, or else we continue with the problem all year.

Individually guided mathematics instruction is not the replacement of a textbook with a set of objectives and a pile of dittoes. Nor should an individualized program become a disorganized, overutilized collection of ditto masters and self-instructional units that are considerably more trouble to locate, run off, and read than they are worth. Individually guided mathematics instruction requires that the teacher direct the instruction of each pupil and encourage each pupil to use manipulative materials and to become actively involved with others in explaining what mathematics means to him.

The new undergraduate mathematics program makes obvious demands on the prospective teacher. If the pupil is encouraged to question, the teacher is obligated to help supply the answer. For a teacher to guide the teaching of mathematics as a system of related ideas, he must *know* mathematics as a system of related ideas. If the university teacher is to individually guide the education of undergraduates through selectivity in approach and creativity in adoption, he must know more mathematics than his students are expected to learn. Too often the end result of an undergraduate program was a teacher whose concept and understanding of mathematics was little broader or deeper than that of the pupils he was to instruct.

The preservice mathematics education program is organized into a set of modules. An example of one of the modules used in the program is shown in Table 8-4.

Table 8-4. Sample Module for CBTE Mathematics Instruction

Department/context: Instructional Organization

Subject/topic: Necessary Training for Instruction, Elementary Mathematics

Title: Using Manipulative Objects in Elementary School Mathematics

Prerequisites: Module #1. Learning theories applied to elementary school mathematics
Module #3. Inductive methods in elementary school mathematics

Behavioral objectives:
(1) The student will be able to describe at least one activity, using Cuisenaire Rods for at least four of the following:
    (a) Developing the concepts of the whole numbers 1-10.

Table 8-4. Sample Module for CBTE Mathematics Instruction *(continued)*

    (b) Adding whole numbers; meaning, facts, commutativity, associativity.

    (c) Subtracting whole numbers; meaning, facts.

    (d) Multiplying whole numbers; meaning, facts, commutativity, associativity.

    (e) Dividing whole numbers; meaning, facts.

    (f) Developing the concept of a fraction.

(2) The student will be able to describe at least one activity, using the Geoboard for at least three of the following:

    (a) Segments—length.

    (b) Angles—congruent, right, obtuse, acute.

    (c) Polygons—convex, concave.

    (d) Area—rectangle, parallelogram, triangle.

(3) The student will describe a method of using base ten place value blocks for developing at least three of the following:

    (a) Base ten numeration system.

    (b) A whole number addition algorithm.

    (c) A whole number subtraction algorithm.

    (d) A whole number multiplication algorithm (1-digit multipliers).

    (e) A whole number division algorithm (1-digit divisors).

(4) Given an elementary school mathematics concept, the student will describe at least two sets of physical objects in the mathematics laboratory and at least one activity using each of those physical objects that can be used to develop the given concept.

Preassessment: None.

Instructional activities:

(1) The student will obtain a set of Cuisenaire Rods and a self-instructional booklet from the Carver Curriculum Materials Center (CCMC) and do the activities in the booklet.

(2) The student will obtain a Geoboard and a self-instructional booklet from the CCMC and do the activities in the booklet.

(4) The student will attend a lecture session in which the instructor shows and demonstrates the many manipulative devices in the math lab.

(5) The student will explore the materials in the math lab doing activities described in the lecture or in the teacher's guides supplied with the materials.

(6) The student will take part in a group discussion of the uses of manipulative objects in general and the strengths and weaknesses of particular manipulative objects.

(7) The student will prepare and teach one or two math lessons using manipulative objects.

Postassessment:

(1) The instructor will select four of the topics listed in Objective (1) and the student will describe at least one activity using Cuisenaire Rods for each of those topics.

(2) The instructor will select three of the topics listed in Objective (2) and the student will describe at least one activity using Geoboards for each of those topics.

Table 8-4. Sample Module for CBTE Mathematics Instruction *(continued)*

(3) The instructor will select three of the topics listed in Objective (3) and the student will describe at least one method of developing each of these topics using place value blocks.

(4) The instructor will select a concept of elementary school mathematics and the student will describe at least one activity for each of two sets of manipulative objects that help to develop the given concept.

An analysis of the treatments, materials, and evaluations of the undergraduate mathematics modules indicates a broad range of use in an activity-centered program. Student involvement is apparent in cooperative activity, direct experience, discussions, individual study, observations, skill development, simulation, and demonstrations. These activities are varied and vital in the preparation of prospective mathematics teachers prepared to function in multiunit schools and to develop individually guided educational programs in mathematics for elementary students.

SCIENCE EDUCATION

Historically, science instruction in elementary schools has been left primarily to the interest, enthusiasm, and enterprising ability of individual teachers. Owing to their limited backgrounds and a paucity of resource materials, teachers attempting to provide science instruction relied heavily on one of a number of textbook series that provided science content for kindergarten through eighth grade. The same instruction was given to all pupils without considering differences in their individual abilities. All learners were treated as though they had identical reading abilities, similar interests in science, and equivalent, prior cognitive experiences related to the science topics covered. They proceeded as a single group through a sequence of topics. It was not uncommon to observe in any classroom several pupils who were not involved because the science instruction failed to provide them appropriate stimuli and challenges. In most classes, children read about natural history in the textbook and learned the names of plants, animals, rocks, earth characteristics, weather, and constellations. The emphasis was typically on teaching the facts and findings of science. Teachers were "tellers" of science who occasionally offered demonstrations designed to illustrate scientific concepts and principles. Science was treated as a mere accumulation of bits and pieces of information. Seldom were children able to examine interrelationships and the processes of science; they gathered observations and experimental data to support what the teacher told them or what they read in their textbooks, not to test ideas and hunches about what they had observed.

During the past decade, new science curricula have been developed that promote direct student involvement in the learning of science processes and concepts. Instead of memorizing the parts of a battery and a light bulb from pictures in their text, children can discover how a battery and bulb can be connected with wires to cause the bulb to light; they are not told how to hook them up, but are given a battery, a bulb, and a wire and the opportunity to test their ideas. Through inquiry, pupils become involved in the basic scientific processes of observing, predicting, and inferring.

Another way in which elementary school children learn the processes of science is through classifying objects. They discover relationships between different objects by classifying them according to size, shape, color, or whatever characteristic they choose. In lieu of being told how to classify the objects according to existing systems, they are asked to classify them in their own way and to indicate the basis for the classification system used.

For example, while studying mealworm behavior, pupils are exposed to opportunities for open-ended short-term as well as long-term discoveries. During short periods, they may discover various patterns of movement and responses to environmental factors such as heat, light, and chemicals. Over longer segments of time they observe the process of metamorphosis as mealworms change to adults from the larval stage.

Having encountered the basic processes of science in the early grades, children are prepared to learn and become involved in the more complex integrated processes of scientific inquiry and problem solving, such as formulating hypotheses, controlling variables, interpreting data, making operational definitions, and experimentation. Children form certain basic relationships of relevant observations—concepts—that prepare them for interpreting or explaining real life phenomena.

In learning the concepts of science—e.g., force, natural selection, and measurement—children interact with the instructional material. Significant concepts are learned gradually as they are revisited at different grade levels. The understanding of some concepts is dependent on knowing others, thus requiring an ordering of conceptual tasks in terms of their dependent knowledge. The mental maturity of the learner must also be considered, because sometimes he is not intellectually mature enough to comprehend certain concepts if these are introduced in the lower grade levels.

Concomitant with an emphasis on child involvement in the learning of science processes and concepts has been a trend toward individualized science programs. Initial ventures toward individualizing science focused on making provisions for pupils, either singly or in groups, to engage in different learning experiences. In one new elementary school science program,[5] each child can elect to explore units entitled "Bones," "Pendulums," "Small Things," "Gases and Airs," or "Light and Shadows," with low-cost laboratory-oriented materials so that he may work alone. The materials are designed for self-pacing, so each individual can pursue the learning experience at his own rate. Bright and curious children are not inhibited by the less intelligent and uninitiated, nor do slower individuals become frustrated and lost if the class proceeds beyond their comprehension rate. Children are not required to examine and explore the various topics to the same depth. Those possessing a greater experience reservoir visualize relationships involving not only fundamental principles, but their application to various situations. Children with limited backgrounds gain success just by discovering basic principles.

Along with multiple grouping and self-paced instruction, auto-tutorial devices have been incorporated whereby pupils are individually given information and directions that are usually given through reading. Child-operated cassette tape players, synchronized filmstrip-tape projectors, slide-tape projectors, and continuous film loop cartridges give those with reading difficulties an opportunity to learn science. Significantly, several teachers have indicated that children who have developed an interest in some aspect of science have been motivated to read about it. To aid learning and retention, individuals can receive repeated exposures to the same material without inhibiting the progress of others. They can also review the material if and when the need arises at a later date.

Most comprehensive of the individualized science programs is the individually prescribed instruction (IPI) science program developed by the Learning Research and Development Center at the University of Pittsburgh.[6] This program features teacher-prescribed science instruction based on individual student pretest results. Each learner not only progresses at his own rate and uses a medium of instruction most congruent with his ability, but conceivably he is also challenged with new learning experiences based on his prior accomplishments and background knowledge. The IPI approach to science instruction is easily accommodated in the IGE instructional model.

Implementation of individualized science instruction in schools has exposed a need for a more comprehensive and different means of preparing prescience teachers for their student teaching experience. Methods courses that concentrated on telling preservice teachers how to teach science and giving them the task of preparing lesson plans for teaching a unit of science are now insufficient and obsolete. All preservice teachers were treated as a single group with no recognition of individual differences and needs. The university classroom instruction failed to relate theory to current situations in public schools.

The multiunit school concept, whereby college and local school personnel are jointly involved in the education of preservice teachers, provides an ideal delivery system for teacher education. College science methods instructors, public school science teachers, and other school personnel combine resources to provide a broad-based preservice teacher education program. Theoretical concepts and innovations in instruction acquired at the university are concurrently examined in local school situations and are discussed with inservice science teachers, affording preservice teachers occasions to observe children learning science in classrooms, to try out new ideas and techniques on individuals, or small groups of pupils, and to examine the results together with practicing science teachers and a university methods instructor. Through these experiences, preservice teachers make a gradual rather than an abrupt transition into their student teaching experience.

The MUS concept has fostered increased inservice education of science teachers in local schools. In several instances instructional innovations initiated by student teachers have been continued by their cooperating teachers after the student teaching experience has been completed. Being involved with college instructors and student teachers during implementation of a new science program has given science teachers background experience and training in the innovation. They are often stimulated to continue it as an integral part of their instructional process. Examples of innovations include student-centered laboratory experiences, individualized instruction, inquiry teaching techniques, and improved questioning abilities. The skills of helping pupils master concepts in science are especially suited to a CBTE program and to IGE/MUS at the elementary level. The example in Table 8-5 of an instructional module for preparing elementary teachers in science bears out this contention.

Table 8-5. Sample Instructional Module, Science Teaching

Department/context: Instructional Organization

Subject/topic: Necessary Training for Instruction, Elementary Science

Title: Inquiry Teaching and Elementary Science Study (ESS)

Prerequisites: The nature of inquiry learning, inquiry teaching

Behavioral objectives:
　　Terminal objective. The preservice teacher will design effective procedures for teaching an ESS unit (e.g., pendulums utilizing inquiry-oriented strategies) and will be able to successfully implement the unit in a fourth, fifth, or sixth grade elementary multiunit school class.
　　Enabling objective 1. Given an opportunity to examine an ESS class kit and associated teacher's guide (e.g., on pendulums) and asked to state the unit objectives, the preservice teacher will include in his response that objectives are to provide children with an opportunity (1) to explore a swinging object, (2) to evolve and test their own ideas, and (3) to develop concepts of their own and modify them according to changing circumstances.
　　Enabling objective 2. Given an opportunity to plan effective procedures for teaching the pendulum unit, the preservice teacher will include in his plan a description of opportunities for children to explore swinging objectives independently, in small groups, or as a total group during various times of the day or during a specified 30- to 40-minute period.
　　Enabling objective 3. Given an opportunity to plan effective procedures for teaching an ESS unit, the preservice teacher will state in the plans a complete listing of all supplies and materials that should be readily available to students during their activity; and will specifically identify any items that require special or advanced preparation, i.e., preparation of pendulum supports.
　　Enabling objective 4. Given an opportunity to plan effective procedures for teaching an ESS unit, the preservice teacher will state all safety precautions to be observed during the student activity.
　　Enabling objective 5. Given an opportunity to plan effective procedures for teaching an ESS unit, the preservice teacher will include a brief preactivity discussion. When asked to state the function of the preactivity discussion, the preservice teacher will indicate that it should arouse student interest by asking them what they think will happen. It is not to be used solely to give directions.

Table 8-5. Sample Instructional Module, Science Teaching *(continued)*

Enabling objective 6. When asked to describe the function of a teacher during an ESS unit activity, the preservice teacher will state that the teacher's functions include discussing specific problems with individual students requesting assistance, to ask pointed and provocative questions, to encourage continued investigation, to give appropriate hints, and to praise students for their work.

Enabling objective 7. Given an opportunity to plan effective procedures for teaching an ESS unit, the preservice teacher will include a postactivity discussion. When asked to state the function of the postactivity discussion, the preservice teacher will indicate that it should guide the students in examining the results obtained from their investigations and the ideas they have gained.

Preassessment: Same as postassessment.

Instructional activities:

(1) Read chapter 3, pp. 37-59, in *Teaching Science Through Discovery*, 2d ed., by Arthur Carin and Robert Sund (Charles E. Merrill Publishing Co., 1970).

(2) Read pp. 16-28 in *Inquiry Techniques for Teaching Science*, by William Romey (Prentice-Hall, 1968).

(3) Read "Messing About in Science," by David Hawkins, in *Science and Children* (vol. 2, no. 5, February 1965).

(4) Select an elementary science study (ESS) unit (e.g., pendulums) and look over the class kit and teacher's guide.

(5) Plan effective procedures for teaching the ESS unit.

(6) Work through the ESS unit activities and at the same time anticipate student responses to each activity.

(7) Teach the ESS unit to a fourth, fifth, or sixth grade class in a multiunit elementary school. Videotape record the class session.

Postassessment:

(1) Answer each of the following questions:

    (a) Describe the function of the laboratory activities in an ESS unit.

    (b) State the function of the preactivity discussion in ESS unit.

    (c) State the function of a teacher during student involvement in an ESS unit.

    (d) State the function of the postactivity discussion in an ESS unit.

    (e) Write out two objectives of an ESS unit in behavior terms.

    (f) List five questions you might ask students while they are working on an ESS unit.

    (g) Outline the components of a class plan for teaching an ESS unit.

(2) Critique the videotape of your teaching the ESS unit with other members of the multiunit team. Describe any changes and innovations you would include if you were to teach the unit again.

SOCIAL STUDIES

The fundamental goal of social studies education is to prepare children to participate as citizens in a democratic society. Paradoxically, social studies instruction in the self-contained classroom has traditionally consisted of children taking turns reading paragraphs in a basal textbook or silently reading the text, then answering the questions at the end of the chapter. Pupils who could not read the textbook were frustrated by a system that made demands on them that they could not possibly meet. They were turned off by an instructional system that made no allowances for individual needs. The pupil not reading on grade level was not the only child to suffer; the more enterprising pupil in a self-contained classroom was tempted to cheat, once he learned that the teacher expected everyone to have the same answers to the questions at the end of the chapter. At the same time, creative children learned the skills of manipulation as they discovered that while round-robin reading was boring, devising ways to make the teacher deviate from the textbook was stimulating.

Project Social Studies, a curriculum reform movement of the sixties, attempted to change the basal-textbook-based, fact-oriented social studies curriculum. There is little evidence that the movement had much impact on the elementary curriculum. In fact, few projects focused on the elementary grades, and those that did tended to be too expensive or limited in scope. Few projects included team teaching or provided a structure to promote individualization.

Many basal textbook publishers found the reform movement to be profitable: it sold new textbooks. However, basal textbooks were "new" only in that the title of the text frequently included a word associated with Project Social Studies (e.g., "concept," "inquiry," "social science").

Social studies in IGE/MUS recognizes that textbooks, basal or otherwise, do not teach citizenship. The responsibility of educating for citizenship is complex and requires the teacher to assume new and diverse roles. In teaching and planning the social studies curriculum unit teachers must assume three roles: (1) teacher/adviser, (2) teacher of social science skills, and (3) planner of curriculum units.

(1) As a teacher adviser, the unit teacher is responsible for guiding a child's personal and social development. Children need someone to talk to and the agenda for such talks must be created by the children. They need to discuss interpersonal conflicts, intergroup relationships, social values, and individual dilemmas. In an IGE/MUS school, each teacher in the unit meets weekly, over a period of two years, with a small group of children in his unit to engage in value clarification,

goal setting, and problem solving. The other children are working independently, or in student-led project groups while the teacher meets with his advisee group. The deliberate inclusion in the social studies program of a structure for dealing directly with the child's experiences in both personal and social dimensions is an important difference between IGE/MUS and the self-contained classroom.

(2) In addition to personalizing the curriculum, social studies in IGE provides the teacher with a practical way of individualizing. For example, there are a number of specific skills in the social sciences that an elementary school child should master: skills such as map, globe, chart, and graph reading, as well as skills related to locating and collecting data, lend themselves to the use of the instructional programming model (i.e., the statement of the skill in behavioral terms, the use of criterion-referenced tests, the formation of task groups based on a common need for instruction in a specific skill). Groups for learning these skills last not longer than three weeks. It should be emphasized that the task groups are not related to ability grouping. In fact the absence of ability grouping is a major characteristic of IGE/MUS.

(3) Perhaps the most well-known aspect of IGE/MUS is the team concept. Unlike the traditional school in which the self-contained or departmental teacher is restricted to his own talents, IGE/MUS curriculum units employ the resources of all the teachers in both the planning and implementation of a curriculum unit. Although the social studies specialist will frequently have the major responsibility in preparing the design, each teacher contributes to planning goal setting, design, grouping, and scheduling, as well as the situational meetings of the IGE planning system. An essential thrust of this planning is to create a learning program that will result in children making decisions such as how and what they will study. IGE/MUS social studies units are characterized by the use of interest grouping, the independent mode, divergent thinking experiences, and student projects.

As has been described, IGE/MUS provides teachers on the team with the structure to change social studies education. By its very nature, IGE/MUS eliminates self-defeating efforts to make social studies more efficient—e.g., delegating to a guidance counselor the responsibility for helping the children develop as concerned, competent citizens, or utilizing ability grouping despite its obvious impact on a child's self-concept—and also erases the naive notion that a field as inclusive as social studies can be departmentalized. If social studies methodologists are enthusiastic about IGE/MUS, it is because they provide (1) a structure and curriculum that are personalized, and (2) an object lesson in democratic behavior.

An example of a module used in the elementary CBTE program is shown in Table 8-6.

Table 8-6. Sample Module, Elementary CBTE Social Studies Program

Department/context: Instructional Organization

Subject/topic: Necessary Training for Instruction, Elementary Social Studies

Title: Social Studies Planning

Prerequisites: None.

Behavioral objectives:
Terminal objective. Students will be able to justify the inclusion or omission in an elementary social studies program of teacher designed curriculum units, concept attainment units, instructional programs for the teaching of social studies skills and/or value clarification exercises.
Enabling objectives. Students will be able to:
(1) Distinguish between introductory developmental and concluding activities.
(2) When given a concept or topic, suggest appropriate introductory, developmental and concluding activities.
(3) Describe the advantages and options available when employing guest speakers, field trips, games, and student-made media.
(4) Describe materials appropriate for value clarification exercises.
(5) Implement the Shaftel and Shaftel process for playing for social values.
(6) List twenty value-clarifying responses.
(7) When given a social action concept, list attributes and examples of the concept.
(8) Distinguish between the goal setting, the design, the grouping and scheduling meeting, and the situational meeting.
(9) Create task groups for social studies skills using WRDR behavioral objectives and Royal McBee cards.

Preassessment: None.

Instructional activities:
Objectives (1) and (2). Means:
(1) Small group discussion to define social studies. Focus questions:
    (a) What courses fulfill your social science requirements?
    (b) What other courses are offered by those departments?
    (c) What do all those courses have in common?
    (d) What would be a synonym word or phrase for social sciences?

Table 8-6. Sample Module, Elementary CBTE Social Studies
Program *(continued)*

    (e) How would you define social studies?
    (f) Closure: Each small group makes a group decision on a topic they would like to plan.
  (2) Lecture:
    (a) The Social Studies Curriculum Unit. Focus: Definition by example of introductory, developmental, and concluding activities.
    (b) The brainstorming technique.
  (3) Practicum: small group brainstorming. Introductory, developmental, and concluding activities for a curriculum unit.
Objective (3). Means:
Independent activity: Read handouts:
—"Team Teaching Elementary Social Studies"
—"Guest Speakers"
—"Field Trips"
—"Student-Made Media"
—"Games"
Objective (4). Means:
Independent activity: View display of value clarification materials in Carver Curriculum Materials Center, including: "Unfinished Stories" (booklet); "More Unfinished Stories" (booklet); "Roleplaying for Social Values" (from text by Bruce Joyce, Marsha Weil, and Rhoada Wald, *Three Teaching Strategies for the Social Studies,* Chicago: Science Research Associates, 1972); "Exploring Moral Values" (filmstrips).
Objectives (5) and (6). Means:
  (1) Independent activity: Read text, Part III, pp. 179-188; complete a role-playing planning form, p. 171; see p. 173 for a completed sample form study handout on value clarifying responses.
  (2) Lecture—value clarification:
    (a) Rationale, relationships to inquiry.
    (b) Types of affective categories, the teacher/adviser in the multiunit school. (During the lecture cooperating professors will review planning forms and note strengths and concerns.)
  (3) Small groups: feedback on planning forms by cooperating professor.
  (4) Small groups: practicum. Students will implement their plan with peers demonstrating value-clarifying responses.
Objective (7). Means:
  (1) Independent activity: read Part I of the text.
  (2) Prepare a poster, haiku, or crossword puzzle on concept attainment.
  (3) Small group discussion.
    (a) Review: concept of concepts.
    (b) Define components of a concept attainment unit.
    (c) Students who wish additional review of concepts will leave with educational psychology professor.
    (d) Display concept attainment creations.
    (e) Discussion: Is this an appropriate learning activity for social studies concept attainment units? for value clarification?

Table 8-6. Sample Module, Elementary CBTE Social Studies
Program *(continued)*

Objective (8). Means:
(1) Large group presentation.
   (a) IGE Planning System—sound filmstrip.
   (b) During the film stops students will simulate the planning meetings focusing on a social action concept.
Objective (9). Means:
(1) Independent activity: read handout on WRSD study skills.
(2) Lecture: The Instructional Programming Model and Its Application to Elementary Social Studies.
(3) Practicum: creation of task groups using Royal McBee notched cards.

Postassessment:
(1) Paper and pencil tests for enabling objectives.
(2) Position paper describing the undergraduates ideal social studies program for the terminal objective. The criteria for evaluation are:
   (a) Definition of basic concepts in elementary social studies; demonstration of understanding of teacher-made curriculum units, the concept of attainment model, instructional systems model, and value clarification.
   (b) Use of evidence to support positions.
   (c) Logical consistency.
   (d) Clarity of thought.
   (e) Inclusion of details related to time and space considerations.
   (f) Articulation of the advantages of team teaching social studies.

SUMMARY

In this chapter we have provided representative, not necessarily ideal, modules in each of the four basic content areas usually found in the school curriculum. Our purpose was twofold: (1) to demonstrate the compatibility of a CBTE approach to these essential areas, and (2) to provide additional samples illustrative of the modular organization of content. In the next chapter we will describe how materials such as these are managed and presented to students.

Notes

1. Hans P. Guth, "The Monkey on the Bicycle," in *Language Arts in the Elementary School*, ed. Hal D. Funk and DeWayne Triplett (New York: J. P. Lippincott Co., 1972), p. 41.
2. Jeannette Veatch, *Reading in the Elementary School* (New York: Ronald Press, 1969).
3. Duane R. Tovey, "Relationship of Matched First Grade Phonics Instruction to Overall Reading Achievement and the Desire to Read," in *Some Persistent Questions on Beginning Reading*, ed. Robert C. Aukerman (Newark, Del.: International Reading Association, 1972), pp. 93-101.
4. Wayne Otto, *Wisconsin Design for Reading Skill Development* (Madison: Wisconsin Research and Development Center for Cognitive Learning, 1970).
5. "Elementary Science Study," McGraw-Hill series (New York).
6. Leopold Klopfer, "Individualized Science: Relevance for the 1970's," *Science Education* 55, no. 4 (1971): 441-48.

Suggested Readings

Carlin, Arthur A., and Robert B. Sund, *Teaching Science through Discovery*. 2d ed. Columbus, Ohio: Charles E. Merrill Publishing Co., 1970.

Engle, Shirley H., and Wilma L. Longstreet, "A Design for Social Education." In Engle and Longstreet, *The Open Curriculum*. New York: Harper & Row, 1972.

I/D/E/A, "The Teacher Advisor Concept." In *Change Program Newsletter* 3, no. 1 (October 1972).

Otto, Wayne, and Eunice Askow, *Rationale and Guidelines* (Wisconsin Design for Reading Skill Development). Minneapolis: National Computer Systems, 1972.

Staff, Analysis of Mathematics Instruction Project, *DMP Sampler*. Chicago: Rand McNally, 1972.

Veatch, Jeannette, *Reading in the Elementary School*. New York: Ronald Press, 1972.

9/ Presenting and Managing the CBTE Program

Castelle G. Gentry
George E. Dickson

There are many elements in any CBTE program, and we have identified them in earlier chapters. Obviously, such a program is a matter of some complexity, and the means of delivering and managing it are crucial to the successful introduction and operation of CBTE. In the following pages our assumption is, and we attempt to demonstrate, that CBTE requires new media and new management techniques.

MEDIA

There have been two major reasons why educators had limited success with new media applications. First, teachers lacked the skills for applying these techniques. This is compounded when teachers of teachers are no more capable than their students in media and other instructional technology skills. Secondly, teachers lacked the skills for determining objectively whether their use of media—indeed, their instruction—had been effective. As long as educators lacked the means to determine the effects of their instruction, they were free to vary their strategies and mediation as they chose. Competency-based programs make visible the process of instruction, and its effect.

Before developing this discussion further, we shall clarify the understandings and the questions we have about educational or instructional technology.

What is Educational Technology?

The field of educational or instructional technology is still in flux. It is an emerging field that borrows from a wide range of disciplines and technologies. Purists make vague distinctions between educational and instructional technology. Others say media is a component of the technology, while some declare it a separate but related concern. Depending on which expert you consult, the definition for the field ranges from "the systematic application of scientific and other knowledge to the solution of educational or instructional problems," to "the presentation of an instructional message through a mechanical or electronic device." The first of these definitions is so all-inclusive that one wonders what remains for the other fields in education. The second is of such small moment that its value is negligible. Our position is that *any techniques or combination of techniques that can be applied to accomplish our instructional and educational objectives more effectively and efficiently* is a technology. Further, we choose to define a medium as "any means by which an instructional message may be presented"—including live teachers.

Regardless of how educational technology is defined, few institutions now require faculty to have skills in the field. For the most part, skills are limited to those acquired during isolated experiences of operating audiovisual equipment and media software production. How can a competency-based teacher education program, in conjunction with the multiunit relationship with the public schools, counteract the lack of media and assessment skills? The lack of these skills remains a limiting factor on the effectiveness of instructional technology.

Effect of a Competency-Based Program on Media

Since the concept of competency or mastery requires that the student exhibit a behavior at a minimal level, it is necessary that the behavior be stated precisely in measurable form. Clearly, if we are to determine whether the student has met the minimal level for the behavior, we must also have a valid and reliable criterion instrument. Assuming that comparative data on means of instruction are analyzed, those means that increase instructional effectiveness and efficiency will continue. Those means that do not will be replaced by alternative means. Logically and practically those successful means that incorporate media and other instructional technology applications can be expected to survive; and users must obviously learn the necessary skills to employ them. By the same token, media techniques that are not successful will be changed or abandoned.

Competency-Based Instruction and Grouping

The requirement of a competency-based program that a student may not move on to the next module until he has mastered the behaviors of his current module, tends to increase the time spread among students. Students who reach competency early will move on to the next module. Students who require extra trials to reach competency will vary as to when they complete the module, depending on the number and degree of their difficulties. This time spread among students makes group instruction difficult, at times impossible. A neat but unlikely solution would be to provide each student with his own tutor. An alternative, and one that distresses many educators, is to automate instruction to permit mediated programs to carry the burden of instruction—in essence, to expand programmed instruction techniques to incorporate both print and nonprint media.

We assume that automation means some self-instructional form using print and nonprint media, and do not equate self-instruction with individualized instruction. Self-instructional programs at present are designed with some normative student in mind. Perhaps in time, through complex branching programs controlled by computers, an individualized self-instructional program might be possible, but we do not expect that level of sophistication in the near future. Instead, we seek to individualize and personalize our instruction through the changed roles of our faculty members. As print and nonprint media take on a greater importance in presenting information, the faculty assumes greater responsibility for the more difficult tasks of advisement, remediation, production and revision of modules, management of instructional resources, and synthesis.

While all these functions are essential, the most challenging and the most interesting is synthesis. Synthesis refers to the process that professors and students go through to integrate the isolated bits and pieces gained from the modules. The guidance of synthesizing activities requires greater subject-matter depth, and far more sophisticated skills of communication, than does the traditional presentation of information. In the latter, the professor has considerable control over the subject matter chosen for discussion, and over the number and kind of questions dealt with by the class. But in guiding the integrative processes designed to help a student synthesize his experiences, the professor must be prepared to deal with the particular content and questions relative to the individual student's condition. We do not know now of any mediated processes that can begin to handle the responsibilities inherent in synthesis, but we do have at our disposal a large number of media techniques that are useful for displaying information and for interacting with the student to some degree.

Mediated Self-Instruction

Although we are aware of the advantages of sophisticated media systems, like those controlled by computer and dial-access mechanisms, their use is limited both economically and programmatically. While some computer programming is used in the management and assessment components of our program, our media systems for instruction are simple but adequate approximations of our needs.

Our self-instructional laboratory uses three types of media: (1) printed program material, (2) synchronized slide/tape programs, and (3) instructional films. Most of the self-instructional modules combine all three. A typical module would have a printed portion containing objectives for the module, directions for completing the module, and a list of assigned or recommended references. The directions might require a student to take the pretest for the module. If the student did not pass the pretest, he might then be directed to read an article. After responding to a question sheet on the article, and checking his answers against a correct response sheet, the student might then be directed to view and listen to a slide/tape. After repeating the question and response routine, he might be directed to a short linear programmed instruction segment. Following that, the student could be required to view an instructional film for which there would also probably be question and correct response sheets. His final direction might be to take the posttest for the module.

If he met the competency requirement, the student would then proceed to the next module. If not, the immediate feedback from the posttest would inform him as to which objectives he had failed to master and possible alternative materials for reaching competency in the behaviors of the objectives. If his deficiency was great enough, or if he so desired, the student could have a strategy conference with his adviser and/or the professor responsible for the module. After following the prescribed strategy the student would retake the posttest or its equivalent.

Faculty Production of Mediated Modules

As mentioned previously, most of the instructional load in the self-instructional modules is carried by slide/tape presentations. Slide/tape was chosen as a major medium partly because of its comparative economy compared with other media, and also because of the ease of production and revision.

With the advent of easily operated automatic cameras and film that can be used with minimum light conditions, most faculty are willing to take their own slides. The new cassette and reel-to-reel tape recorders, with their built-in slide synchronization capability, can also be operated successfully after only a few minutes' instruction. The capability to synchronize the slides and tapes, so that the slide advances automatically, is important; automatic synchronization enables the student to watch and take notes without having to advance the slides himself. It also prevents the disorienting problem, often encountered in unsynchronized slide/tape presentations, of the audio portion getting behind or ahead of the appropriate slide.

Usually, the most time-consuming task in revising a slide/tape presentation is redoing the audio tape. The slides, for the most part, can be easily rearranged, deleted, or augmented.

The use of instructional films creates special problems, and we do not ordinarily use them in our self-instructional modules unless they provide information or techniques not possible or practical through still photography or other media forms, or unless the university owns the film. High rental fees restrict film use; in a traditional program a sixteen-millimeter instructional film would be used for a day or two, but with the individual pacing of a competency-based program, the film might be needed for weeks until all the students passed the point of the film's program sequence. As more and more instructional films are put into an eight-millimeter format, their lower cost will make it more reasonable to purchase rather than rent.

The specific nature of our objectives enables us to be critical about the value of a film. We do not often wish to have our students view all of a film. Much of the content is either redundant or filler material, and unnecessary for the student's understanding. The short, single-concept film is generally more useful. With the almost daily improvement in Super 8 film systems and their ease of use and editing, in the near future we should be able to begin to produce short films for our own specific needs. At present, videotape substitutes for film production, and in some cases goes beyond film capabilities.

The Use of Television in Instructional Modules

We have the use of several small, portable television systems. Besides the short vignettes of teaching skills and strategies in the single concept mode, they find their major use in microteaching. Our microteaching technique involves the video recording of a prospective teacher carrying out some specified teaching task, followed by a critical viewing of the video tape with a faculty member. The portable television systems are usually operated by faculty or under faculty supervision.

In addition to the portable systems, we use the university's professional instructional television installation. It is primarily budgeted for mass instruction, but the staff anticipates that it may be used in self-instructional modules at a later date when some form of dial-access capability becomes practical.

Instructional Simulation and Gaming

Our teacher preparation program emphasizes field experiences. A major concern about our former program was that the often theoretical campus classroom activities were isolated from the practical world of the public school classroom. One could hear about an instructional event, one could discuss it, one could see a teacher deal with the event, or one could deal with the event oneself. And in that order of importance.

One of the problems of learning in the field is that a student may have to wait a long time before he observes the desired student and teacher behaviors. Consider the instance where the purpose in visiting a public school classroom is to see the application of pupil control techniques. If the teacher visited is a successful classroom manager, there is less likelihood that the occasion for exhibiting controlling behavior will arise. But if we observe a poor manager's classroom, we may see many instances calling for pupil control, but few examples of appropriate treatment being applied. It is also difficult for the neophyte to separate out the cues indicating the need for control. An accomplished manager can perceive such cues, and might act on them before the need is apparent to others. In fact, where the cues are very subtle, the manager's reaction might be missed entirely, or at best be misconstrued by the prospective teacher.

A set of media techniques that may not only adequately substitute for a "real" experience, but in some cases prove a better alternative, is called instructional simulation. Very simply, instructional simulation is the process of abstracting the important characteristics from a situation, and putting them in a form that will encourage the student to interact with them. Chess is an example of simulated battle. A wind tunnel simulates a wide variety of aerodynamic conditions. A television program may simulate a teacher, and so on. To illustrate an appropriate use of simulation dealing with pupil control problems, imagine the following situation.

On entering the simulation facility, a student is given an advance organizer, which informs him that he is about to see a short filmed episode of a classroom setting. His task is to spot instances where disciplinary action would be appropriate and to recommend disciplinary measures. He is told to give the projectionist a signal when he is ready to view the film. At a predetermined point the projectionist stops the film and the prospective teacher writes a description of the event requiring pupil control, and his measure for correcting the problem. At his signal the film continues, presenting a solution chosen by a group of professional educators and their reasons for choosing that solution.

In one sitting, a prospective teacher might have an opportunity to see and practice dealing with several different instances of undesirable pupil behavior, or he might look at simulated instances of other classroom problems (i.e., spotting cues that indicate the need for remediation). To experience those same instances a student might have to observe in a classroom for days or even weeks. It would also be difficult to get the immediate feedback provided in the simulated situation. Considering the short time that we have to prepare prospective teachers, simulated experiences may not be ideal, but they may be the only reasonable alternative. We anticipate that a significant percentage of field experiences will be handled through simulation.

The Use of the Teacher Education Center[1] Concept and Instructional Media

The multiunit program requires a recognition that our responsibility for teacher preparation does not begin and end with formal courses on campus. Public schools and the university are both subsystems of the larger educational system. The multiunit concept is supported by the teacher education center concept.

The teacher education center serves many purposes for both preservice and inservice teachers. As we will demonstrate, media is an important means for carrying out the functions of such a center, including consultation, demonstration, instruction, and production.

The majority of the learning stations in the teacher education center laboratory are one-person carrels equipped with a synchronized slide/tape unit. Any teacher or prospective teacher in the area or on campus can use the self-instructional modules. We envision that students will eventually have their own playback equipment at home. At such time they could borrow modules, much as they now borrow library books. Given high speed duplication equipment, we may soon make it possible for a student to have his own copy of a mediated module.

The curriculum materials demonstration unit of a teacher education center has available a broad range of media, both print and nonprint. It is the purpose of this unit to make preservice and inservice teachers aware of instructional materials and their applications. Materials include instructional films, filmstrips, audiotapes, disc records, transparencies, slide sets, simulation games, programmed textbooks, and a plethora of other printed media. Because of storage and retrieval priorities, more and more printed media are being stored on either microfilm or microfiches. Besides a continuously updated catalog, a newsletter is periodically sent to preservice and inservice teachers, informing them of new acquisitions.

The instructional equipment operation and production laboratory serves both pre and inservice teachers as well as college faculty. A major reason that teachers and prospective teachers don't make more use of media is simply fear of the hardware of instruction. Our program requires prospective teachers to develop at least minimal operative skills for: slide projectors, filmstrip projectors, overhead projectors, film projectors, audiotape recorders (both cassette and reel-to-reel), and portable television systems. Teachers and prospective teachers also develop skills and receive guidance in producing mediated materials for their specific instructional needs.

The larger concept of instructional technology, which is as much process as it is materials and equipment, is taught both as content and process. To a large extent, the latter is taught through modeling by the faculty. Each of our professional education instructional teams has a media person whose responsibility it is to encourage, and to help develop, instruction that makes appropriate use of an expanding instructional technology.

MANAGEMENT

The competency or mastery concept governing our CBTE program requires measurable objectives for essential knowledge and skills and public criteria for determining the degree to which students attain them. The basic unit that our management-information-evaluation system depends on is a three-way match among behaviorally stated objectives, strategies for accomplishing the objectives, and criterion items that indicate how well the objectives have been met. These basic units not only provide the evaluative data needed at the micro level but also at the broad programmatic level. A comparison among and across these units provides useful information about people and the program. We concentrate first on the changes that exposure to our program may cause in beginning teachers and then on changes that they bring about in their pupils, with greatest concentration on the former. Using this focus, comparisons among and across the above units indicate the degree to which learners acquire necessary knowledge and reveal particular skills which have been learned. When related to the overall goals of the program, similar comparisons will be a source of information for making decisions about program irrelevancy and deficiency. The data for all of these purposes must be in such a form that their analysis will point to (1) individual student needs that are not being met by the instructional program and (2) elements of the instructional program that need revision.

The functions of any management process are planning, organizing, coordinating, controlling, and assessing (appraising). These functions are accompanied by the management components of analysis, design, operation, feedback, and revision. *Analysis* defines the needs, tasks, variables, and constraints related to program objectives. *Design* develops the factors relevant to the solution of problems. *Operation* is the process of physically setting up and running a management-information-evaluation system to solve problems. *Feedback* provides information on the success of problem-solving operations in all components of the system. *Revision* is the refinement or the changes necessary to continue meeting program objectives, or to generate new needs and tasks for the successful operation of the program. The entire effort is a process that must be thought of as cyclical and ongoing.

Since our basic purposes are to implement and then operate a CBTE program, management is needed for program development, installation, maintenance, and revision. To achieve these purposes management allocates various resources, develops a procedure for handling information, provides a communication network to distribute information, and concerns itself with the various logistical problems of the system.

Given the unequal and interactive effects of technological and sociological evolution, management-information-evaluation systems are often at a low level of approximating an ideal system. In Chapter 10 we describe an ideal system of evaluation and management, but we have begun our efforts at a much lower level. In moving toward the ideal management system we are guided by the concept of successive approximations, which was discussed in Chapter 5. A good management operation requires considerable resources of personnel, materials, space, equipment, and time, and scarcity of these have prevented us from creating an ideal instructional and management system immediately. The survival and continued refinement of our program, operating from a base of limited resources, requires a pragmatic approach.

Assessment is the key component for a management system under the restraint of successive approximations. Our efforts to develop a CBTE program focus on assessment and on decisions about assessment outcomes. Change in our instructional and management system depends on the assessment of objective data and on the revision processes channeling that data. In a sense we are required to manage by objectives because the instructional program is by definition competency based. The ongoing collection and assessment of data from our management-information-evaluation system results in continuous changes in the instructional system and in management needs as we move closer to an ideal CBTE program.

Managing and Evaluating Student Progress

Perhaps the most effective way of presenting our initial, admittedly incomplete, CBTE managing-information-evaluation system will be to indicate what a student does as he goes through the process. Preassessment and postassessment for each module take place in a testing laboratory, which is a part of the teacher education center. A student who wishes to begin a particular module goes to the laboratory and asks to take the pretest for that module. On entering the testing laboratory, he exchanges his university identification card for the appropriate test, and takes it in a supervised carrel station. Answers are put on IBM punch cards or answer sheets for machine scoring. In constructed response examinations and performance checklists, the faculty member giving the examination uses the same type of scoring sheets to indicate how well the student has met the criteria specified.

All data are then put through a special computer program, the Competency-based Teacher Education Assessment and Revision Component, which analyzes test data for student advisement and program revision purposes. Information is secured on each objective per student, as the objective is linked with a "criterion item." The student is given immediate feedback on the examination from a laboratory assistant; the information also goes to his adviser. If the examination has been a pretest, the results can determine what parts or behaviors of the module the student has already attained, or the terminal skill and knowledge that he has already achieved. He can then enter at an appropriate point in the modules available for the course he is taking. If the student lacks entering skills and knowledge, the laboratory assistant will direct him to a prerequisite module or indicate that he is ready to begin the activities of the module under consideration.

If the student has some of the skills or knowledge taught by the module, the laboratory assistant will inform him of the objectives remaining. Thus the student can concentrate on the objectives he has not learned and ignore those that he has pretested out of. A student who has not successfully passed the pretests is directed to the appropriate entering point of the module to carry out the indicated learning activities. On completion of these, he returns to the testing laboratory for postassessment procedures. The feedback from this effort goes directly to the student and his adviser and provides information such as his performance on the objectives attempted and the stage at which objectives and modules have been completed. Since rapid feedback is provided, immediate module recycling or progression is possible.

Other useful information on students in the program has been included in the material input to the computer, other than test responses. These are the student's identification number, his adviser's code, the module cluster or course number, the specific module being worked on, the number of estimated hours spent in preparing for a posttest, a ranking by the student of the appropriateness of the module objectives, and the strategy used to teach the objective.

The computer program provides two types of readouts to faculty. One type goes to the instructional team member who is the student's adviser. This information is computer data reduced statistically from accumulated student data, and goes to the adviser at least once a week or more often if needed. On the basis of such information, the faculty adviser can determine how to be of assistance to a student having difficulty. He is able to pinpoint troublesome objectives and to examine the activities that the student went through to master the objectives. For example, if he finds that his student took half the time to prepare for the posttest that successful students took, this could be an indication that insufficient time was spent on the instructional activities. Those cases where the students' attitudes were negative about the objective or the learning activities would suggest a different instructional approach. By pinpointing the objective and the strategies for teaching it, the adviser-instructor is able to offer alternative means for learning the objective, or he can direct the student to another faculty member who can recommend alternatives. This process prevents the accumulation of error and negative affect by getting to the student quickly with a workable solution to his problem.

The second type of computer program readout goes to the instructional team that has primary responsibility for any module. Again, these statistically reduced data provide considerable information about student successes and difficulties with module (program) objectives and activities. Objectives can be reexamined in terms of relevancy and clarity and instructional strategies can be inspected for defects. This provides opportunities for module revision before students are again exposed to them. Student exposure to revised modules can then be reviewed to learn if the revisions had the desired effect.

The two computer readouts deal only with data collected while the student is in the CBTE portion of the program. They do not use the considerable external data that could be extremely useful in advising students or revising program components, such as outcomes of general education courses or specialized courses taken in the college of arts and sciences, or university data on student characteristics (e.g., age, sex, high school GPA, etc.). Computer programming that will incorporate such data is being developed. It is also anticipated that certain data could be collected from participating public and parochial educators about the effectiveness and efficiency of various program components. This information too will eventually be put into the computer for the generation of more complete program information.

The intent of our first CBTE management-information-evaluation system effort is to provide data to aid the effective advising of students and to identify potentially ineffective, inefficient, and irrelevant portions of our program, so that corrections can be made. It must also indicate necessary changes in CBTE organization and management. We think the continuous process of assessment and revision now begun will bring us closer to an ideal management-information-evaluation system, and, more importantly, to a valid and reliable program for preparing teachers.

An additional significant spinoff from the accumulating data bank of our present system is the obvious opportunity for educational research. To be able to compare the effects of relating the variety of student characteristics to the variety of learning strategies has great promise for identifying the most appropriate learning strategies for individual learning styles.

SUMMARY

We have discussed some of the new means of instruction prescribed for a CBTE program, as well as some of the procedures for managing this more complex instructional program. We believe it is necessary to use a computer program to provide necessary data on schedule. The next chapter describes an ideal evaluation model for CBTE and the actual, practical procedures used in evaluating CBTE and IGE/MUS.

Notes

1. The teacher education center concept is fully discussed in Chapter 11.

Suggested Readings

Cook, Desmond. *Management Control Theory as the Context for Educational Evaluation.* Columbus, Ohio: Educational Program Management Center, The Ohio State University, 1970.

Corrigan, R. E., Associates. *A Systems Approach for Education.* Anaheim, Calif.: R. E. Corrigan Associates, 1969.

Forrester, Jay. *Principles of Systems.* Cambridge, Mass.: Wright-Allen Press, 1968.

Hartley, Harry J. *Educational Planning-Programming-Budgeting: A Systems Approach.* Englewood Cliffs, N.J.: Prentice-Hall, 1969.

10/ Evaluation and Feedback for CBTE and IGE/MUS

Stephen Jurs

H. Eugene Wysong

Evaluation is a crucial component in the total development and implementation of the program. Evaluation provides an information feedback system that describes the accomplishments and needs of the program, and its procedures and results help personnel clarify their goals and make decisions which maximize the probability that their goals will be achieved. Data collected through evaluation can be used to diagnose program strengths and weaknesses and to communicate the significant events in the program to others.

Evaluation does not label a program as "good" or "bad." It is a dynamic process of providing information that facilitates communication and understanding among the people concerned and helps the program to change in the direction of the planned objectives. Evaluation should be identified within the plans of the total CBTE/IGE/ MUS program so that the procedures and results will be effective in facilitating communication, decision making, and change. Evaluation procedures need to be planned well so that appropriate measurement strategies (i.e., pretesting and posttesting) can be used and so that data collection techniques will not interfere with other activities of the program. Evaluation is a tool of decision makers, a way of viewing planned educational change.

Almost any new educational program goes through four basic developmental stages, which might be described as (1) planning, (2) implementation, (3) growth, and (4) adjustment. Each stage has special needs, and the purposes of evaluation may be different at each stage.

THE ORIGINAL EVALUATION MODEL

Our original evaluation design for the Ohio model competency-based teacher education program was an amalgamation of the Context, Input, Process, Product (CIPP) and Evaluative Programs for Innovative Curriculums (EPIC) evaluation models developed by Drs. Daniel Stufflebeam and Robert Hammond. Their combined model is represented in Figure 10-1, and provides a general design for evaluation procedures that can be adapted to various innovative programs in education. The general logic of the model stresses the relationship of evaluation to decision making, as indicated in Figure 10-2.

In the Hammond-Stufflebeam model four types of educational decisions are necessary and sufficient to provide information and knowledge of the educational decision situations to be served: (1) planning, (2) structuring, (3) implementing, and (4) recycling. *Planning decisions* specify the changes that are needed in a program. *Structuring decisions* specify operationally defined objectives; general program strategies; and method, personnel, facilities, budget, schedule, organization, and context—for use in effecting desired changes. *Implementing decisions* are those used in carrying through an action plan. *Recycling decisions* determine the relation of outcomes to objectives and help decide whether to continue, terminate, evolve, or drastically modify the operation under way.

These four kinds of educational decisions require four kinds of evaluation: (1) context evaluation, which provides information for planning decisions; (2) input evaluation, which provides information for structuring decisions; (3) process evaluation, which provides information for implementing decisions; and (4) product evaluation, which provides information for recycling decisions. The context

Figure 10-1. Hammond-Stufflebeam Evaluation Model

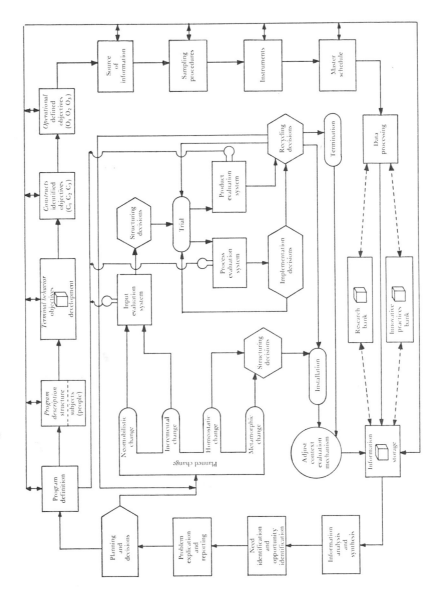

Figure 10-2. The Relationship of Evaluation to Decision Making

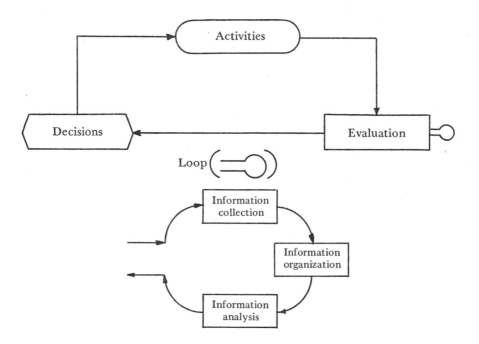

evaluation system is continuous and systematic, while the input, process, and product evaluation mechanisms are ad hoc, put into effect only when it is desired to bring about changes within the system for which adequate supporting information is not already available. In relation to a CBTE teacher education program, context evaluation indicates the need for change within the program, input evaluation helps determine how the change is to be effected, process evaluation aids in the day-to-day implementation of the change, and product evaluation identifies the outcomes of the change effort.

A full explanation for the evaluation model in Figure 10-1 is found in the report of the Ohio Elementary Teacher Education Model Program.[1] The following discussion provides a brief explanation, to indicate the general structure of a design for educational evaluation.

Fundamentally, the model design provides for a continuous, systematic, monitoring type of program evaluation, as well as ad hoc process and product evaluations. The outer loop of the figure represents a continuous, systematic context evaluation mechanism, which provides information to the planning body of the system for use in making decisions to change the system or to continue with present procedures that are serving important objectives effectively and efficiently. Context evaluation consists of four major subsystems: (1) program explication, (2) data collection, (3) information processing and storage, and (4) planning. These are indicated, respectively, at the top, right, bottom, and left sides of Figure 10-1. If the operations in the context evaluation process indicate that there are no discrepancies between the intentions and actualities or between possibilities and probabilities of the educational program under operation, the planning body would likely make choices which would result in a "steady-as-you-go" or a continuous satisfied CBTE program state. However, if the context evaluation indicates that the program is deficient in some way, the decision-making group would decide to bring about some changes in the program to correct the deficiencies. These changes represent the ad hoc evaluation process, as represented by the inner portion of Figure 10-1. The changes could be of four types:[2]

(1) *Metamorphic change,* based on decisions to effect large changes in the program supported by a high level of relevant understanding on how to bring about such changes;

(2) *Homeostatic change,* based on decisions to effect small changes, again supported by a high level of relevant understanding;

(3) *Incremental change,* based on decisions to effect a small change supported by a low level of relevant understanding; and

(4) *Neomobilistic change,* based on decisions to effect large change supported by a low level of understanding.

Depending on the types of change that result from planning decisions, different evaluation procedures are necessary. In any event, input evaluation study is first done to identify and evaluate strategies and procedures that could be used to effect the desired changes and assist all decision makers in designing change procedures. Process and product evaluation are then included to aid in decisions pertaining to trial or pilot phases of the program. Process evaluation provides information for implementation decisions needed for efficient operation of the trial. Product evaluation goes on simultaneously throughout the trial process in conjunction with process evaluation, and supports recycling decisions that could lead to reformulation of the change to be brought about, a modification in either strategy or procedure, termination of the change effort, or installation of the total program. In the case of installation, obviously the context evaluation mechanism would be adjusted to allow for systematic monitoring of the new element in the total system.

The small loops attached to each of the evaluation systems represent the elements of evaluation design concerned with focusing, information collecting, information organization, information analysis, information reporting, and evaluation administration.

This model for evaluation is an excellent conceptualization of the entire process. However, it is one thing to design a model and quite another to put that design into operation. In our feasibility study of the Ohio model, we determined that implementation of the CIPP-EPIC evaluation model would require an outlay of $1,750,000. Since these funds have not been available, the model remains a goal and a guide to what is desirable in evaluation.

EVALUATING THE OHIO MODEL CBTE PROGRAM

The development of our CBTE program is an ongoing process. Our initial implementation has been merely an approximation of the program that was designed, and the same can be said for our evaluation efforts. Much of the potential of the program and of the sophisticated procedure for evaluation cannot be realized until program operations have run for several cycles and difficulties have worked themselves out.

Two distinct types of evaluation are necessary to ensure that the difficulties do get worked out and do not remain as long-term encumbrances on the program. Evaluation first identifies deficiencies and successes. It will not indicate the *cause* of these deficiencies and successes; hence whenever deficiencies are found, a second phase of adjustments will be necessary. Without evaluation, deficiencies could persist without remedial attention. Evaluation is more than an accounting of what happens. It provides information to diagnose whether the program is operating as expected. Evaluative data will ensure that program development proceeds in an organized manner based on the best available data.

Formative Evaluation

Evaluation that is concerned with the continuous development of new curricula has been termed formative evaluation. "The role of formative evaluation is to discover deficiencies and successes in the intermediate versions of a new curriculum."[3] Hence, formative evaluation is a primary concern as the program is implemented.

Evaluation for Program Development

In our CBTE implementation evaluation for program development has taken place at two levels: the module level and the program level. Evaluation within each module is similar to any systematic evaluation of instructional units. Between-module evaluation is concerned with articulation and efficiency across the entire sequence of modules. Program level evaluation is more than aggregated evaluations, for it includes module-to-module integration as well as other program level considerations.

Module Diagnostic Evaluation

Evaluation at the module level focuses on providing information on whether particular modules need revision. The modules are based on a match among the objectives, the means for achieving the objectives, and the criterion. Module evaluation must provide information about all three of these components, but emphasis is on the criterion performance of the students.

Evaluation information that serves as a diagnostic of module problems includes student reaction both to the objectives of the module and to the means for attaining these objectives. Adverse reaction to either suggests a need for one or two intensive follow-up evaluations, one to judge the worth of objectives and the other a process evaluation to identify whether intended classroom activities were actually implemented.

Data about criteria concentrate on the adequacy of criterion instruments and the performance of students relative to the criteria. Item analyses and reliability estimates for criterion tests are made available to module producers. Such data help determine whether test scores are accurate enough to warrant alternative decisions about students, and also suggest which items might be revised in subsequent administration of that test.

Student performance yields diagnostic information relative to the entire module. For example, there is obviously a problem when too few students successfully complete the module within the estimated time limits. The exact cause will not be known, but some of the more obvious possibilities can be investigated. It may be that the criterion level of the test was set too high for most students. The means might also be inadequate for bringing students up to the specified performance level. Perhaps time estimates were too short. Only careful research untangles such complex causal networks; evaluation merely pinpoints where such research would be desirable and reveals some of the relevant data.

Program Diagnostic Evaluation

Evaluation of module-to-module interrelationships is necessary. An evaluation of the system of modules provides information about the adequacy of the system design. The sequence of modules, including the perceived prerequisite modules, is analyzed in terms of the student performance in that sequence. Minimum competence criteria, time estimates, and faculty load requirements for recycling are then established on the data base of the initial implementation effort.

Again, such evaluative data will probably not determine the cause of any system deficiencies, but these data are diagnostic to the extent that they pinpoint problem areas within the complex of modules. For example, within-module evaluation reveals, in a particular module, when students do not reach a criterion level within reasonable time limits. The within-program (i.e., between modules) evaluation can relate this situation to criterial performance of these same students on prerequisite modules. In this way the module-to-module integration is monitored. Perhaps early modules with too low minimum competence criteria will look good in terms of within-module evaluation (over the short term), but long-term weaknesses appear as the module is analyzed in terms of the entire sequence of modules.

EVALUATION FOR ADMINISTRATIVE PURPOSES

An evaluative system is also used as a management information system for administrators. When organized appropriately, routinely collected data provide administrators with a data base that is more detailed and more up-to-date than are usual, less systematic information sources.

Program Accounting

Module data can be aggregated to provide necessary information for planning and budgeting. Rational decisions about the program require complete descriptions of the progress of the students; the numbers of students in each module and their projected rate of progress must be monitored as the flexibility of individualized progress takes place. Staff needs in terms of presenting modules, recycling modules, and student advising become much more complex as students proceed through the program at their own pace. Traditional information sources are not adequate, but the evaluation system keeps track of the appropriate data as a matter of course. What is required to yield appropriate administrative feedback is a different means of compilation and reporting of the obtained data.

Student Accounting

At present student records are kept by both the instructors and the central office. Quarterly updates allow academic advisers to help the student plan his schedule so that he completes his program in the most expeditious manner.

The program evaluation system provides an improved feedback system for students and advisers. Advisers can better understand the progress of each student through his set of modules, and they obtain this information more frequently than in end-of-quarter reports. This amount of information is more than is needed for most students, but it facilitates advising of certain students, thus making better use of an adviser's time.

IMPLEMENTING EVALUATION PROCEDURES

The evaluation component in CBTE programs is as integral a part of the total program as is the instructional component. Program revision and program accounting provide a continuously improving effort to maximize effective student learning. Implementation of the evaluation system requires the development of a network to parallel and complement the instructional system. The evaluation effort necessarily addresses the questions of what data should be collected and what persons ought to have access to the data.

Data to be Collected

The data that have to be gathered to provide an adequate description of the program and students are somewhat more extensive than that presently collected in typical teacher education programs. Typical information required in a CBTE system includes at least the following kinds of data:

(1) *Student characteristics.* Characteristics such as previous grade point average, aptitude test scores, student's course load, etc., ought to be kept up-to-date so that unexpected performance on module tests can be analyzed in terms of these variables.

(2) *Module characteristics.* A complete description of each module is essential to its evaluation. Included in this description is the estimated time for completion, the prerequisite modules, the activities and materials used to teach the module, and the criterion performance required of the student.

(3) *Test characteristics.* The evaluators need to have copies of all pretests and criterion tests, with scoring keys. Only then can item analysis be run and reliabilities be computed so that decisions about students that are based on test scores take into account the relative accuracy of the scores.

(4) *Student ratings of modules.* The feedback system provides the reaction of the students to the module. After completing each module, students should have the opportunity to rate the quality of the instruction, the quality of the materials and activities, and the perceived worth of the module objectives themselves.

(5) *Faculty rating of modules.* Faculty working on modules need to provide input about those modules to the evaluation system. Perceptions of how well modules appear to be working, estimated revisions of modules, and time and material constraints are shared with evaluators so that the work of the evaluators is not out of phase with that of the faculty.

Schedules of Data Collection

The flexibility of individualized programs is perhaps their greatest asset. Unfortunately, this flexibility creates a difficult task for the evaluation system monitoring student progress. The unit to be tracked through the system is the individual, rather than the class. Individual students will not all be ready for criterion assessment at the same time for the same module, and they must be tested when ready. Thus, there must be continuous rather than periodic collection of criterion test data.

The mechanics of implementing such a system are complex. Test materials must be prepared in advance and be available to the evaluators. The scoring of tests, compilation of test performance for subsequent item analysis, and updating of student progress records must be done continuously.

Reactions of students to modules are gathered as soon as the student completes the posttest. The perceptions of the faculty about modules may be gathered less frequently, perhaps after an adequate number of students in any block have completed a module.

Clearly, the staff and space requirements for continuous data collection are greater than in traditional programs. However, the benefits of such a flexible program outweigh increased costs.

Audiences for Dissemination

The several purposes for which evaluative data are gathered may at times appear to be in conflict. For example, the administrator's accounting of program performance and the module developer's determination of revision needs can be based in part on the same data, but each interprets the data differently. At issue is whether certain kinds of information ought to be withheld from certain audiences within the system. One option is to have all information available to all audiences. Another is to have each audience in the system receive only the information for which it is responsible, i.e., separate reports tailored to particular needs. Probably the best compromise is to prepare separate reports for the various audiences but to establish policies through parliamentary action on the sharing of this information. When each party understands the data on which program decisions are made, cooperation is enhanced.

Separate reports need to be generated for administrators, advisers of students, instructional teams, etc. While the evaluators have access to a great deal of essential information about the program, they do not share in the decision-making power. The evaluator's stance is neutral. His role is to provide as much data as the system demands for making these decisions.

Evaluation Staff Needs

The evaluation system requires different kinds of expertise. The personnel needed are:

(1) A system design coordinator, whose responsibility is to provide the overall plan for logistical operations in terms of data gathering and processing, and generating reports;

(2) A statistics and measurements person, to oversee the development and validation of instruments and conduct within-system experimentation, e.g., identifying learning styles or aptitude-by-treatment interactions;

(3) Data processing personnel, including computer programmers, to develop programs to automate as much of the record keeping as possible;

(4) Clerical assistants and secretarial help, to tabulate data and prepare summary reports.

Several of these job descriptions may be assumed by one person, depending on the scope of the program.

In addition to the personnel listed, the evaluation system must be directed by a person familiar with each of the above responsibilities, who communicates well with all users of the system—administrators, the instructional staff, program developers, and students—so that program needs can be translated into ongoing functions of the evaluation system.

THE USE OF EVALUATION RESULTS

The data compiled and reported by the evaluation unit can be applied to a wide variety of problems. For each module in a competency-based system, the following areas are the minimum that can be assessed:

1. The evaluative data must pinpoint those modules with which students are having the most difficulty; additional study can then take place to see whether the difficulty is due to program deficiencies.

2. Evaluation identifies the factors that influence student performance in modules which have been indicated as problems.

3. Data on the performance of different kinds of students in the

modules allows the construction of expectancy tables so that students at different levels of proficiency can assess their chances of success on subsequent modules.

4. The progress of the many kinds of students through the series of modules identifies rates of work and alternate materials that maximize criterion performance for particular student types. Such aptitude-by-treatment interactions would suggest tailoring the individual's program specifically to his strengths and weaknesses.

The evaluation data can also be put to many uses at the program level. Among these is the monitoring of student progress through a flexible, individualized program for purposes of present budgeting and budget projections for the future. Improved feedback to advisers about student progress facilitates the student-adviser relationship; the quality of advice should improve as advisers are provided with more detailed and more up-to-date information about students. Finally, the large amount of information about student activities, materials used, and student progress provides a complete and accurate description of the instructional program. This description will be useful for communications with prospective students, parents of students, other schools, and accrediting agencies.

EVALUATING THE IGE/MUS PROGRAM

People who are involved in the IGE/MUS program will naturally make evaluative judgments based on their own perceptions. Parents and members of the board of education will judge the value of the program basing their decisions on whatever information is known to them. This information may only be hearsay or may be about an isolated incident. School administrators will make decisions based on their own perceptions of what is occurring in the program. Lack of valid information has not stopped people from evaluating programs in the past and will not stop them in the future. The question is not, "Should we evaluate the IGE/MUS program?" but "How shall we and how completely will we evaluate the program?"[4]

Evaluation in the Program Planning Stage

The planning stage of a program begins when someone believes that a new concept, activity, or program is preferable to what currently exists. The most important tasks to be accomplished in the program planning stage are to

—Define the program innovation at least well enough so that it can be described generally;

—Describe the general purposes the program should be able to accomplish;

—Determine if the populations to be served have the need to accomplish those purposes for which the program would be designed;

—Define specific product objectives, within the general purposes;

—Describe the program activities that should be performed to accomplish the desired objectives;

—Identify resources needed to perform the program activities;

—Identify barriers that would impede implementation and growth of the program;

—Make a decision to implement the new program.

Evaluation procedures are helpful in accomplishing some of the tasks in the planning of various stages in the IGE/MUS program. Probably the most important question is, Do the populations to be served have a need that might be met by the IGE/MUS program? Evaluation procedures are useful in assessing program needs. The following are some questions that can be asked in such an assessment to determine whether there is need for IGE/MUS:

—Are some students not achieving basic skills in reading, math, or language arts because individually prescribed learning experiences cannot be provided?

—Do some students have negative attitudes toward learning and school because they do not relate to instruction planned for the majority of students?

—Do some students have limited comprehension of science and social studies concepts because their learning experiences are restricted to vicarious group learning experiences of a self-contained classroom?

—Are some teachers at a plateau in their development because they are not stimulated through interaction with fellow teachers?

—Are some teachers dissatisfied and frustrated because they are required to teach subjects for which they are unprepared?

—Are some parents unhappy because their children are exposed to only one teacher? Do they consider this teacher to be incompetent?

—Are some parents unhappy because the classroom teacher cannot or will not provide special individualized help for their children?

—Are some children being retained (failed) and repeating a grade level?

Additional questions might be raised and answered by a program needs assessment.

The objectives to be accomplished in the IGE/MUS program must be defined. Objectives can be categorized into product objectives and process objectives. Product objectives are those planned outcomes judged to be desirable results of the program, for example, increased learning, improved attitudes, greater satisfaction, and greater competency. Process objectives are those planned activities that are conducted for the purpose of accomplishing the product objectives. Process objectives include a description of activities to be performed by people in the program and those conditions that are to be provided by the program. For the accomplishments of the product and process objectives to be measured, they must be adequately defined during the program planning stage.

The resources that can be allocated to the program must also be assessed. Certain personnel, material, and facility resources are required for the IGE/MUS program. The following questions need to be answered:

—Will a sufficient number of classroom teachers be willing and ready to participate in the implementation of the program?

—Will paraprofessional staff be available?

—Will nearby universities provide cooperation and support?

—Can individualized instructional materials be made available?

—Can physical facilities for large group instruction be made available?

—Can provisions be made so that teachers will have time for instructional planning?

—Is inservice education of staff provided for?

Another task is to assess the barriers that might impede implementation and growth of the IGE/MUS program. A determination should be made on whether some forces in the schools or community might resist change. For example, are personnel policies of the school or agreements with teacher associations in conflict with staff provi-

sions of the IGE/MUS program? Will the teaching staff oppose
change? Will lack of administrative leadership or university cooperation be a hindrance?

The ultimate task in the program planning stage is to make the
decision whether to implement the proposed IGE/MUS program or
not. The evaluation procedures should not only provide information
that can be used to make this decision, but should also provide a
means for people to become informed and to communicate their
ideas.

During the program planning stage, the evaluation procedures
emphasize: (1) definition of product and process objectives, (2)
assessment of system needs and resources, and (3) the survey of
potential barriers. Plans should be made to meet any pretesting provisions for future evaluation purposes. Eventually, evaluation should
determine whether or not the product objectives of the IGE/MUS
program are being accomplished. Base-line data for this are collected
before the actual beginning of program development (see description
of the fourth stage, p. 232).

Evaluation in the Program Implementation Stage

The implementation stage is the period when plans for the program are put into action. The major tasks in this stage are to:

(1) Identify and organize the specific staff, material, and facility
resources to be utilized in the program;

(2) Stimulate the beginning of program activities and use of resources;

(3) Coordinate the functioning of all program activities toward
accomplishing product and process objectives;

(4) Change practices that are not consistent with objectives, or
modify objectives when considered desirable from empirical evidence.

Evaluation procedures can be used to obtain feedback on what is
happening in the program from the participants. For example, are
the planned activities (i.e., process objectives) being carried out? Are
the units able to plan their instructional strategies adequately during
planning sessions? Are paraprofessional staff used appropriately? Are
provisions made in each unit for meeting reading, science, math,
social studies, language arts, and guidance needs?

During program implementation evaluation techniques are used to help staff clarify their thinking about objectives of the IGE/MUS program and about their responsibilities in the program. The product and process objectives are listed in the form of an inventory checklist, on which the staff indicates their perceptions of which planned objectives are being accomplished. This process gives feedback information on the current state of affairs and also helps the staff recall the program objectives.

Evaluation in the Program Growth Stage

During the growth stage of the IGE/MUS program, the participating staff members become competent in their new roles and grow in their understandings and skills. They develop new working relationships as they participate with others in planning and providing instruction for the pupils. They become accustomed to new materials, facilities, and procedures.

The major tasks to be accomplished in the program growth stage are to

(1) Clarify the product objectives;
(2) Clarify or modify the process objectives (roles and responsibilities);
(3) Establish channels of communication and cooperation among all people affecting the program;
(4) Improve competencies and skills.

Many of the evaluation tasks conducted during implementation are also appropriate in the program growth stage. In addition, efforts should be made to communicate to various publics the evaluation data that describe what is being done in the program. Parents, administrators, staff, and university personnel need to know the accomplishments and needs of the program.

Evaluation techniques are used to identify needs of staff for inservice education. A list of product and process objectives can be used as a checklist on which staff can indicate which objectives will require them to receive new training.

Evaluation in the Program Adjustment Stage

The program adjustment stage occurs after most of the planned process objectives have been accomplished. At this stage, the program is functioning at least at a minimal level of adequacy. This could be described as a period of stability; however, "stability" does not adequately communicate what takes place during this stage. Adjustments continue to be made even after the program is functioning well. They are needed when staff members leave and new people are employed. New curricular ideas and materials require adjustments, as do new pupils. Adjustments will be made as new evaluation information is obtained, and occur throughout the life of the program. If the program is judged to be unsuccessful in accomplishing the product objectives, the ultimate adjustment could be discontinuation of the program.

The two main tasks in the adjustment stage are to

1. Use evaluation procedures and results in facilitating communication and cooperation; and

2. Adjust the program as a result of evaluation data or changed conditions.

Certain evaluation procedures and strategies can be helpful during the program adjustment stage. The most difficult question to answer is, Are the product objectives of the program being accomplished? If the program is truly in the adjustment stage, most of the planned program activities are being performed. Evaluation of the product objectives is appropriate only after the program has been functioning for a reasonable period of time. A mistake too often made is the attempt to show product accomplishments before the program is adequately under way. Time is needed for a new program to progress through the first three stages of development, and a product evaluation conducted too early is disappointing and meaningless. However, as noted in the discussion of the first stage, plans for evaluating attainment of product objectives should be made early because baseline data are often needed in product evaluations. In addition, the procedures for obtaining feedback information on the fulfillment of the process objectives should be continued.

Various evaluation strategies can be used to determine if the IGE/MUS program is meeting the product objectives. A pretest-posttest design could be used to determine if the product objectives are being accomplished to a greater extent after IGE/MUS program operations than before the program began. For this, data must be collected during the planning stage or early in the implementation stage. A pretest-posttest control group design could be used, in which data is collected before and after implementation in the school with the IGE/MUS program and in a comparable school that does not have the program. Another strategy is the posttest control group design, in which a comparable control group would be used but only posttest data would be collected. Another evaluation design, less experimental, is to describe the product objectives in behavioral terms and determine whether or not the behavioral objectives are being met. This design will give the information needed by a school but it does not give data for comparing the relative effectiveness of IGE/MUS program with other programs.

Content to be Evaluated in the IGE/MUS Program

What should be evaluated in the IGE/MUS program? The content to be evaluated can be categorized into product objectives and process objectives. As stated earlier, product objectives are those planned outcomes that are desired to be the end results of the program. Product objectives are usually described in terms of understandings, attitudes, skills, appreciations, values, competencies, satisfactions, etc., which are gained by students, parents, teachers or others involved in the program. Product objectives are derived from a system of values which defines what is desirable and what is not desirable.

Process objectives are those activities and provisions that are designed to attain the product objectives; they are usually described in terms of activities performed by the program staff, fulfillment of roles and responsibilities, amount of time spent in certain experiences, materials and facilities being used, kinds of instruction given, nature of policies being followed, etc. Process objectives are considered valuable only to the extent that they contribute toward the accomplishment of product objectives. The establishment of process objectives should be based on empirical evidence or on logical reasoning that would indicate their value in attaining the product results.

In planning evaluation procedures, the sources of information must be carefully identified. Various data sources are needed to obtain information that will determine the extent to which the product and process objectives are being accomplished. The people who are to accomplish the product objectives must be identified, and so must the sources for fulfilling the product objectives.

Figure 10-3 provides a model of data sources that can be used to

Figure 10-3. Data Sources for Evaluating the Product and Process Objectives of the IGE/MUS Program

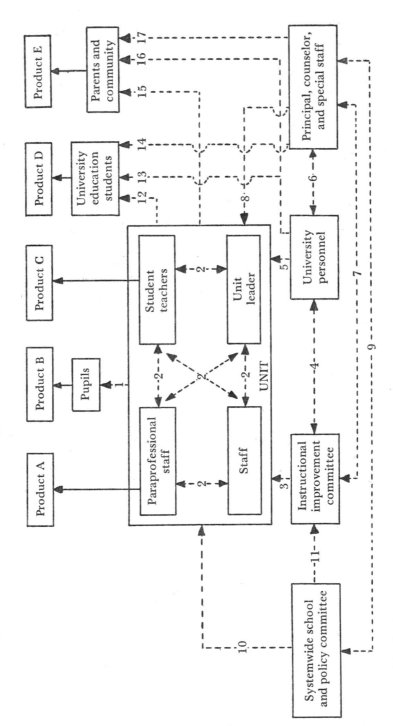

Process objectives ------
Product objectives ———

plan data collection for evaluating the product and process objectives of the IGE/MUS program. The model identifies the people who are to realize the various kinds of product and process objectives. Each line identifies a content area for possible evaluation. Each solid line represents a progression toward the accomplishment of product objectives. Each broken line represents process objectives that influence various elements in the IGE/MUS program and concern the ultimate accomplishment of product objectives; the broken lines can be activities, provisions, or other services that influence the program or the beneficiaries of the program. The possible data sources for measuring product objectives are labeled by letters, and the possible data sources for measuring process objectives are numbered.

The following are examples of general product objectives that might be established for the IGE/MUS program:

Product objective A: Staff teachers, unit leaders, paraprofessional staff, and student teachers develop understandings, competencies, and satisfactions in the IGE/MUS program.

Product objective B: Pupils develop better understandings, skills, and attitudes; experience less failure; attend school more; participate more in class experiences.

Product objective C: Student teachers develop teaching competencies, satisfactions, positive attitudes.

Product objective D: University undergraduate education students attain objectives of competency-based teacher education program.

Product objective E: Parents and people in the community understand and have positive attitudes toward school program.

The following are examples of general process objectives that might be established for the IGE/MUS program:

Process objective 1: Students spend more time in instructional activities, receive more individualized instruction time, receive more variety in educational experiences, receive more individual attention.

Process objective 2: All staff members of the unit carry out their responsibilities in the unit.

Process objective 3: The instructional improvement committee makes decisions that support the units.

Process objective 4: Instructional improvement committee and university personnel assist each other.

Process objective 5: University personnel contribute through in-service education to building the competencies of the unit staff.

Process objective 6: Principal, counselor, resource staff, and university personnel assist each other.

Process objective 7: Principal, counselor, resource staff, and instructional improvement committee serve one another.

Process objective 8: Principal, counselor, and resource staff aid the units.

Process objective 9: Principal, counselor, resource staff, system-wide school personnel, and systemwide policy committee serve one another.

Process objective 10: Systemwide school personnel and system-wide policy committee support personnel in the units.

Process objective 11: Systemwide school personnel and system-wide policy committee provide information and support to instructional improvement committee.

Process objective 12: Units provide environment for helping university education students to develop understandings.

Process objective 13: University personnel assist education students to participate in IGE/MUS program.

Process objective 14: Principal, counselor, and resource staff assist university students.

Process objective 15: Units assist parents and community to understand growth of children in IGE/MUS.

Process objective 16: University personnel meet with parents and community to explain IGE/MUS.

Process objective 17: Principal and resource staff help parents understand school accomplishments and needs.

Of course, each of the above general objectives must be expanded and defined more specifically to fit the needs of the particular school in which the IGE/MUS program is being conducted.

Procedures and Instruments for Evaluating the IGE/MUS Program

When planning procedures and instruments for evaluating the IGE/MUS program, the purposes of evaluation and the content to be evaluated must be considered. The evaluation procedures may be accomplishing different purposes within each of the four program development stages. Also, consideration must be given to whether product or process objectives are being evaluated. The basic purposes of the evaluation procedures and instruments are to

1. Assist people to make decisions and changes that will be more effective in producing desired outcomes;

2. Assist participants in the program to achieve better understanding and cooperation;

3. Assist in providing information that can be communicated to the various publics who should know the accomplishments and needs of the program.

The specific procedures and instruments used should be able to accomplish the purposes of the evaluation at a particular stage of program development, and should be reasonable in terms of cost. The benefits received from the evaluation process should be worth the expenditure of staff time and the cost of materials involved.

When evaluation procedures are being conducted during either the implementation stage or the growth stage, the *content* of the evaluation will be focused on measuring the attainment of the process objectives of the functioning unit. The *purposes* of the evaluation will be to make decisions or adjustments to improve the functioning of units so that the staff of each unit can clarify their understandings of the process objectives to be accomplished. The following procedures and instruments can be used:

—Develop a survey inventory based on the established process objectives for the functioning unit.

—Ask each unit staff member to use the inventory to provide information on the extent to which each process objective is being performed.

—Summarize the results of each inventory.

—Share and discuss the total results with all members of the units.

—Agree on how improvements in the units might be made.

When the program is in the adjustment stage, one purpose of evaluation is to determine whether or not the students have a positive attitude toward school. A pretest-posttest control group design can be used, along with a school attitude instrument. Before the beginning of the IGE/MUS program, data are collected from students in the IGE/MUS school and in a matched control school. Posttest data are collected after the program is functioning adequately.

Comparisons are then made to determine if the change between the pretest and posttest data in the IGE/MUS school is more positive than the change in the control school.

Various techniques and instruments can be used to evaluate the accomplishments of product and process objectives. Data are collected by use of the following kinds of instruments:

Observational reports
Survey inventories
Open-ended questionnaires
Interaction analysis techniques
Individual interviews
Group interviews
Standardized norm-referenced tests
Standardized criterion-referenced tests

Adjective checklists
Q-sort techniques
Student records
Teacher turnover records
Teacher promotions records
Records on student transfers
Records of student failures
Student attendance records
Teacher attendance records

SUMMARY

In this chapter we first considered the proposed role in evaluating CBTE program activities of the Context, Input, Process, Product model. Since the CIPP model is not now operational, other types of evaluation now in use with the CBTE program were explained. This was followed by the delineation of procedures and instruments to evaluate the school-based IGE/MUS program. The purposes of the chapter have been to answer the questions:

Why evaluate?
What can be evaluated?
How can the evaluation be done?

Answers to each of these three questions are needed if program evaluation is to be a meaningful and positive force in influencing program improvement.

This completes our presentation of the several elements of the CBTE, IGE/MUS program. In the next chapter, we shall describe the comprehensive model that encompasses all of these elements.

Notes

1. George E. Dickson et al., *Educational Specifications for a Comprehensive Elementary Teacher Education Program*, vol. I, The Basic Report (Toledo: The University of Toledo, October 31, 1968), pp. 209-35.
2. Ibid., pp. 219-23.
3. Michael Scriven, "The Methodology of Evaluation," in *Perspective of Curriculum Evaluation*, AERA Monograph Series on Curriculum Evaluation, no. 1 (Chicago: Rand McNally, 1967), p. 51.
4. For an actual evaluation of one IGE/MUS program, see H. Eugene Wysong and Michael LaBay, *Evaluation Report on The Multiunit School Project at Martin Luther King, Jr., School* (Toledo, Ohio: Center for Educational Research and Services, University of Toledo, 1970).

Suggested Readings

Alkin, Marvin C. "Evaluation and Decision Making." *Planning and Changing* 3 (winter 1973): 3-15.

Guba, Egon G. "Evaluation and Change in Education," National Institute for the Study of Educational Change. Bloomington: Indiana University, May 1968.

Randall, Robert S. "An Operational Application of the CIPP Model for Evaluation." *Educational Technology* 9 (July 1969): 40-44.

Schmuck, Richard, et al. *Handbook of Organization Development in Schools.* Eugene, Oregon: Center for Advanced Study of Educational Administration, 1972.

Stufflebeam, Daniel, et al. *Educational Evaluation and Decision Making.* Itasca, Illinois: F. E. Peacock Publishers, 1971.

Stufflebeam, Daniel. "The Relevance of the CIPP Evaluation Model for Educational Accountability." *SRIS Quarterly* 5 (spring 1972): 3-7.

Thomas, J. Alan. *The Productive School: A Systems Approach to Educational Administration.* New York: John Wiley & Sons, 1971.

11/ A Comprehensive Model for Educational Renewal

George E. Dickson

In the preceding chapters we have identified and described all the elements in our particular effort to change the teacher education system. In this chapter we shall attempt to provide a comprehensive overview of the entire CBTE project with all essential interrelationships. Again, we should note that the project is changing even as this is written.

ORGANIZATION AND OPERATION OF THE MODEL, PERSONNEL, AND FACILITIES

Competency-based teacher education, its corollary, competency-based education, and individually guided education/multiunit schools have previously been explained. The matter now before us is the way in which these particular innovations can be brought together into a comprehensive educational system. Our solution to this problem is shown in Figure 11-1. This figure represents a successful combination of educational programs, institutions, personnel, and facilities, joined together by a concept and facility called a teacher education center.

Figure 11-1. A Comprehensive Model for Educational Reform and Renewal

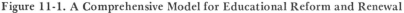

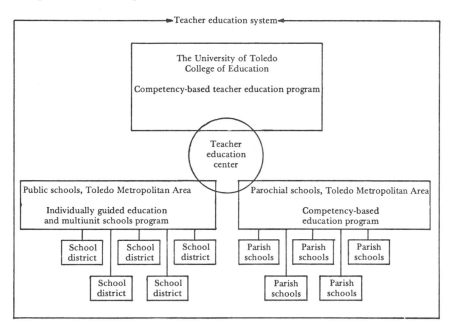

The comprehensive model in Figure 11-1 describes and directs a process for the improvement of teacher competency, both preservice and inservice. All programs, institutions, personnel, and facilities are linked together for the benefit of children. We attempt to deal with educational complexity by considering any component or factor that is involved in the educational process; whatever occurs in one unit or facility affects all the others. Ultimately, all such activity results in educational change in school districts, parish school districts, and the individual schools within those districts.

The first important linkage involves educational programs. The college CBTE program cannot exist without its relationship to the new and changing educational programs in the public and private schools, and their programmatic efforts are in turn bound to the evolving college-based program. Competency-based education in

parochial schools and IGE/MUS in public schools have had a reciprocal and vital effect on the development of CBTE for preservice and
inservice teacher training.

As with programs, so with institutions. The College of Education
does not operate successfully without reciprocal ties to the public and
private school sectors. It is our experience in the Toledo area that all
three can work with and do affect each other. The Toledo public
schools are interested in the CBE curriculum guides produced by the
parochial schools, which are becoming involved in IGE and MUS. Both
are connected with the University of Toledo CBTE program. The
college has been instrumental in developing CBE and IGE/MUS in
schools, and separation of any institution from the others would
inhibit program development.

Personnel in each institution are also linked in many ways through
program development and implementation. We have mentioned the
involvement of college personnel in public and private school operations. Teachers from both public and private schools have taken special
classes and institutes offered by the college. All personnel have met and
served together on committees. Interchange will increase with the
full-scale operation of a teacher education center. In terms of educational personnel, the system for teacher education improvement is
continuous and comprehensive.

Facilities in the teacher education system are no less interconnected.
However, the sharing of facilities between public and parochial schools
is not yet as developed as it is between these institutions and the
College of Education. The college freely uses classrooms and other
school facilities for instruction and demonstrations; teachers and administrators from the schools have equal access to college facilities.
One institution may borrow equipment and materials from the other
with no formal arrangements needed.

THE TEACHER EDUCATION CENTER

The concern of all institutions and personnel involved in educating
teachers is to maximize interrelationships to promote educational
change. The teacher education center has been developed to achieve
this goal. The teacher education center model is represented in
Figure 11-2.

A teacher education center is both a concept and a facility. As a
concept, it is the primary institution to facilitate the implementation

Figure 11-2. A Model for a Teacher Education Center

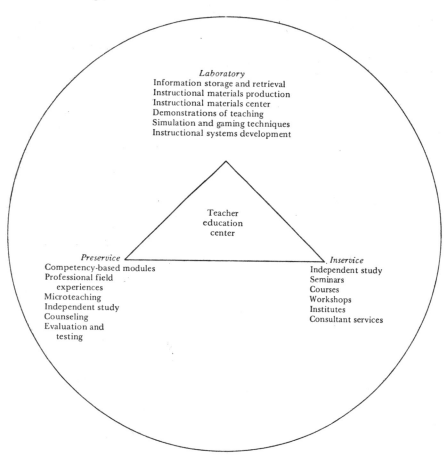

of IGE and CBE in the schools and CBTE in the university. The center has various roles:

(1) It provides the connecting unit through which subsystems of the educational system relate to each other.

(2) It aids in implementation of IGE/MUS, CBE, and CBTE.

(3) It helps provide the inservice and preservice training and re-education necessary for the implementation process, ranging from individualized instruction to workshop or institute experiences.

(4) It creates delivery systems to prepare and disseminate information about educational innovation and trends.

(5) It provides opportunities for consultation on school and university educational problems, from individual exchanges to teaching team meetings.

(6) It provides evaluation and testing services for all teacher center users, as well as program evaluation.

(7) It aids in developing strategies for gaining acceptance of innovative instructional processes in schools or universities.

Essentially, the teacher education center becomes the vehicle for educational change in which change can be designed and where teachers can solve daily problems associated with instruction, teaming, and a host of other issues.

As an educational facility, the teacher center provides—as a minimum—the following:

—A broad collection of print and nonprint instructional resources, a curriculum materials collection;

—The opportunity for instructional materials production;

—The development of an information storage and retrieval system to guide center users to available educational resources;

—A microteaching laboratory to enable college faculty and pre and inservice teachers to observe and analyze their own teaching behavior;

—Model demonstrations of teaching techniques and practices, real and simulated;

—A simulation and gaming laboratory to provide instructional, learning, and motivational techniques.

As a laboratory the teacher education center makes possible the gathering together of instructional materials and equipment in one location for a wide variety of educational uses.

The basic functions of a teacher education center are consultation, demonstration, instruction, production, and evaluation. To carry out these tasks, the center requires six major divisions: management, consultation, resources, production, learning programs and instruction, and evaluation and testing.

(1) *Management* is responsible for coordinating, supervising, and administering all activities within the teacher center.

(2) *Consultation* deals with specific instructional or educational problems requiring expertise not usually available in the schools. The major function would be to analyze and aid in clarifying the perceived problems of center users. Such analysis and clarification would provide both the consultants and those seeking help with data to recommend specific individual or school utilization of teacher center resources to

solve a wide range of educational problems, ranging from those as simple as analyzing a specific teacher behavior with the goal of providing improved teaching skill, to complex efforts such as devising a new curriculum.

(3) The *resource or curriculum materials* division provides a wide variety of print and nonprint instructional resources. Its major feature would be an efficient information and storage retrieval system for such media, and consultation on how to use it effectively.

(4) *Production* serves as a training area to practice and learn instructional media production skills, in order to develop inexpensive and noncommercial teaching materials.

(5) *Learning programs* provide instructional opportunities to develop teacher knowledge and skills through various forms, e.g., self-instructional modules, seminars, workshops, and institutes. This division would be equipped with one-person carrels with self-instructional media. Teaching demonstrations would also be provided.

(6) *Evaluation and testing* carry out objective pre and posttesting of CBTE students. This division would provide timely feedback of testing results to students and faculty.

In England teacher centers have performed an additional function of providing educators with a place for casual conversation, discussion, and informal social activity. A teacher center should have a coffee room and, eventually, a social program for teachers, faculty, and students.

The teacher education center should be located on a university campus or in a nearby school. It must be readily accessible to college students planning to become teachers as well as to all types of school personnel. In the Toledo area, several schools (four to six) have joined together to develop mini teacher-centers which provide collections of instructional materials and related preservice and inservice activities for the schools involved. Mini-centers should have a clear relationship with the major university teacher education center. As extensions of that center, they make possible even closer, more productive relationships among different educators, curriculums, and ways of utilizing teaching materials.

The concept of a comprehensive model for educational reform and renewal involving the use of the teacher education center can be extended statewide. Figure 11-3 provides a possible statewide consortium model. In this model the state department of education would

**Figure 11-3. A Statewide Consortium Model for
Educational Reform and Renewal**

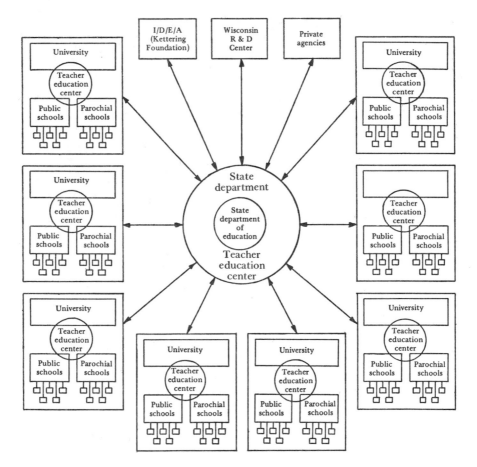

operate a state department teacher center, an enlarged version of the university teacher education center. Each state university or college would have its own teacher education center providing the university with connections to the public and parochial schools in the regional area served by the university. Assuming that the state department of education is concerned with developing individually guided education, multiunit schools, and competency-based education, the state center would have available to it consultation from private agencies, including the Wisconsin R & D Center and I/D/E/A of the Kettering Foundation.

Interchange between the state department teacher center and regional teacher education centers would permit the development of a state-wide planning-implementation effort for IGE/MUS and CBTE. Such a statewide model involving MUS has already begun in Ohio; the Ohio State Department of Education adopted in June 1972 a plan to develop and evaluate multiunit schools in Ohio which incorporates the regional center concept. Coordinating communication links have been established among the intrastate regional centers and with the generic agencies. Each regional teacher education center will provide accurate data for the communications system being developed, and all teaching materials banks will be housed both in the regional centers and in the central materials bank of the state department of education. This development has promise as a statewide strategy for educational innovation.

Whatever local needs dictate, a teacher education center must be. However, under any circumstance the center will be able to call into service the resources of a variety of organizations and individuals to improve education. This should result in better education for children together with acceptance by educators of the idea that all programs can be improved by cooperative efforts.

SUBSYSTEMS FOR BASIC COMPREHENSIVE MODEL DESIGN

The University CBTE Model

Chapters 2, 3, and 5 described our efforts to design, determine the feasibility of, and implement our CBTE program. We shall now describe our existing program and how it operates at the elementary and secondary teacher education levels.

Figure 11-4 presents a model of our competency-based teacher education program. The original Ohio model program design has obviously influenced the present result. Beginning with the minimal option four program for preservice teachers, the faculty has accepted the original ten goals for teacher education of the basic design and subjects, topics, and many of the behavioral objectives derived from those goals for the five contexts. As stated in Chapter 5, the faculty did not accept all of the behavioral objectives from the option four program. These objectives did, however, provide the essential core of the program on which further development was based, first with the process system approach, then with operations under the systems

Figure 11-4. A Model of a Competency-Based Teacher Education Program

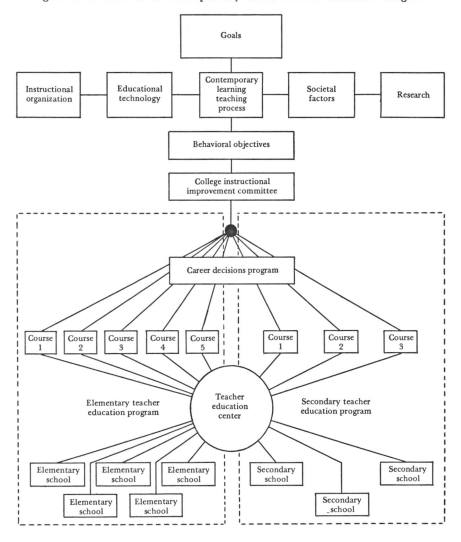

process coordinators, and finally through the establishment of the college instructional improvement committee (CIIC).

We see the development of our teacher education program as a system of successive approximations of the original ideal design. As we develop we implement; implementation is now a process of successively approximating a more nearly ideal CBTE program. Program development and implementation efforts are never finished. What is now described as our competency-based elementary and secondary teacher education program is that particular program currently in existence. What the program becomes one, two, and five years from now will represent our continued efforts to approach the ideal as we respond to a changing world.

College Instructional Improvement Committee

The college instructional improvement committee was the third administrative leadership unit designed to further CBTE development and implementation. Clearly, no system is fixed or complete in its conception and operation: modification and renewal are essential to a dynamic program. The CIIC replaced the three systems process coordinators and the coordinator for the career decisions program. These coordinators had served model development purposes on an ad hoc basis for approximately two years, but the time arrived to move from ad hoc operations toward further internalizing the development-implementation process within the regular administrative structure of the college.

The primary reason for this was simply the growth of the program. As courses and modules were offered in a more regular and less experimental format, program demands of budget, personnel, supervision, assignment, etc., became overriding concerns for the coordinators, tending to divert their energies from developmental efforts. The coordinators did not have the final authority to handle budgetary and personnel problems. This authority rested primarily with the administrative structure of the college: the dean's office and staff, division directors, and department chairmen. Authority for curriculum matters flowed from the dean directly to the division directors and department chairmen. Consequently, as the program gained form and substance, it was necessary to involve the individuals more closely in CBTE implementation.

The CIIC therefore had not only to involve those in the college who administered curricula matters, but it also needed to include those in leadership positions in the development-implementation effort. We had long been cognizant of the unusual success of the instructional improvement committee (IIC) in MUS development, and it seemed a logical, coordinate idea to adapt this administrative and planning concept from the multiunit school plan and incorporate it into college operations.

The CIIC consists of the directors of four college divisions (curriculum and instruction; foundations of education; educational leadership development; and health, physical education, and recreation), the chairmen of the departments of elementary education, secondary education, educational technology and media, educational psychology, and social foundations, the director of student field experiences, the team leaders from each instructional team (seven now, to be expanded later as more teams are needed), two student representatives, and two school representatives. The dean serves as committee chairman. The committee numbers twenty-two persons, which is admittedly large but necessary for our present purposes. The committee has all the necessary personnel to continue planning and administering our CBTE program.

The CBTE program is divided into two major parts: the elementary teacher education program and the secondary teacher education program. Each part operates separately and yet relates to the other at two points: the Career Decisions Program and the teacher education center.

Career Decisions Program

The Career Decisions Program is common to both the elementary and secondary CBTE programs. This program provides an introduction to the world of professional education by providing opportunities for students to make three basic career decisions: (1) whether they wish to become a teacher and if they are suited for teaching, (2) on what educational level they should teach, and (3) the subject matter area of specialization. The fundamental rationale is the belief that a student should get as much information as possible about teacher roles in a variety of school settings, the organization of schools, the social and community influences that affect school programs, and the realities of teachers' professional life-styles, before he makes a commitment to the profession of teaching. This information must be made available to each student early in his college career, while he is still able to change his program or modify his objectives so as not to be forced to extend his college career beyond the usual four-year period.

The Career Decisions Program attempts to merge the conceptual and experiential components of teaching. The conceptual component deals with teaching and learning strategies, the problem of educational gains and losses, the distinction between description and explanation, techniques of modifying behavior, and inquiry and value clarification. The experiential component is aimed at enabling students to recognize teaching and learning strategies as they are utilized in the classroom, to judge the effectiveness of those strategies in terms of their practical consequences, to observe how subject matter can be made meaningful to students, to assess the effectiveness of behavior modification techniques used in the classroom, and to provide an "experience" in personal introspection, value clarification, and value analysis. All this needs to be related to career choice, one's future pupils, oneself, and the contemporary issues of the education profession.

Career decisions is a two-quarter, eight quarter hours-credit, program required of all students entering the College of Education, taken during the freshman or sophomore years. The first course consists of eight modules, the second has three. Each student spends two hours per week on campus in small group classroom instruction and one hour in large group instruction. He is also required to provide one full morning or one full afternoon per week in a related school experience as a career decisions aide (CDA). Each CDA prepares a written contract listing his duties and responsibilities for his two quarters of service. His contract is approved by the cooperating teacher and his university seminar instructor. CDA experiences are evaluated on a form by the cooperating teacher. CDA experiences are of a wide variety with children of different socioeconomic levels and in different geographic settings for limited teaching activities. Time is equally divided between work on campus and activities in schools.

The first eight modules of the Career Decisions Program concern:

(1) Professional interest areas, involving job entry requirements, educational supply and demand, working conditions, and other pertinent information;

(2) Identification of and experience with brainstorming, buzz sessions, panel discussions, sensitivity sessions;

(3) Planning and organizing the career decisions aide experience, including the compilation of a list of CDA activities and means to analyze various expectations for personal relationships and verbal communication between CDAs and cooperating teachers and pupils;

(4) Taking audiometric tests, a speech-articulation test, and the Strong Vocational Interest Inventory, including analysis of results plus comparisons of congruencies of results with persons in various occupations that emphasize some aspect of teaching;

(5) Correctly understanding and distinguishing identifying charac-

teristics between self-contained classrooms and multiunit school operations;

(6) Experiencing ways of modifying behavior; selecting a specific personal behavior to be changed and then using positive reinforcement and/or extinction;

(7) Noting examples of various forces operating in school and in the surrounding neighborhood, such as those affecting teachers and teaching and involving influences of parents, colleagues, noninstructional personnel, race and/or ethnic groups, special purpose agencies, teacher organizations, status considerations, etc.; and

(8) The evaluation of experiences associated with being a career decisions aide.

The three modules in the second course are all devoted to inquiry and value clarification in teaching. These modules not only provide competencies in value clarification and analysis, they also promote introspection about career decisions. The modules aim at helping the students become value investigators and decision makers, not to rebel or devalue present society but to identify choices and create alternatives.

Staffing for the Career Decisions Program is from the faculties of the four divisions: educational foundations; curriculum and instruction; educational leadership; and health, physical education, and recreation. Each career decisions course is taught by an interdisciplinary team of four to six faculty and several graduate assistants. The faculty teams serve as teachers and as undergraduate advisers. The adviser relationship continues after the student leaves career decisions until the junior year, when he is assigned to an adviser from the faculty operating the elementary and secondary teacher education programs.

The Career Decisions Program provides a screening device through which students and the college can mutually accept or reject one another based on objective criteria, both cognitive and affective. For those who remain in the program, a foundation has been provided from which more intensive educational experiences can be generated. Moreover, it provides continuity in the remainder of the student's undergraduate program.

All the foregoing is based on the assumption that the primary task of colleges of education is not to produce teachers who will move smoothly into existing school structures, but teachers dedicated to experimentation, with intellectual curiosity and the maturity of judgment to nurture whatever is educationally viable and to alter or eliminate whatever is educationally weak.

The Preservice Elementary CBTE Program

The elementary CBTE program consists of four basic components: general education, career decisions, the professional year program, and area of specialization. The CBTE portion of the program is limited to the five professional courses on the teacher education model (Figure 11-4) labeled course 1 through course 5. The Career Decisions Program has been presented above. General education consists of 94 quarter-credit hours in English, mathematics, social science, art, music, health and physical education, and psychology. Social science, English, science, and mathematics courses consume 69 quarter-hours of this total general education requirement. The area of specialization requires a minimum of 20 additional quarter-hours in a subject matter area of student choice. There are also 22 quarter-hours available for electives, which are usually used to strengthen the subject matter specialization area. The total program calls for 192 quarter-hours for graduation with a bachelor's degree.

Professional education requirements total 56 quarter-hours, with career decisions using 8 quarter-hours of this total. The remaining 48 quarter hours are divided among five courses: elementary teaching and learning 1, 2, 3, 4, and 5. The first four courses are offered for 8 quarter-hours each and the last calls for 16 quarter-hours. These five courses use a competency-based modularized format.

The fundamental principle underlying the progress of the student through the program is that module achievement should be held constant, not time. A student may work as rapidly or as slowly as he chooses, but he cannot progress to the next module until he has demonstrated competency at the prerequisite stage.

The use of traditional course numbers and credit allocation is observed to provide the registrar with information compatible with the university system for recording credit. Grades are given for successful completion of the modules in a course because of the current university requirement for grades and student interest in grades. Since modules can only be passed or failed, the grade depends on both the quality of work and the amount of work contracted in completing the module. The faculty wishes to go to a pass-no credit system of grading, which will likely occur as soon as it can be arranged and agreed on by all parties.

Students who do not complete modules are recycled (i.e., repeat) through the module a second time. Failure to complete modules on a second trial and general difficulty with a number of modules usually results in students being counseled out of further teacher education work or separation from the program. Students who complete less than 50 percent of the modules in any course during the regular term will be rescheduled for the entire course at another date. Students with a few modules to complete at the end of the course term may continue in the next course with the understanding that they will complete the missing modules of the previous course on their own time. Our present experience indicates that slightly more than 90 percent of all students successfully complete all modules in each course and proceed to the next experience. (Approximately fifty to one hundred students are enrolled in each course.)

The first four courses are offered two half-days a week, with each half-day four clock hours. Course 5 is offered on a full-day basis five days a week and includes what is usually known as student teaching.

Each course and set of modules is field-based, that is, efforts are made to ensure that what is introduced in college relates to actual practice. Thus, each course in the elementary program requires an in-depth experience in a school setting where the student can demonstrate selected competencies while working with elementary pupils. Students are assigned to work in multiunit schools in the Toledo metropolitan area, under the supervision of the instructional team responsible for the particular course in which they are enrolled.

Each multiunit school with college students assigned to it as career decision aides, participants, or student teachers is assigned a college facilitator. The college facilitator assigned to a school is also a member of an instructional team. The facilitator participates on the elementary school instructional improvement committee and coordinates all student field experiences in that school. Facilitators carry at least a half-time load for their activities in schools. In addition to aiding students assigned to the school, they help teachers in the school develop their roles as classroom teacher educators. They further aid the school faculty in implementing IGE/MUS.

The facilitator typically has the following responsibilities:

(1) Coordinating the field component of team modules and the planning of these experiences with personnel in the schools;

(2) Continuing implementation of IGE/MUS through mutual agreement to attend IIC and unit meetings, to provide or obtain other needed school inservice activities, plus informal meetings with teachers when requested;

(3) Coordinating the career decision aide activities in the school;

(4) Supervising the student teaching program in the school, including the supervision of student teachers assigned to the school;

(5) Providing training and supervision to unit leaders so that they can assume a major responsibility for direct supervision of students in all field experiences.

All courses in the program are the responsibility of teams of regular faculty members who represent the disciplines of educational psychology, curriculum and methodology, educational media and technology, and the social foundations of education. Each team consists of four to six persons for each course assisted by a minimum of three graduate assistants. The courses are arranged sequentially and can begin as early as the first quarter of the junior year. At present the interdisciplinary teaching teams work with the same group of students through their first four quarters in the professional program (courses 1-4); they provide instruction and serve as the students' advisers. Each team spends four to five hours per week in planning sessions outside of regular class schedules. Team planning includes not only the team members but also student representatives from the elementary education course and selected personnel from the public schools to which the students are assigned. Elementary education specialists can be brought in for special instruction when necessary with particular modules. There are now three elementary instruction teams, which will be expanded to four and later six teams to accommodate the entire sequence of courses.

The initial modules came from the original Ohio teacher education design, with its five contexts. The first major task was to select from that original study those specifications perceived to be most relevant to an elementary (as well as a secondary) teacher education program. Instructional areas considered necessary but not included in the original study required further generation of behavioral objectives.

The basic objectives for the entire effort were: (1) to write objectives for the major context areas in a measurable form, (2) to write criterion measures for the behavioral objectives, (3) to write modules in a common format, (4) to sequence modules in terms of prerequisite, concurrent, and successor modules, (5) to PERT (program evaluation review technique) the instructional development events, including periodic revisions, (6) to pilot test the individual modules, (7) to revise the modules on the basis of the evaluation data from the pilot test, (8) to form instructional teams with specific goals, (9) to design a strategy for accomplishing the goals, (10) to design a management system for implementation and coordination of the program, and (11) to fully implement the program.

All the above objectives have now been met. The modules[1] in the present courses, by title, are as follows:

Elementary Teaching and Learning 1

  (1) Performance Skills in Inquiry
  (2) Group Process
  (3) Value Clarification
  (4) Value Conflict among School Roles
  (5) Social Class Values and School Behaviors
  (6) Teacher Professionalism and Accountability
  (7) Instructional Media: Operation of Audiovisual Equipment
  (8) MUS/IGE: Context of American Public Education
  (9) MUS/IGE: Organization of a Multiunit School
(10) MUS/IGE: Operation of a Multiunit School
      (Above three include observation of a multiunit school.)
(11) Instructional Systems Design

Elementary Teaching and Learning 2

  (1) Learning Theory and Motivation
  (2) Identifying and Specifying Behaviors
  (3) Observing and Recording Behaviors
  (4) Behavioral Objectives
  (5) The Structure of Knowledge: Bloom's Cognitive Domain
  (6) Instructional Media: Components for Effective Planning of Instruction and Skills in Instructional Planning
  (7) Children's Literature: Picture Books for Children
  (8) Children's Literature: Poetry for Children
  (9) Developmental Stages and Motivation in Children
(10) Tutorial Experiences in School

Elementary Teaching and Learning 3

  (1) Instructional Media: Instructional Simulations and Games

(2) Instructional Media: Preparation of Inexpensive Materials
(3) Behavior Modification and Management
(4) Mathematics Elementary School: Learning Theory
(5) Mathematics Elementary School: Using Manipulative Objects
(6) Mathematics Elementary School: Mathematics Content in Elementary School
(7) Children's Literature: Folk Literature
(8) Children's Literature: Realism and Fantasy
(9) Language Arts: Diagnostic Procedures in Reading
(10) Language Arts: Creative Experiences in Language Arts
(11) Problem Solving
(12) Small Group Instruction: Practicum

Elementary Teaching and Learning 4

(1) Teaching Science and Social Studies
   (a) Concept attainment and evaluation
   (b) Bridging interdisciplinary content
   (c) Value clarification and humanistic encounter
   (d) Individualized instruction
(2) Unit Planning for Science-Social Studies
(3) Field Experiences (with the unit plan)
(4) Selection and Utilization of Educational Media in Unit Planning and Teaching

Elementary Teaching and Learning 5

(1) Orientation
   (a) Rules
   (b) Criteria
   (c) Particular pupil characteristics
(2) The Individualized Unit of Instruction
(3) IGE Planning Skills
(4) Gaining Acceptance and Respect
(5) Instructional Activities 1 to N.
(6) Synthesis and Evaluation

Demonstrated competence in the pre-student-teaching modules, both at the knowledge level in course content and at the application level in the field component of CBTE, should provide an opportunity to redefine the role of the student teacher as it exists in a traditional teaching training sequence. As a result of the field-based professional sequence modules, the experiences that a student teacher has in the final laboratory experience should more closely approximate those of a regular teacher. The student teacher's role should change from that of a passive observer, limited participant, presenter of materials, and conforming instructor to that of a full, functioning teacher, diagnostician, and decision maker.

However, in this process of induction into full teaching responsibility, the student teacher is entitled to supervision and feedback by both the classroom teacher and university personnel. It is also understood that this period of teacher training offers opportunity for analysis, growth and refinement of skills acquired within the professional block preceding student teaching.

Terminal performance objectives that we have identified for elementary teachers require the student to:

(1) Identify important knowledge, skills and concepts with respect to specific subject matters and needs of elementary children;

(2) Translate those instructional goals into behavioral objectives;

(3) Create preassessment instruments appropriate to the subject matter and the students;

(4) Develop strategies for implementing and evaluating instructional procedures in the classroom;

(5) Implement those strategies and evaluate their effectiveness;

(6) Evaluate and revise those procedures in light of the feedback gained from the pupils' performance.

The particular role of Elementary Teaching Learning 5 (formerly student teaching) includes two major functions:

(1) To refine terminal performance objectives of previous modules in a continuous teaching situation;

(2) To synthesize the terminal performance objectives learned in previous modules to create a continuous student teaching experience.

To aid the faculty and cooperating teachers supervising Elementary Teaching Learning 5, checklists of criteria are developed to include criteria for skills, techniques, and knowledge in the following areas: design, implementation, evaluation, and revision. These criteria are largely the terminal performance criteria of the modules that have been taught prior to the student teaching experience.

The observation and evaluation of Elementary Teaching Learning 5 is organized and directed by the checklist of terminal performance objectives. The procedures followed by both college-based supervisors and cooperating school teachers include that:

(1) They will have a clearly stated plan from the student for each of their observations.

(2) The criteria relevant to the plan objectives and strategies will be applied while observing the students carrying out the particular activities of that plan.

(3) After each observation, the student will be provided feedback in terms of how well he has met the criteria for the particular competencies observed.

(4) Student teacher and observer will determine appropriate strategy for refining competencies in question.

(5) Final determination of whether or not the student has met the criterion list will be made by the cooperating teacher and college supervisor, on the basis of data collected using the common criteria.

Elementary Teaching Learning 5 includes a weekly seminar to permit extensive analysis and refinement of teaching behaviors by the several students, with the assistance of both college and public school support staff. This provides a cadre of interdisciplinary, interinstitutional expertise with resources beyond the reach of the best college supervisor of the usual model, which featured one junior faculty member and twenty student teachers from five or more schools.

The module titles indicate faculty concern with professional academic disciplines; teaching, teaching skills and methodology; and the educational technology and media techniques and materials necessary for effective subject matter presentation. Such is the first CBTE approximation of the Ohio model. Additional information on modules and the program resulting from them will be provided in Chapter 12.

The Secondary CBTE Program

The present secondary CBTE program has drawn heavily from the original elementary design, but has also developed its own individuality. The CBTE portion of the program includes only professional education courses and totals 40 quarter hours, 8 of these being the Career Decisions requirement. The remainder of the work for a baccalaureate degree in secondary education—152 quarter-hours—is devoted to subject matter specialization and general education.

It is difficult to conceive of a single organizational plan for professional education that will encompass the wide variety of program features found in middle schools, junior high schools, and senior high schools. The differences in educational philosophy, student populations, and organizational patterns of secondary schools are profound. The present professional program for secondary education tries to recognize and combine "what is" and "what is desired" for an effective program.

The effort has been to provide a mix of teacher behaviors, school and curriculum organizational patterns, and student outcomes that vary from school to school. The general approach has been to try to identify a minimal core of modules and to sequence them across two courses, to comprise the program. Each course consists of 8 quarter hours and meets four clock hours mornings or afternoons two days a week. The final course calls for 16 quarter hours of credit, which includes student teaching.

At this writing the secondary education faculty has a special working relationship with two large junior high schools to develop differentiated staffing and team teaching operations (comparable to the multiunit school concept). However, the activities of students and faculty in other secondary schools utilize the usual organizational and instructional situation. Thus the field portion of the secondary CBTE program is based on a classification scheme for considering the behavior of a potential teacher in the field. This general classification of needed secondary education student behavior is as follows: (1) organizing and planning classwork, (2) classroom management, (3) developing a motivating environment, (4) instruction, (5) evaluation, (6) guidance and counseling, (7) professional activities out of school, (8) interpersonal behavior, and (9) school-community relations.

The classification allows us to focus on tasks associated with the general teacher role. Sample categories of participant and student teacher field behavior are then developed as a process for selecting field behavioral objectives within the instructional modules.

The entire secondary education faculty has worked as two large teams to plan and operate their CBTE program (beginning in fall 1973, the faculty will divide into three teams of five, seven, and two faculty members). Unlike the elementary program, university facilitators are not assigned to secondary schools. Secondary faculty members supervise students in their field experiences, and through this effort come in contact with secondary school personnel and work with them for the general benefit of the students under supervision as well as for the inservice program development desired by the school. More definite role expectations would legitimize the outcomes sought by university supervisors.

The secondary education courses are composed of modules developed by the secondary education faculty. All courses are team taught with specific teams assigned to each course. Interdisciplinary secondary faculty members (curriculum and methods, educational technology and media, social and philosophic foundations, and educational psychology) differentiate functions relative to module requirements across all courses. In this arrangement all faculty members work in schools as well as on campus.

The secondary professional education courses are titled Secondary Teaching and Learning 1, 2, and 3. Secondary Teaching and Learning 1 consists of seven modules, course 2 has nine modules, and course 3 has nine modules. The titles of the modules for each course are:

Secondary Teaching and Learning 1

(1) Behaviors and Inferences
(2) Components of an Instructional Model and Module
(3) Behavioral Objectives
(4) Hierarchial Structures (Bloom's Taxonomy, Cognitive Domain)
(5) Assessment and Evaluation
(6) Analyzing the Learning Setting
(7) Field Performance: A Synthesis

Secondary Teaching and Learning 2

(1) Designing, Implementing, and Evaluating an Instructional Unit in a Major Methods Area
(2) Analysis of Teaching Behaviors
(3) Instructional Strategies
(4) Instructional Media Production, Selection, Evaluation, and Equipment Operation
(5) Behavior Modification
(6) Methods of Teaching English and Reading in Secondary Schools
(7) Methods of Teaching Social Studies in Secondary Schools
(8) Methods of Teaching Mathematics in Secondary Schools
(9) Methods of Teaching Science in Secondary Schools

Secondary Teaching and Learning 3

(1) Instructional Design
(2) Questioning
(3) Lecture-Recitation as a Teaching Strategy
(4) Guided Discussion as a Teaching Strategy
(5) Inquiry Teaching
(6) Educational Media and Technology

(7) Classroom Tests—Cognitive
(8) Classroom Tests—Affective
(9) Self-Evaluation and Personal Qualities Checklist

Secondary Teaching and Learning 1 aids students in differentiating between pupil behavior and teacher inferences about pupil behavior, assessing pupil needs in the classroom, instructional goal identification (behavioral objectives in the cognitive, affective, and psychomotor domains), and evaluating and analyzing instructional goals. Opportunities are provided students to apply the concepts and skills learned in field settings. The emphasis in Secondary Teaching and Learning 2 is the design, implementation, and evaluation of actual teaching. A microteaching clinic is utilized to help students acclimate themselves to teaching performance and to gather first hand data about such performance.

Since students entering Secondary Teaching and Learning 3 have already field tested some basic teaching concepts and skills and identified areas of potential strengths and weaknesses in their teaching repertoire of behaviors, they begin what has been known as student teaching with greater confidence and higher expectations and standards for performance. This experience is viewed as an extension of previous field experiences and a time for further polishing and development of skills. Specific behavioral competencies are utilized which will be demonstrated by preservice students within the ten-week period. No specific teaching strategy is dictated as "best"; what is required is that a variety of instructional strategies will be demonstrated. A weekly seminar accompanies the school and teaching experiences undertaken by students; the seminar has the following objectives: (1) to provide an extension and sophistication of skills previously learned (questioning skills, test construction, classroom management, etc.); (2) to introduce additional professional information (school laws, associations and unions, interviewing, etc.); (3) to enable further microteaching experience when needed; and (4) to provide analysis of teaching using audio-video tapings of student teacher performance. The entire experience is oriented toward the notion of accountability—that teachers should be evaluated on the basis of what happens to pupils in the teaching process.

Similarities and differences are noticeable in the modules for the secondary and elementary professional education courses. In both there is concern for educational methodology and the teaching of subject matter. However, both need continued development to approximate a more ideal program.

A final examination of Figure 11-4 indicates that the course module instruction is related to the schools through the teacher education center. As previously indicated, module testing and evaluation and considerable instructional effort connected with modules occurs in the teacher education center. The elementary and secondary CBTE programs are basically joined through teacher education center operations. Otherwise, the programs are distinct except that they both utilize the Career Decisions Program as their initial point of entry.

Public Schools Model, IGE/MUS

A public school model for IGE/MUS and university CBTE relationships is presented in Figure 11-5. The figure presents a typical elementary multiunit school operational plan, with two exceptions. First, multiunit schools in the extended Toledo area (which includes other school districts) operate through the Metropolitan League of Multiunit Schools (MLMUS), and in Toledo public schools through the Multiunit Schools for Teacher Education Committee (MUST).

The Metropolitan League of Multiunit Schools (MLMUS) consists of representatives from fifteen elementary schools in five public school districts and the Toledo diocese. Nine of these schools are in the Toledo public school system, two in the Sylvania city schools, and one each in the Oregon, Ottawa Hills, Northwood, and Toledo diocesan school districts. These schools range from those in affluent suburbs to those in the Toledo inner-city. MLMUS is a USOE Title III project, funded for three years, which began operation during the school year of 1972-73. The program objectives for the first year of operation were:

(1) To establish an instructional materials center;

(2) To demonstrate teacher planning skills according to planning competencies that are established and approved by the MLMUS policy planning committee;

(3) To develop an inservice training plan for teachers, principals, and aides;

(4) To increase the knowledge and skills of administrators and teachers in developing individually guided education;

Figure 11-5. A Public School Model for IGE/MUS and University
Teacher Education Relationships

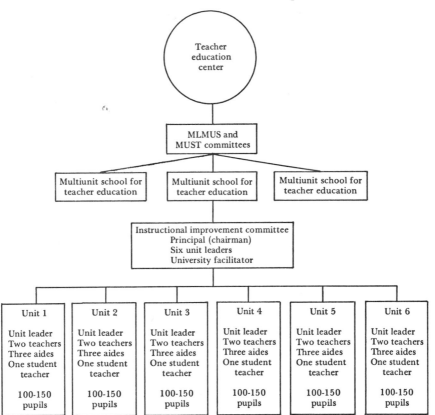

(5) To expand the concept of multiunit organization in the Toledo area;

(6) To establish the MLMUS as a functioning organization;

(7) To collect student achievement data in reading and mathematics to establish a cognitive baseline for comparing pupil achievement in multiunit schools and nonmultiunit programs;

(8) To disseminate the activities of the MLMUS.

The College of Education participates with MLMUS and is a vital part of project efforts. Three University of Toledo professors are paid in part by funds from MLMUS, and the entire university staff concerned with developing the elementary CBTE program have volunteered their services to facilitate the development of multiunit schools in the Toledo area. At the present time, thirteen College of Education faculty facilitators are working in MLMUS elementary schools and participating in meetings of each school's instructional improvement committee. College faculty have also made various presentations and instructional efforts with MLMUS personnel, who at the beginning of the 1972-73 academic year totaled 232 teachers who have received inservice training. The college also provides students in undergraduate teacher training to the multiunit schools in the league; these students serve as aides, participants, and student teachers.

The Toledo Junior League of Women has adopted IGE/MUS as a major project. Each week thirty-four women volunteer their services for a half-day to work in an instructional material center in an elementary school or as a teaching assistant. It is a goal of the Junior League of Women to provide sufficient experience with IGE/MUS and to increase the number of volunteers, eventually resulting in the recruitment of other adult teaching assistants and also providing needed aides for IGE/MUS operations.

The MLMUS is establishing IGE/MUS activities across school district boundaries, including the needed program dissemination and the development and implementation of program evaluation. The director of the league serves half-time with the project, and is fully supported by the Toledo public schools. The league also employs an instructional materials center director and secretary.

The organization known as Multiunit Schools for Teacher Education committee (MUST) was a forerunner of MLMUS. This committee was formed when four elementary schools in the Toledo public school system who were experimenting with IGE/MUS identified common interests in the development of their programs, personnel, and the field-based teacher education activities. The four principals of the schools, the college faculty facilitators in each school, and two teachers from each school formed the MUST committee as a voluntary effort. The committee had no funds for operation, but its members clearly perceived a need for planning and communication if the development of IGE/MUS was to succeed in the elementary schools of Toledo.

MUST became a coordinating and steering body for IGE/MUS development in the Toledo public schools. It has now been operating for four years. A unit leader from one of the schools has been elected chairman. From the outset MUST refused to accept negative responses to proposals designed to establish multiunit schools. Rather, it established a communications network and functions as a clearinghouse and sounding board for new ideas. It experiments with various factors such as modes of lesson presentation, choice of materials, and grouping of students. MUST has been known to act as a vigorous advocate with the central office of the Toledo public schools, individual schools, and the university when questions have remained unanswered and problems have not been solved.

MUST has an inherent ability and authority to create change. The strength of the committee lies in its combination of top personnel from the university, school administration, and the MUST schools. These people come to MUST meetings with educational improvement in mind and they are ready to act and field test new ideas. The MUST committee has accomplished such things as securing adequate time for group planning for IGE/MUS teachers as a part of the school day. Committee members and career decisions program personnel from the university wrote the career decisions aide handbook, provided to all students enrolling in career decisions. The committee has developed a written constitution, publishes a newsletter, and led in developing the Title III program for MLMUS.

Interestingly, MUST did not dissolve with the creation of the Title III MLMUS program but remained a strong and viable force for educational development in the Toledo city elementary schools. The present MUST committee comprises teacher representatives from eleven elementary schools, the central school administration, the University of Toledo, the Junior League of Women, and university students. Meetings typically consist of thirty to forty persons and topics cover a wide range of subjects. Minutes are published. Excellent liaison has been established between MUST and MLMUS. Dialogue between teachers, professors, administrators, and students has been institutionalized. Toledo teachers in IGE/MUS schools have taken the lead in educational planning and development through the MUST committee.

The cooperative relationship of the university with IGE/MUS schools is clearly indicated in Figure 11-5. The multiunit schools are more than organizations and operations for individually guided education; they are also equally concerned with and established as units for field-based teacher education. The university facilitator serves as a member of the instructional improvement committee in each multiunit school. A university student teacher is assigned to each multiunit, again indicating the interrelationships between the university and a multiunit school at the classroom level.

The IGE/MUS operation in the Toledo area is similar to that of IGE/MUS schools elsewhere in the country. Important differences in our program are the teacher education relationships and activities in such schools, which are a unique contribution to the IGE/MUS concept.

Diocesan Schools and CBE Model

The Catholic diocesan schools of the Toledo area comprise more than fifty schools, from the Indiana state line to Sandusky, Ohio, and from the Michigan-Ohio border south to Lima, Ohio. These schools are both urban and rural, and their problems are typical of those facing all schools in America today. For example, minority and other interest groups found the curriculum geared to students much different from their own children. Often school work was too analytic and middle-class-oriented, or teachers had arbitrarily decided that children who failed to handle this type of curriculum had learning disabilities that limited their learning to simple tasks. The Toledo diocese was committed to the proposition that all children had the right to learn the basic skills necessary for participation as active citizens in our society. Recognizing that there had been no recent systematic revision of curriculum in their school system, they contacted the College Center for Research and Services (CERS) in 1970 to provide inservice support to their faculty preparatory to an extensive curriculum development project. CERS entered into an agreement with the diocese which provided long-term consultive service. The plan included inservice training in competency-based education for key administrators, supervisors, and teachers. Diocesan school personnel organized into subject-matter-area groups to determine what the curriculum should include and how it should be organized, using a CBE format. They decided that the project would last five years and would include not only curriculum development efforts but the collation and creation of needed teaching materials, field testing of curricular plans, and revisions and subsequent publishing of workable curriculum modules in all subject areas for grades one through eight. The logical outcome of the entire effort was the development of competency-based curriculum guides.

With the aid of consultants from CERS, various task groups of supervisory and teacher personnel from the diocese were provided instruction on competency-based education and procedures whereby broad statements of goals could be translated into behavioral objectives, suggested learning activities, teacher techniques, evaluation procedures, and the resources necessary for the instruction prescribed. In this way a large number of concepts and generalizations were developed for all subject areas over all eight grades. From these concepts a series of sequenced instructional objectives were developed. Materials and resources were recommended that were available and appropriate for achieving the objectives. Suggested teacher techniques and learners activities were provided for meeting each objective. Since teachers were encouraged to develop their own evaluation procedures, no pretests or posttests were provided. The guides were written in a modified module format with opportunity for users to substitute their own activities and means for meeting curricular objectives.

Diocesan personnel working on the project were provided with inservice courses on developing and evaluating the modules and determining the appropriateness of the concepts, objectives, and methods suggested. Curriculum guides were completed for art, music, social studies, science, mathematics, language arts, guidance, and drug education in the elementary health curriculum.

The diocese is now field testing the curriculum guides in designated pilot schools, to obtain both process and product evaluation of the curriculum materials. On the basis of the field tests portions of the guides are being revised. This process will be repeated until at the end of five years all guides will have been evaluated and changed so that the CBTE elementary curriculum can be implemented throughout all diocesan schools.

The diocese has begun its education renewal efforts with curriculum development. There was originally little interest in developing multiunit schools and using a differentiated staff, team teaching approach to elementary education. However, with the completion of the curriculum guides, the diocese has begun to consider the value of

IGE/MUS and is now experimenting with MUS in two elementary schools. It is expected that more schools will come into the multiunit structure as time passes because the implementation of their new curricular program is facilitated more effectively with a differentiated staffing, team teaching organization than a self-contained classroom organization.

SUBJECTIVE REFLECTIONS ON THE COMPREHENSIVE MODEL

Through a process of change centered around teacher education we have attempted to deal with educational complexity and have tried to "put it all together" for the benefit of children and youth. The question may now be asked, Has this been accomplished in our comprehensive model for educational renewal? The answer cannot be immediate because time is needed to experience and evaluate the results of our efforts, but the first signs of what may be the answer and what is to come are now available. They tend to be positive, even promising.

Recently, the Associated Organizations of Teacher Education (AOTE), affiliated with the American Association of Colleges for Teacher Education, conducted an organizational survey of current issues in teacher education.[2] This survey was an attempt to determine what the basic and relevant issues of teacher education were in 1973 by polling the representatives of the twenty prestigious organizations affiliated with AOTE.

The responses from this survey indicated that the following were the major issues of education, listed in the order of their importance:

(1) Inservice and preservice education.

(2) Involvement of teacher education in schools.

(3) Curriculum, methods, innovations, the place of subject matter.

(4) Nature and role of teaching: objectives and philosophy.

(5) Certification.

(6) Performance-based (competency-based) teacher education.

(7) Admission, selection, and screening.

(8) Financing.

(9) Relationships of school and society.

(10) Decision making: roles of various organizations, agencies, and persons.

(11) Evaluation and accountability.

(12) Supply and demand.

(13) Educational technology.

(14) Equal educational opportunity: ethnic groups, inner-city schools.

(15) Career education.

(16) Affective education, human and humane teaching.

(17) Individualization and open education.

(18) Staffing problems and paraprofessionals, roles, differentiated staffing, modifications of traditional teaching roles.

(19) Research in teacher education.

(20) Unionization and negotiations.

If these are indeed the basic issues confronting teacher education today, we submit that our comprehensive model for educational renewal and change has addressed itself in some degree to every issue. The heaviest emphasis of our model is on the very issues considered the most important by the AOTE: the continuum of preservice and inservice education, the involvement of teacher education in schools, innovations in curriculum and methods of teaching, a consideration of the nature and role of teaching, competency-based teacher education, selection and screening processes, the relationships of school and society, decision making, evaluation and accountability, educational technology, equal educational opportunity, career education, affective education, individualization, staffing considerations, and research.

The only issues our model does not touch on significantly are those that would usually be outside of comprehensive efforts such as ours, i.e., certification, financing, supply and demand, and unionization and negotiations. Nevertheless, the model is concerned with these issues in certain ways. It should be noted that the application of our comprehensive model in the Toledo area has been primarily accomplished through the creative application of local revenues and limited outside funding; multimillion dollar transfusions have not been needed for the development of our model nor will they be for its continued implementation.

Obviously, we have been dealing with the fundamental concerns of teacher education and education generally as indicated by the AOTE survey. The degree of our success is presently unknown, and must depend on the continuing collection and analysis of data from many sources.

SUMMARY

In this chapter we have described the organizational structure that supports the CBTE program. New policy-making bodies were described and ways of developing channels of communication and influence were suggested. These were related to the substance of CBTE—the modules of the professional teacher education program. The structure discussed in these pages can be viewed as the skeleton that supports the entire program. Finally, comparing the comprehensive model to a list of vital issues facing teacher education, we note that it is directly responsive to a majority of these issues and indirectly responsive to some few beyond the scope of CBTE.

The next chapter concerns our plans to maintain the vitality of CBTE by providing for assessment and renewal.

Notes

1. All actual modules cannot be reproduced in this chapter. They can be obtained by contacting the authors. This applies to both elementary and secondary modules.

2. Associated Organizations for Teacher Education, *Issues in Teacher Education, Organizational Survey, 1972-73,* mimeographed (Washington, D. C.: the Associated Organizations for Teacher Education and the American Association of Colleges for Teacher Education, 1973), pp. 1-37.

Suggested Readings

Saxe, Richard, ed. *Educational Comment, 1969: Contexts for Teacher Education.* Toledo, Ohio: The University of Toledo, 1969.

Nussel, Edward J., John F. Ahern, Dennis E. Hinkle, and George E. Dickson, eds. *Educational Comment, 1971: The Ohio Model and the Multi-Unit School.* Toledo, Ohio: The University of Toledo, 1971.

Inglis, Joan, ed. *Educational Comment, 1972: Field-Based Teacher Education Emerging Relationships.* Toledo, Ohio: The University of Toledo, 1972.

12/ Field Testing, Modifying, and Renewing a Comprehensive Model

George E. Dickson
Richard H. Hersh
Hughes Moir
Richard W. Saxe

An operating comprehensive model for educational change, represented by competency-based teacher education, competency-based education, and individually guided education and multiunit schools, has been presented, examined, and explained. It is a strategy for the preparation of educational personnel, both preservice and inservice, combined with curricular change and development that is heavily process oriented. Hence the substance of our program is constantly evolving and emerging from the employment of program strategies and processes. Although the model is still in a state of becoming, it is even now superior to previous programs.

We wish to emphasize that our comprehensive model has not been a preoccupation with a limited aspect of education. We have concerned ourselves with the whole of education and all individuals engaged in the educational process. We have tried to develop varied approaches to educational change while remaining consistent in our attention to educational objectives. Our model is ambitious and innovative. It combines program prescription and flexibility. We have created initial procedures for objective feedback that bring to our efforts a self-correcting, up-to-date aspect. We understand that what has now been developed and initiated will not remain the same year after year; for us education is and shall be a changing, self-renewing process. As a strategy for preparing educational personnel, our model has considerable potential to bring about needed education reform, given intelligent leadership and adequate support.

But any strategy devised for bringing about educational change has many problems, and our model is no exception. Chapter 5 indicated some of these, and their solutions, which we encountered in our first efforts to develop and implement CBTE. Over time other problems, both educational and political, have emerged. For example:

—What are the generally agreed-on knowledge, performance, and product criteria essential in CBTE programs?

—How are such criteria identified?

—How are such criteria to be validated to establish that we have the right criteria, as well as to provide the methodology to further a validation process?

—How does one assess teaching behavior and pupil learning?

—How can a CBTE program in all its complexity be managed?

—What is the optimal procedure for sequencing modules in a CBTE program?

—What constitutes acceptable mastery of the objectives in a CBTE program?

—How are working arrangements with schools and various organizations associated with schools best facilitated in a CBTE program?

These are some of the problems connected with CBTE, IGE/MUS model development. We do not perceive such problems as insurmountable and are confident that our model has the potential to deal with all these and others.

Karl Massanari has said that the power of competency-based teacher education resides in the fact that it pushes educators in necessary and appropriate directions. He identifies these directions as the following:

—We are forced to ask the right questions at the right time (e.g., What is the role of the school? What are needs of children and youth? What kinds of teachers do we want to prepare? What competencies do these teachers need? How can we be sure that teachers are competent? How should we evaluate competency?).

—We are required to define professional roles more clearly.

—We must design preparation programs in their totality and in their relation to a conceptualization of professional roles.

—We must relate preparation programs more closely to the schools and to the profession; in training programs the relation of theory and practice is more systematic and schools are utilized.

—We are required to explicate program objectives in relation to the professional roles that have been identified and defined.

—We must design instructional systems that support the achievement of the specified competencies and relate instruction and learning to objectives.

—We must individualize and personalize instruction, and instructional characteristics we have enunciated for decades.

—We are required to develop and use new kinds of training materials, draw on the resources of educational technology, and utilize field situations to field test and validate such materials.

—We must develop new types of management systems for students and their records, human resources, and field resources.

—We are forced to define problems more clearly.

—Both formative and summative research become necessary to keep programs regenerative and open.

—The base for decision-making is broadened to involve teachers, administrators, students, and the community.

—We are asked to be truly accountable for what we are doing.

Finally, Massanari indicates that we are being pushed in all the above directions at the same time with dynamic and synergistic effects that generate power and give CBTE strategy real potential for improving teacher education.[1]

IMPLEMENTATION UNDER WAY

The directions identified by Massanari on the ways in which CBTE is pushing teacher educators have certainly been not only evident but applicable in the development of our comprehensive model. We have been compelled to deal with all the effects mentioned. We also learned that planning for instruction is a necessary but not sufficient condition for learning to take place; the operationalization of such planning, in the ultimate revision of goals and means, is also required. We have now arrived at a stage at which description and analysis of our first year of implementation have resulted in further revision of the program. The principle of successive approximations has been a useful tool to implement what first appeared to be well-developed plans. The reality of work weeks extending well beyond forty hours, the logistics of team teaching, developing and organizing the instructional modules including their field-based components, and the press of normal instruction duties, writing, and research work have required compromise. We have learned that we are not so much agents of change as we are partners of change with other institutions and individuals. Each developmental effort has affected all parts of the program, and overall program coordination, administration, and communication were important concerns throughout the entire year.

Delivery Systems

The delivery system for the elementary teacher education program consisted of three interdisciplinary, instructional faculty teams handling four groups of students. One team was to plan for and instruct two separate groups of students—one group just entering the professional program and the other group in their final term. Membership of both instructional teams and student groups remained fairly constant through the developmental year, with minimum changes due to faculty reassignment and student attrition. Each team spent a minimum of four to five hours each week in group planning sessions. Talking about and planning for team teaching was as difficult as implementing the process. The elementary teams spent much time on the immediate problems of developing and integrating the particular components of the instructional program for which they were responsible.

The secondary education faculty utilized two teams, each responsible for a specific set of modules. They met once a week to plan objectives. Some of the first modules developed for the secondary program were found to be unrealistic in terms of the time required for mastery, comprehensibility, and usability. The secondary teams had planned to have modules in final polished form for student use, but soon realized that lack of pilot efforts in field situations made much of what was intended insufficient. Immediate revision of modules began; this took place in working retreats of one day or weekends at the homes of various faculty members.

The data management system that was to provide immediate student feedback on all modules before and after they were taken was not yet complete, and pre and posttests of the more sophisticated modules required hand scoring, which placed further burdens on faculty team members. Members of both elementary and secondary teams had occasional doubts about what was being delivered to their students, but as the 1972-73 academic year passed various components of the program began to fall into place.

Progress in Instructional Development

A wide variety of modes of instruction characterized the practices of each instructional team. Initially, the most frequently used team method was large group presentations using lectures and discussions. As the year developed emphasis was increasingly placed on small group instruction and the use of self-instructional materials, as these were produced.

Personal and academic advising patterns changed dramatically. As close and continuous interpersonal team relationships developed students identified more and more closely with members of the instructional teams. Students consistently sought out team members for advice rather than their assigned advisers.

A persistent problem was the integration of each of the modules into an effective unified program. A great deal of faculty time was spent simply learning about each other's disciplines and objectives. To provide assistance to students and teachers in cooperating schools, educational psychologists and sociologists had to become familiar with general and specific curricular methodology and materials. Curriculum specialists and methodologists had to become sufficiently familiar with particular aspects of learning principles in instructional procedures to aid students. At times students indicated that they had some difficulty in arriving at a synthesis of teaching concepts and skills because the relationships among modules were not apparent to them. Instructional teams remedied this in two ways. First, as each team moved from one course or block of modules to another, the members attempted to reorder the sequence of modules that comprised the block or course, using data from the team that was responsible for the course during the previous quarter, as well as their own professional judgment and expertise. In this way each successive team built on the work of the preceding team to achieve a better sequence of modules for each course and a more ideal overall program. Secondly, as each team member learned more about the specific instructional objectives and disciplines outside his own area of knowledge and developed a broader understanding of the program as a whole, he was better able to synthesize for himself, and for his students, the interrelated components of the program.

Students came to see that initial nonmastery of modules did not result in failure but rather in recycling. Some students had smug smiles as they pretested out of certain modules and were able to walk out of class to pursue others while classmates remained behind. An interesting phenomenon took place in grading: students refused to accept grades of C or B as they completed modules and continued to recycle until they reached A criteria. Even though the team upgraded the completion criteria for an A by 50 percent the following quarter, students still refused to accept less and the proportion of A grades remained the same. Once students became aware of our objectives and the criteria for meeting them, they began to realize that they were no longer committed to a normal curve grading system. Their attitude was that additional recycling time was not wasted effort, since no guessing game existed. This behavior also indicated that students were willing to take advantage of a college program that allowed for different time dimensions in completing course work—a major ingredient in the process of individualizing instruction.

Students began to approach individual faculty team members for help and discussion, not in the usual adversary relationship typifying fear and distrust but in what we perceived as a more honest and open manner. Students willingly joined team planning sessions or offered open criticism as well as praise in class. Students became involved in the instructional-learning process; the passive approach changed to one of doing. While the faculty looked for data to rationalize their shortcomings, the positive events involving students provided more than sufficient incentive for the faculty to revise, revise, and revise again their instructional modules.

The year's implementation effort also tested another hypothesis about modules. Our original planning suggested the need to sequence modules by using a task analysis paradigm. In several cases our analysis proved correct, as in the teaching of behavioral objectives before test item construction. But we also learned that students who missed classes or sometimes skipped modules for one reason or another were able to achieve mastery in modules that we thought required prerequisite skills. This convinced us that students can deal with several modules concurrently or in an order which they rather than we choose. Obviously, more research is needed to validate module sequences.

A major area neglected during the first quarter of our implementation process was the writing and implementing of field modules. While field experiences were always required with each set of modules, these were not at first specified in such a way as to require specific performance, which would enable us to measure significant student progress or mastery in the field. In our efforts to get the program under way, we simply did not have time to wrestle with this problem. In theory we agreed that our students should, as a terminal performance, be able to operationalize what they had learned in previous modules in their classrooms. Thus, field experiences, especially student teaching, would be an application level extension of our classwork on campus.

In the latter half of the initial implementation year we began the task of writing specific field component modules to link earlier modules to teaching performance in the classroom. In this effort we moved one step closer to our ideal of approaching Turner's level two,[2] which requires that teachers be evaluated in terms of their pupil's short-term learning. We began to require that each student, prior to and during student teaching and in cooperation with his supervising teacher, submit pre and posttest data with objectives etc. that demonstrated that his pupils had exhibited behavior to meet the objectives. This was of course not the only criterion for success, but it was a necessary condition. How often and at what minimum level of sophistication module objectives must be met is obviously arbitrary. We have not reached concensus on this matter.

Finally, it should be noted that team teaching, whether in higher education or in elementary or high school, demands not only personal commitment and professional expertise, but also the ability on the part of the instructional team to work together effectively in a coordinated manner. This requires common sharing and trust in one another for support and mutual effort to complete tasks. Time is required in large measure for any group of people to achieve a high level of team cohesiveness and effectiveness. As the second year of the program begins, each team having completed one full program cycle, current team behavior indicates to us that our faculty has learned the art of team teaching.

Progress in Linking Preservice and Inservice Education

We have repeatedly emphasized that our comprehensive program recognizes the need for a direct and continuous link between pre and inservice training. The beginning teacher as well as a student teacher requires an environment that reinforces what he learned previously in his training period.

We have begun a sophisticated inservice effort, which brings teachers together to learn the language and criteria of our modules as well as how to model certain teacher behaviors. This is accomplished in several ways. Inservice courses are specifically designed for and provided to a designated target school(s) wishing to cooperate with the university in training teachers. We utilize university faculty facilitators—faculty members who are assigned various responsibilities in a particular school or schools, as was indicated in Chapter 11. With the emergence of the Toledo Metropolitan League of Multiunit Schools, we assigned three university staff members to work with this league to coordinate and provide inservice training and workshops to these schools on an as-needed basis. Each of these individuals is also a member of an elementary instructional team. In 1973-74 there will be four league representatives, one in each subject area (language arts, mathematics, social studies, and science).

Through formal and informal inservice training, classroom teachers are truly becoming teacher educators with major responsibility for teaching and evaluating the field experiences of preservice teachers. The major role of the college facilitators has already shifted from preoccupation with student supervision to that of aiding teachers in becoming better instructors and supervisors.

We not only have developed vital communication links with teachers and administrators in the field, but this has been done through the development of a total educational system. Cooperating teachers now come to the university, and we go to them for various purposes. Besides taking university courses, they act as resource persons in our classes for the benefit of students, and they also enlist the aid of students for various classroom duties and experiences.

Progress in Developing Content Expertise

One of the perennial problems in teacher education has been that of assuring student competence in a particular subject matter discipline. We know that course hours in and of themselves do not guarantee competence. We are now in the process of forming coalitions with members of the liberal arts faculty who are willing to prepare objectives in their courses that will facilitate the teaching of that content by those students going into teaching. This effort is at present limited, but it is a beginning cooperative effort between arts and sciences and education faculty that may result in adding content specialists to education teaching teams, thus making our program an intercollege as well as an interdisciplinary effort.

Current Status

We have reached a point in our CBTE program where we have a set of modules that have been revised at least twice and have remained stable enough to continue being used in the 1973-74 program year. We feel we can now devote ourselves more to gathering data on the effects of particular modules (in terms of both cognitive and affective outcomes), sequences of modules, and relevance of the modules to teaching in real classrooms. Data is needed from our students in the field as well as from the inservice teachers with whom they come in contact as to which modules are necessary or unnecessary, and what needs to be subtracted from or added to the total program. After a year of trial, we continue to believe that an interdisciplinary team approach is viable. The personal and professional growth of each member of the team has been enormous. We found that it is more difficult to actually teach and practice team teaching than it is to lecture about it. We have acquired new respect for the classroom teaching teams in the schools with which we work.

It is more difficult to individualize instruction than it is to talk about it. It is more difficult to write behavioral objectives, especially at the higher levels of the taxonomy, than it is to tell others how to do so. It is more difficult to develop pre and posttests matched to objectives than it is to require this of others. The process of CBTE and all its related components are as critical to the learning process in becoming a teacher as is the content of the learning itself. We have begun to realize the power in the concept of modeling, often referred to in educational psychology books but rarely demonstrated. We have learned that hypocrisy is always with us, forced on us by the demands of reality, but honesty includes the willingness to openly admit such hypocrisy and behave in a way that minimizes it. Students understand this and accept us more for what we are rather than what we have told them educators should be. In this sense our efforts have led to a much more humane and personalized program.

We are aware of the criticism CBTE has received from those who seem to react automatically to words like behavioral objectives, modules, pre and posttests, as being the essence of nonhumanism. The concern for humanism in education is proper and should not be disregarded. Individuals should be given every opportunity to maximize their individuality and power of individual choice, and to minimize external imposition. Traditional teacher education programs and, indeed, almost all of present university course work is truly antihumanistic. The secrecy of program objectives, the capriciousness of faculty criteria, the lock-step of quarters or semesters, and the refusal to acknowledge that individuals have different needs in learning is the essence of traditional education in teacher training and the liberal arts. All this is well documented. But, based on our experience as well as on information from other CBTE programs around the country, we now have some evidence to suggest that students perceive such programs to be more humane than traditional training. Competency-based teacher education:

(1) Tells students in advance what faculty expectations are;

(2) Defines criteria;

(3) Allows for individual differences in time needed to learn;

(4) Provides individual choices in meeting objectives;

(5) Uses a data feedback system for diagnostic rather than for punitive purposes;

(6) Allows for student input in selecting objectives and means;

(7) Provides more meaningful field experiences for practice in order to learn from failure as well as from success; and

(8) Calls on the faculty themselves to model appropriate teaching behavior.

There is really no contest. Those who understand the human uses of technology and science, as suggested by Mumford[3] and Fuller,[4] understand that a systematic and scientific approach need not negate those attributes we hold to be uniquely human.

NEEDED FUTURE DEVELOPMENTS

As with any new program, our first year of full operation has resulted in periods of ambiguity, satisfaction, trial and error, and failures and successes. As we look ahead, a number of concerns and developments are apparent.

Staffing presents a definite problem for the future. Our current staff was selected on the basis of an undergraduate program that no longer exists. The new program with its greater emphasis on extensive involvement with public schools, its commitment to support the Metropolitan League of Multi-Unit Schools, the gradual decrease of enrollments in teacher education reflecting a national trend, with its financial implications—all require a review of new faculty roles and revised strategies for staffing instructional teams.

We have been successful in linking teacher education efforts at the elementary level to multiunit schools, but problems occur in similar linkages at the secondary school level. Two school systems in the Toledo area have indicated interest in developing a multiunit school organization and concept at the secondary level. We look forward to such development, but recognize that it will be difficult in schools that are organized around specialization in subject matter.

We have been unable to arrange for or to utilize facilitators at the secondary education level, as was possible in elementary schools. This has increased our difficulties with inservice education at the secondary level. The teacher education center must be the unit through which working relationships and linkage are developed between the university and the schools. Our center needs further development.

Another major problem is the effective integration of individual program components—instructional modules, field experiences, performance criteria, etc. (i.e., the content of the program)—into a unified, synthesized, coherent, articulated whole. To this end we have analyzed existing modules that reflect certain faculty preferences against the original Ohio model design specifications to guide module revision. This analysis has indicated that we are presently treating the broad contexts of educational technology and instructional organization satisfactorily, neglecting some aspects of the contemporary learning-teaching process (such as social learning and child development), and that we are paying insufficient attention to the contexts of societal factors and research. The latter area is the most neglected and there need to be modules developed based on teacher behavior and teacher characteristics research. In short, the objectives of the program and the instructional strategies utilized must be constantly revised and shifted in the light of new data.

We need to conduct research and acquire data to provide us better evidence on how to link teacher behavior to pupil outcomes. With all the interest and effort involved in CBTE, a basic unanswered concern remains: What is to be accepted as evidence of successful performance of teacher candidates in CBTE programs? There is no common and satisfactory list of crucial skills and behaviors which a majority of educators agree that teachers must possess in order to perform reasonably well in existing classrooms. The most complex problem confronting CBTE developers and implementors is the identification of criteria to determine behavioral objectives for and by which to assess the effectiveness of trainees and teacher training programs. This is known as the criterion problem. No one can provide an all-purpose answer to the question because the answer must be situation-specific. Our present research base is rather thin in this area, and there are complex technical issues. Nevertheless, the validity of any CBTE curriculum can only be established through research that relates teacher behavior to pupil behavior. Criterion judgments are now being made on an a priori basis, utilizing some results of past teacher behavior research. Our creation of behavioral objectives is a first comprehensive attempt to establish such criteria. Our evaluation efforts offer promising procedures for pertinent criteria establishment, enumeration, and validation. Only in the real world with real teachers, both students and inservice, will effective teacher behaviors be identified, tested, and proven relevant.

The present comprehensive program uniquely accommodates students attending college on a full-time basis. In such a program, commonly using the regular eight-hour day, we have no difficulty in securing field experiences for students in schools and other agencies. However, when part-time, evening, and summer session educational programs are considered, it becomes far more difficult to provide adequate, appropriate, and needed student field experiences. We are currently working on the problem of how to shift a full-time day session CBTE program into a part-time effort. Many of our students go to college on a part-time basis and there is no reason why their instruction and college experiences should be markedly different from those enjoyed by their full-time colleagues. This problem must be solved if CBTE efforts are to be relevant for all students.

Of related concern is the development of the relationship of the preceding professional year to the student teaching experience that immediately follows. Another potential problem is the relationship of student teaching to any internship following a fourth year of college.

In the development and adoption of our model, time, rather than commitment or effort, has become our most precious commodity. Time is needed to learn new roles and to adapt to new responsibilities. New working relationships require a period for adjustment. The transition from what was toward the ideal comes in short steps and requires planned choices based on mutually agreed-on priorities. The 1972-73 academic year has been called a developmental or implementation year. We now realize that 1973-74 and each succeeding year will continue to be developmental, a process of continuing to adapt to constant change.

New developments will be guided by the constant feedback of data revealing discrepancies between where we are and where we ought to be—between our real program and our ideal program. As we indicated in some detail in Chapters 9 and 10, evaluating and managing the program take on a new importance. They become more like "directing" than "monitoring" processes. We have an excellent technical model but have not resolved this important issue operationally to our satisfaction. Much work still needs to be done.

Colleagues who helped prepare this case history of a CBTE program continue to press for revisions of their reports. That is as it should be, for the situation now is not as it was when they first prepared their descriptions. The program described here no longer exists—at least not in the same manner as described. This constant reorientation-revision process in response to new data is a very real pressure on personnel. We believe that they can handle the stress and that it can become more a source of stimulus than of concern. But we need to reexamine this assumption as we proceed.

ON TRANSFER

There is nothing unique in our comprehensive CBTE, IGE/MUS program except the exact combination of the several components of the program as arranged in this university, these schools, and these communities. This is not to detract from the importance of any part of our program, but simply a relinquishment of any claim to special knowledge, special resources, special anything.

Having made this disclaimer of unique status, we must quickly make the paradoxical request that no one should attempt to replicate our program—that is, our program, *exactly*. Special, local conditions make our program uniquely suited to our place at this time. The chances of those conditions being identical anywhere else are highly unlikely.

Although the entire program cannot be replicated, this does not mean that the processes followed in developing the program should not be similar, nor that important elements as they took shape in our program could not be readily adapted or even adopted. Of course, we believe in the integrity of our entire system for our purposes, but even in our own situation we have seen the possibilities of different means to similar ends. For example, one group of cooperating elementary schools moved directly to competency-based education without the prior reorganization of personnel required by multiunit schools. Logically, we would have preferred to have the general education content of preservice teachers reorganized either before or concurrently with the professional education component. So, our comprehensive model is a unique response to our needs and resources.

Among important elements that may be transferred to other institutions and programs with similar purposes are, for example:

—The teacher education center concept.

—A process of module development.

—A plan and a structure to coordinate schools and university programs.

—A plan to compose interdisciplinary teaching teams of university faculty.

—The role of facilitator.

—A plan to merge preservice and inservice education of teachers.
—A teaching laboratory concept.
—A data management system.

This is an impressive list, but it is only a partial inventory of important but not unique elements that form the comprehensive model in existence at this moment. We have also identified several of our needs, the answers to which we would unhesitatingly adapt and incorporate in our model should we learn that someone else has made the necessary discovery or invention. Our ultimate goal requires us to avoid overidentification with materials and practices which our own experience or that of others has revealed to be less than optimal.

SUMMARY

The CBTE program staff have reviewed progress to this date compared with the ideal design formulated in 1968. Although much remains to be done, the general impression is one of satisfaction with activities currently under way and optimism for their continued success. It seems unlikely that professionals elsewhere will attempt to duplicate this particular project in its entirety. However, we stand ready to cooperate with and aid others who wish to adapt program elements or program development processes to their own situations.

The final selection in this report is a view by a professional teacher educator not affiliated with the project but who has closely observed implementation procedures. It is followed by bibliographies of selected references in the areas of CBTE, IGE, and MUS.

Notes

1. Karl Massanari, address to the Regional Invitational Conference on Performance-Based Teacher Education, San Diego, California, May 14, 1973. The entire address appears in the *Journal of Teacher Education* 24, no. 3 (fall 1973).

2. Richard L. Turner, "Relationships Between *Teachers for the Real World* and the Elementary Models Programmatic Themes and Mechanisms Payoff, Mechanisms and Costs," in *The Power of Competency-Based Teacher Education: A Report,* ed. Benjamin Rosner (Boston: Allyn & Bacon, 1972), pp. 198-201. Turner's chapter in the above book deals with six criterion levels, defined as follows:

Criterion Level Six is concerned with the effects of a training program on improvements in teacher knowledges and understandings. Criterion Levels Five and Four are concerned with the effects of teacher training on improvement in pedagogic skills under laboratory or simplified training conditions. (Level Five differs from Level Four in that the teacher need not perform before live students; simulation experiences are acceptable; and demonstration of one teaching skill is required rather than a broader range of teacher behavior, specified for Level Four.) Criterion Level Three addresses itself to the effects of training on a teacher's behavior under actual classroom conditions. The concept of pupil change as a criterion of teacher effectiveness is introduced at Criterion Levels Two and One. Criterion Level Two is concerned with changes in pupil behavior that can be effected in a relatively short time period (one to two weeks) and under actual classroom conditions. Criterion Level One is concerned with the long range effects of teacher behavior on changes in pupil achievement and well being. (Committee on National Program Priorities in Teacher Education, Benjamin Rosner, chairman, *The Power of Competency-Based Teacher Education,* final report, USOE Project no. 1-0475 (Princeton, N.J.: Educational Testing Service, July 31, 1971, p. 5.)

3. Lewis Mumford, *The Myth of the Machine* (New York: Harcourt, Brace & World, 1967).

4. R. Buckminster Fuller, *Operating Manual for Spaceship Earth* (Carbondale, Ill.: Southern Illinois University Press, 1969).

Epilogue: A Time for Change

Howard Coron

Carping is easy. Grappling with the realities of an issue is another matter—a risky business at best. As communities across the nation demand proof of teacher effectiveness, educational institutions know that they must begin to look within to respond to the challenge. For some time the teacher education "establishment" has failed to produce evidence of its effectiveness in training school personnel. Paralleling this, public school personnel have failed to produce evidence of their effectiveness. Now is the time for change!

Unfortunately, the 1970s are increasingly seen as a period of economic limitation—even poverty—in education. Many educators are struggling with these and other constraints on their effectiveness. Many constraints are real; some are imaginary. The public and its legislative representatives are demanding accountability from educators, but at the same time show no great desire or support for the appropriate changes. The demand and the constraints are both real. Imaginary constraints appear to grow out of an inability of educators to see themselves as having control over their own realm of proficiency. They have tended to build high walls around their private domain, shutting out the real world.

In the last few years the University of Toledo has begun to breach these walls. With limited funds, little outside support, but a willingness to risk public failure, a group of ambitious educators has chosen to develop a new style of teacher education. Their choice—a competency-based approach to teacher education coupled with individually guided education and multiunit schools—has placed them in the forefront as innovators. It has also left them open to close scrutiny and sharp criticism.

There is little evidence that the development of specific teaching competencies automatically leads to improved pupil learning, nor that defining these competencies ensures more effective results from teacher trainees. There is much less likelihood that training institutions will obtain adequate financial support to develop competency-based teacher education programs. All this has not stopped the University of Toledo from designing and implementing a comprehensive program to accomplish a particular educational change.

AN INCENTIVE GRANT

In 1971 the Sears Foundation, recognizing the private sector's responsibility to energize efforts to strengthen teacher education, decided to award grants for innovative urban teacher preparation programs. The basic objective was to stimulate and accelerate the planning and development of new teacher training programs with small incentive grants of $10,000. Proposals solicited were to:

(1) Focus on the preparation of teachers for schools serving low income populations;

(2) Indicate evidence of cooperation among all the significant parties associated in the program, i.e., representatives of teacher training institutions, school systems, the community, teacher associations, and students;

(3) State that, if courses are involved in the plan, their content and articulation with the goals of the program should be clarified;

(4) Specify approaches to the task of assessing teacher performance; and

(5) Contain a careful management plan of operation.

Preference was given to proposals that indicated a sharp awareness of the politics of urban education, an awareness of potential in the real world of education but also cognizant of its limitations.

On the first reading of the proposals, the University of Toledo received overwhelming support from the Guideline Committee.[1] The specifics that attracted this support had to do with the history of the institution in developing the Ohio Model Elementary Teacher Education Program, and the fact that the model program insisted that all groups of educational personnel who were actively involved in the education, induction, and support of new teachers had to undergo training or retraining programs that dealt realistically with the contexts of educational change. The Guideline Committee's considerations and the University of Toledo's proposal appeared to be an excellent fit. A competency-based program of teacher education was joined with the development of individually guided education and multiunit schools, utilizing a teacher education center concept for inservice training as well as the portal school concept for the Teacher Corps program then operating at the University of Toledo. While the Ohio model was originally developed as an elementary teacher training program, the proposal extended the program to include preparation of secondary teachers. Full implementation was projected for 1972. In all ways the proposal by the University of Toledo indicated their readiness for a breakthrough to new approaches for urban education teacher training that could revitalize the profession.

In addition to awarding the grant to the University of Toledo, the Sears Foundation financed periodic site visits throughout the planning year by one of the consultants who designed the guidelines. The project was to have more accountability to the funding agency than simply the use of periodic reports. The University of Toledo project consultant (the writer) made four site visits and reported to all concerned parties. This close contact with the project enabled the consultant and the coordinators of the project to meet more fully various deadlines for the planning period, and enabled the consultant to play more of a supportive than an evaluative role. Through his work the consultant became committed to the success of the project.

RISK-TAKING—A STEP IN THE PROCESS OF CHANGE

On the surface, the tasks set out by the University of Toledo faculty would not seem threatening, but it soon became apparent that the team members continuing to design and plan the implementation of the program, whether individually or in groups, were taking some risks. As each step of the program planning progressed, it was more evident that the faculty members were going to have to make public their thinking, their instructional objectives and module content and, most painful, accept the challenge of the accountability of their own teaching competency.

Such risk taking was handled by creating an environment in which individuals felt safe. It was obvious that the tasks the group had set for itself were important on both the professional and personal level. The participants agreed about the ineffectiveness of their current teacher education program. The difficulty was to help individuals fully analyze all problems without feeling overwhelmed and resorting to placing the blame on the administration, public school personnel, or their colleagues. The process called for evaluating available opportunities, making thoughtful choices, and accepting full responsibility for the decisions made.

The coordinators of the project assumed responsibility for completion of various tasks but their main goal was to achieve total staff involvement. They helped staff members accept changes in program and work style without feeling excessively threatened. The coordinators' complicated role reinforced productive behavior, lessened possible threats, and eliminated nonproductive behavior.

CHANGE-IN-PROGRESS

Some of the University of Toledo faculty who had been involved in the original design process of the Ohio model needed new persuasion of its validity. Many staff members needed initial awareness of the significant components involved in competency-based teacher education. The entire undergraduate faculty had to receive intensive inservice training in the fundamentals of CBTE. The varied levels of commitment or lack of commitment to this new teacher training process were quite apparent. Faculty had differing perceptions of what teachers or teacher trainers do, or of what really happens in the public schools. The faculty evidenced concern about changing their present working style for new faculty roles. Individual teaching in university self-contained classrooms, with little or no accountability to fellow staff members, was being altered to team planning and teaching, including the development of instructional modules connected to one another in logical sequences. At times the process of change was obviously painful. Some challengers aggressively questioned everything; others reacted by incipient withdrawal behavior and complete nonparticipation. There were many behavior variations within these extreme reactions.

CHANGE NECESSITATES COMMUNICATION

As faculty efforts progressed it was apparent that an improved communication system would be needed to link all participants. The three project coordinators were department heads and had existing channels to the university administration, coadministrators, departmental faculty, and students. In addition, the already functioning formal links to school districts, multiunit schools, and various committees within and without the university were utilized. But simultaneously to change the content as well as the structure of the total undergraduate teacher training program required a revision of the existing communication system. The major purpose of this effort was to provide responsive and effective feedback to all its various constituencies. This was primarily accomplished through innumerable task-oriented, formal, small-group, one-to-one, and divisional meetings. Correspondence was sent immediately after all meetings and reactions were requested and received, overcoming the time lag.

Still, this in itself was not quite enough. The information interaction that gave the program much-needed impetus to reach fruition also developed for coordinators, faculty, and administrators those skills necessary to deal with the sensitivities of their colleagues. On some occasions coordinators closeted themselves with individuals who had obviously felt hurt by their fellow faculty members' probing attitudes and behavior. The coordinators countered such feelings by positively reinforcing the faculty members' contributions, suggesting alternative ways of presenting the material, and in some instances shielding the injured party by taking on themselves the brunt of the criticism.

CHANGE TAKING EFFECT

Various groups of faculty members participated in retreats to write measurable behavioral objectives, develop training modules, and formulate implementation procedures. At the first retreat, education faculty made beginning efforts to list potential module titles, prerequisites, pretests, behavioral objectives, means for assessing objectives, directions to students, references, and posttests. By the second retreat a mutually acceptable work pattern developed and faculty members were willing to develop the skills and products needed for a competency-based program, a process they were reluctant to cope with in the beginning.

This spirit of cooperation, communication, and work did not simply happen. Progress was arduous and at times discouraging, but the entire group became a part of the decision-making process and the best thinking of the faculty was utilized for the benefit of the program. This also ensured greater feasibility for implementating faculty decisions. One area of vital concern was the financial feasibility of the program. Administrative representatives of the college reviewed faculty planning progress and assured members that the parameters of their planning were financially realistic.

The pattern was now set. Total college participation was more than norm. Several organizational process schemes were presented to the faculty for the implementation and continued development of the new program. These proposals were clearly tentative ways of looking at the program as a process-in-progress. There were no hidden agendas. Explanations were provided for all and commitments to any particular scheme were minimal in the continued hope that faculty would devise strategies ever more acceptable to the group.

CHANGE MAKES THE DIFFERENCE

As the project developed, faculty became involved to the point where almost the total undergraduate teaching faculty participated in some aspect of the program. Instructional teams were formed, made up of faculty from the departments of elementary education, educational psychology, social foundations, educational media and technology, secondary education, and health and physical education. These teams were responsible for planning, team teaching, and supervising the campus courses and field components of the program. Here was innovation in itself. Some faculty members who had rarely visited the public schools before were now requiring of themselves field supervision of students and firsthand knowledge of the school-teaching-learning situation. Faculty teams were now responsible for all instruction contained in the modules for the entire length of both the elementary and secondary professional teacher education program.

Developments were also under way to create procedures for assessing the effectiveness of the training modules. Modules were pilot tested, written, revised, tested, and revised again. A management system for implementation and coordination was devised. University of Toledo faculty members were invited by various other institutions of higher learning and school groups to prepare and operate workshops in developing CBTE programs.

CHANGE, A CONTINUOUS PROCESS

Good human relations alone are not sufficient to effect lasting change. The change needed in teacher education must be organized so as to ensure continuous evaluation and growth. This is evident in the design and operation of the Toledo CBTE IGE/MUS program. It has a self-help concept; people have learned to work together; all are accountable to each other and to the program. This program should survive future problems, for it has been developed to grapple continuously with the process of change.

Persons involved in a project benefit greatly from the Hawthorne effect of importance and excitement that accompanies participation in a new experience. They also suffer a kind of myopia that causes them to perceive events in the most favorable manner possible. For this reason it was thought important that analysis by a careful, objective "outsider" be a part of this document. This observer has had an opportunity to view the Toledo comprehensive CBTE IGE/MUS program in all of its ramifications. He advises other innovators that the process by which an innovation is implemented is no less important than the very substance of the innovation.

Note

1. Members of the Guideline Committee who later became site visitors to the institutions selected were: Dr. Lawrence Barnett, Center for Urban Education, now at the University of Wisconsin–Milwaukee; Dr. Richard Wisniewski, University of Wisconsin–Milwaukee; Dr. Anthony LaDuca, Center for Urban Education; Dr. Howard Coron, New York University; and Dr. Donald Orlovsky, University of South Florida.

Selected Reading

Otten, Jane, ed. *An Experiment in Planned Change.* Washington, D. C.: American Association of State Colleges and Universities, 1973.

Selected Bibliographies

This listing is provided to assist educators who wish to become informed about the development of competency-based teacher education. The professional literature is expanding rapidly. Most of the entries are quite recent. None is more than a few years old.

We have attempted to keep a sharp focus on the descriptors of "competency-based" or "performance-based" teacher education. Those who are familiar with the topics will realize that there are several other elements invariably associated with competency-based programs. More information could be obtained by organizing a search guided by terms such as field centered, individualized instruction, modules, management information systems, differentiated staffing, multiunit schools, and systems approach. However, many entries under these descriptors will not pertain to competency-based programs, so they were not used to prepare this list.

Sources consulted include the *Education Index,* the *Current Index to Journals in Education, Research in Education* (ERIC), and the files of miscellaneous materials accumulated by members of the Model Teacher Education program at the University of Toledo. Materials shown with an ED number are abstracted in *Research in Education.*

COMPETENCY-BASED TEACHER EDUCATION

Allen, Wendell C., et al. "Performance Criteria for Educational Per-
    sonnel Development: A State Approach to Standards." *Journal
    of Teacher Education* 20, no. 2 (summer 1969): 133-135.
American Association of Colleges for Teacher Education, Performance-Based Teacher Education Series. Washington, D.C.: The association, 1972-1973:
>   #1. "Performance-Based Teacher Education: What Is the State
>   of the Art?" by Stanley Elam.
>   #2. "The Individualized, Competency-Based System of Teach-
>   er Education at Weber State College," by Caseel Burke.
>   #3. "Manchester Interview: Competency-Based Teacher Edu-
>   cation/Certification," by Theodore Andrews.
>   #4. "A Critique of PBTE," by Harry S. Broudy.
>   #5. "Competency-Based Teacher Education: A Scenario," by
>   James Cooper and Wilford Weber.
>   #6. "Changing Teacher Education in a Large Urban Univer-
>   sity," by Frederic T. Giles and Clifford Foster.
>   #7. "Performance-Based Teacher Education: An Annotated
>   Bibliography," by AACTE and ERIC Clearinghouse on
>   Teacher Education.
>   #8. "Performance-Based Teacher Education Programs: A Com-
>   parative Description," by Iris Elfenbein.
>   #9. "Competency-Based Education: The State of the Scene,"
>   by Allen A. Schmieder (jointly with ERIC Clearinghouse
>   on Teacher Education).
>   #10. "A Humanistic Approach to Performance-Based Teacher
>   Education," by Paul Nash.
>   #11. "Performance-Based Teacher Education and the Subject
>   Matter Fields," by Michael F. Shugrus.
>   #12. "Performance-Based Teacher Education: Some Measure-
>   ment and Decision Making Considerations," by Jack C.
>   Merwin.
*Analytic Summaries of Specifications for Model Teacher Education
    Programs.* Systems Development Corporation, Falls Church, Va.
    Washington, D.C.: Government Printing Office, October 1969.
    ED 037 422.

Andersen, D. W., J. M. Cooper, M. V. DeVault, G. E. Dickson, C. Johnson, and W. H. Weber. *Competency Based Teacher Education.* Berkeley, Calif.: McCutchan Publishing Corp., 1973.

Andrews, Theodore. *New Directions in Certification.* Denver, Colo.: Improving State Leadership in Education Office, September 1970. ED 043 796.

————. "Certification Reform: The Search for Better Folk." *New York State Education* 57 (February 1970): 17-19.

Arends, Robert L., John A. Masia, and Wilford Weber. *Handbook for the Development of Instructional Modules in Competency-based Teacher Education Programs.* Syracuse, N.Y.: Syracuse University, Center for the Study of Teaching, January 1971. ED 050 009.

Association of Teacher Educators. *Performance-Based Certification of School Personnel.* Washington, D.C.: NEA, 1971.

Bhaerman, Robert D. *Which Way for Teacher Certification?* AFT QUEST, paper no. 2. Washington, D.C.: American Federation of Teachers, 1969. Also in *American Teacher* (February 1969). ED 032 269.

Bloom, B. S., et al., eds. *Taxonomy of Educational Objectives: Handbook I, The Cognitive Domain.* New York: David McKay Co., 1956.

Bloom, B. S., J. T. Hastings, and G. F. Madaus. *Handbook on Formative and Summative Evaluation of Student Learning.* New York: McGraw-Hill, 1971.

Burdin, Joel L., and Lanzilletti Kaliopee. *A Reader's Guide to the Comprehensive Models for Preparing Elementary Teachers.* Washington, D.C.: ERIC Clearinghouse on Teacher Education and the AACTE, 1969.

Burdin, Joel L., and Margaret Reagan, eds. *Performance-Based Certification of School Personnel.* Washington, D.C.: Association of Teacher Educators and ERIC Clearinghouse on Teacher Education, 1971. ED 049 152.

Cooper, James. "Current Trends in Teacher Education Curriculum." *Journal of Teacher Education* 23, no. 3 (fall 1972): 312-317.

Daniel, K. Fred. "Performance-Based Teacher Certification: What Is It and Why Do We Need It?" Paper prepared for a training program for teacher education leaders, Miami Beach, Fla., May 19-22, 1970. ED 045 551.

Darland, D. D. "The Role of Professional Organizations in Performance-Based Teacher Education." Editorial comment, *Journal of
Teacher Education* 23, no. 3 (fall 1972): 275-276.

Dickson, George E. *Planning for a Performance-Based Teacher Education Program: A Final Report.* Toledo, Ohio: The University
of Toledo, College of Education, August 1972.

—————. *Planning a Prototype Teacher Center for Ohio.* Toledo,
Ohio: The University of Toledo, College of Education, June
1972.

Dickson, George E., Gilbert F. Shearron, Gary E. Cooke, and Nancy
Hensel. *Early Childhood Education and Competency-Based
Teacher Education.* Storrs, Conn.: University of Connecticut,
National Leadership Institute, Teacher Education/Early Child-
hood, June 1973.

Dickson, George E., et al. *The Feasibility of Educational Specifications for the Ohio Comprehensive Elementary Teacher Education Program. Phase II, Final Report.* Toledo, Ohio: The University of Toledo, 1970. ED 042 721.

Drummond, William H. "The Meaning and Application of Performance Criteria in Staff Development." *Phi Delta Kappan* 52, no.
1 (September 1970): 32-35.

*Elementary Teacher Education Models, Phase II Feasibility. Journal
of Research and Development in Education* 3, no. 3 (Athens,
Ga.: University of Georgia, College of Education, spring 1970).

Florida Department of Education, *Florida Catalog of Teacher Competencies.* Tallahassee: Florida State University, 1972.

Gage, N. L., ed. *Handbook of Research on Teaching.* Chicago: Rand
McNally, 1963.

Houston, W. Robert. *Performance Education: Strategies and Resources for Developing a Competency-Based Teacher Education
Program.* Albany: New York State Education Department, Division of Teacher Education and Certification and Multi-State
Consortium on Performance-Based Teacher Education, 1973.

—————, and Robert B. Howsam. *Competency-Based Teacher
Education.* Palo Alto, Calif.: Science Research Associates, 1972.

—————, et al. *Developing Learning Modules.* Houston, Tex.: University of Houston, College of Education, 1971.

Hoyt, Donald P. *Identifying Effective Teaching Behaviors.* Manhat-
tan, Kan.: Kansas State University, December 1969. ED 039
197.

Inglis, Joan D., ed. *Field-Based Teacher Education: Emerging Relationships, Educational Comment, 1972.* Toledo, Ohio: The University of Toledo, College of Education, 1972.

Johnson, Charles E., and Jerold P. Bauch. *Competency-Based Teacher Evaluation Guide.* GEM bulletin 70-3. Athens, Ga.: University of Georgia, College of Education, 1970. ED 042 698.

———. *Criteria for Validating the Feasibility of the Components of a Model Teacher Education Program.* GEM bulletin 69-24. Athens, Ga.: University of Georgia, College of Education, 1969. ED 040 920.

Johnson, Charles E., and Gilbert F. Shearron. *Selected Teacher Performance Specifications Generally Applicable to Teacher Education Curricula.* GEM bulletin 69-1. Athens, Ga.: University of Georgia, College of Education, 1969. ED 040 924.

Johnson, Charles E., Gilbert F. Shearron, and David Payne. *Specifying Assumptions, Goals and Objectives for a Competency Based Teacher Education Program.* GEM bulletin 71-1. Athens, Ga.: University of Georgia, College of Education, 1971.
[Note: Charles E. Johnson and Gilbert F. Shearron have authored a series of GEM publications, all of which may be of interest.]

Joyce, Bruce, et al. *Materials for Modules: A Classification of Competency-Oriented Tools for Teacher Education.* New York: Columbia University, Teachers College, June 1971. ED 057 016.

Kay, Patricia M., et al. *Performance Based Certification.* New York. City University of New York, New York Office of Teacher Education, June 1971. ED 056 991.

Krathwohl, D. R., et al., eds. *Taxonomy of Educational Objectives. Handbook II, The Affective Domain.* New York, David McKay Co., 1956.

LeBaron, Walt. *Systems Analysis and Learning Systems in the Development of Elementary Teacher Education Models.* Washington, D.C.: Government Printing Office, 1970.

Massanari, Karl. *Performance-Based Teacher Education: What's It All About?* Washington, D.C.: AACTE, April 1971. ED 055 972.

Nussel, Edward J., John F. Ahern, Dennis E. Hinkle, and George E. Dickson. *The Ohio Model and the Multi-unit School, Educational Comment, 1971.* Toledo, Ohio: The University of Toledo, College of Education, 1971.

Rosner, Benjamin, ed. *The Power of Competency-Based Teacher Education.* Boston: Allyn & Bacon, 1972.

Saxe, Richard W., ed. *Contexts for Teacher Education, Educational Comment, 1969.* Toledo, Ohio: The University of Toledo, College of Education, 1969.

Shearron, Gilbert F., and Charles E. Johnson. *A Prototype for a Competency-Based Proficiency Module.* GEM bulletin. Athens, Ga.: University of Georgia, College of Education, 1969. ED 042 693. (See note under Johnson, Charles E.)

Sikula, John P., ed. *Teacher Education for an Urban Setting, Educational Comment, 1973.* Toledo, Ohio: The University of Toledo, 1973

Simon, Anita, and E. Gil Boyer, eds. *Mirrors for Behavior, an Anthology of Classroom Observation Instruments.* Philadelphia, Pa.: Research for Better Schools, 1967.

Smith, B. Othanel, ed. *Research in Teacher Education: A Symposium.* Englewood Cliffs, N.J.: Prentice Hall, 1971.

Smith, B. Othanel, et al. *Teachers for the Real World.* Washington, D.C.: AACTE, December 1968.

Teacher Education Models. Journal of Research and Development in Education (Athens, Ga.: University of Georgia, spring 1969).

Travers, Robert N. W., ed. *Second Handbook of Research on Teaching.* Chicago: Rand McNally, 1973.

The United States Office of Education Elementary Models:

Allen, D. W., and J. M. Cooper. *Model Elementary Teacher Education Program.* FS258:58022. Washington, D.C.: USOE Bureau of Research, 1968. (University of Massachusetts Model Project.)

DeVault, M. Vere. *Wisconsin Elementary Teacher Education Project.* Madison: University of Wisconsin, School of Education, 1969. (University of Wisconsin Model Project.)

Dickson, G. E. *Educational Specifications for a Comprehensive Elementary Teacher Education Program* (vol. I, The Basic Report; vol. II, The Specifications). OE-58023. Washington, D.C.: USOE Bureau of Research, 1968. (University of Toledo Model Project.) ED 025 427, ED 025 426.

Houston, W. Robert. *Behavioral Science Elementary Teacher Education Program.* FS5.258:58024. Washington, D.C.: USOE Bureau of Research, 1968. (Michigan State University Model Project.)

Hough, J. *Specifications for a Comprehensive Undergraduate* and *In-service Teacher Education Program for Elementary Teachers*. FS5.258:58016. Washington, D.C.: USOE Bureau of Research, 1968. (Syracuse University Model Project.)

Johnson, C. E., G. F. Shearron, and A. J. Stauffer. *Georgia Educational Model Specifications for the Preparation of Elementary Teachers*. FS5.258:58019. Washington, D.C.: USOE Bureau of Research, 1968. (University of Georgia Model Project.)

Joyce, B. R. *The Teacher Innovator: A Program to Prepare Teachers*. FS5.258:58021. Washington, D.C.: USOE Bureau of Research, 1969. (Columbia University Teachers College Model Project.)

Schalock, H. D. *A Competency-Based, Field Centered, Systems Approach to Elementary Teacher Education*. FS5.258: 58020. Washington, D. C.: USOE Bureau of Research, 1968. (Northwest Regional Laboratory, Oregon, Model Project.)

Southworth, H. C. *A Model of Teacher Training for the Individualization of Instruction*. FS5.258:58017. Washington, D.C.: USOE Bureau of Research, 1968. (University of Pittsburgh Model Project.)

Sowards, J. W. *A Model for the Preparation of Elementary School Teachers*. FS5.258:58018. Washington, D.C.: USOE Bureau of Research, 1968. (Florida State University Model Project.)

Weber, Wilford A., James M. Cooper, and W. Robert Houston. *A Guide to Competency-Based Teacher Education*. Westfield, Texas: Competency-Based Instructional Systems, 1973.

INDIVIDUALLY GUIDED EDUCATION

Askov, Eunice Nicholson. *Assessment of a System for Individualizing Reading Instruction*. Report from the Individually Guided Instruction in Elementary Reading Project. Madison, Wis.: Research and Development Center for Cognitive Learning, March 1970. ED 040 840.

Blount, Nathan S., et al. *The Effect of a Study of Grammar on the Writing of Eighth-Grade Students*. Report from the Individually

Guided Instruction in English Language, Composition, and Literature Project. Madison, Wis.: Research and Development Center for Cognitive Learning, December 1968. ED 036 515.

Buegen, Joan, Ira Kerns, and Norman Graper. *Individually Guided Education: Principal's Handbook.* Dayton, Ohio: Institute for Development of Educational Activities, 1971.

[Note: A complete series of thirteen IGE publications and related audiovisual aids is published by I/D/E/A, P.O. Box 628, Far Hills Branch, Dayton, Ohio 45419.]

DeVault, M. V., et al. *Teacher's Manual: Computer Management for Individually Guided Education in Mathematics and Reading.* Madison, Wis.: Research and Development Center for Cognitive Learning, 1969.

DiPego, Gerald. *Individually Guided Education: Unit Operation and Roles.* Dayton, Ohio: Institute for Development of Educational Activities, 1970.

Edling, Jack V., ed. *Case Studies: Individualized Instruction.* Stanford, Calif.: ERIC Clearinghouse on Educational Media and Technology, June 1970. ED 041 452.

Esbensen, Thorwald. *Individualizing the Instructional Program.* Duluth, Minn.: Duluth Public Schools, August 1966. ED 016 003.

Gibbons, Maurice. *Individualized Instruction: A Descriptive Analysis.* New York: Teachers College Press, Columbia University, 1971.

Goodlad, John I. "Educational Change: A Strategy for Study and Action." *Journal of Secondary Education* 46, no. 4 (April 1971): 156-166.

Howes, Virgil M. *Individualization of Instruction: A Teaching Strategy.* New York: Macmillan Co., 1970.

Individualizing Instruction: A Selected Bibliography. I/D/E/A bibliography series. Dayton, Ohio: Institute for Development of Educational Activities, 1968. ED 030 619.

Jablonsky, Adelaide. *A Selected ERIC Bibliography on Individualizing Instruction.* ERIC-IRCD urban disadvantaged series no. 2. New York: ERIC Clearinghouse on the Urban Disadvantaged, January 1969. ED 027 358.

Kennedy, B. J. *Motivational Effects of Individual Conferences and Goal Setting on Performance and Attitudes in Arithmetic.* Technical report no. 61. Madison, Wis.: Research and Development Center for Cognitive Learning, 1968.

Klausmeier, Herbert J., et al. *Individually Guided Education in the Multiunit Elementary School: Guidelines for Implementation.* Madison, Wis.: Research and Development Center for Cognitive Learning, August 1968. ED 024 994.

Klausmeier, Herbert J., E. Schwenn, and P. A. Lamal. *A System of Individually Guided Education.* Practical paper no. 9. Madison, Wis.: Research and Development Center for Cognitive Learning, 1971.

Klausmeier, Herbert J., et al. *A System of Individually Guided Motivation.* Madison, Wis.: Research and Development Center for Cognitive Learning, January 1970. ED 039 619.

Klausmeier, Herbert J., et al. *Individually Guided Motivation: Goal Setting Procedures to Develop Student Self Direction and Prosocial Behaviors.* Madison, Wis.: Research and Development Center for Cognitive Learning, March 1970. ED 039 551.

Klausmeier, Herbert J., et al. "Individually Guided Motivation: Developing Self Direction and Prosocial Behaviors." *Elementary School Journal* 71, no. 6 (March 1971): 339-350.

National School Public Relations Association. *IGE: Individually Guided Education and the Multiunit School.* Washington, D.C.: NSPRA, 1972.

Pooley, Robert C., and Lester S. Golub. *Concepts and Objectives for Learning the Structure of English in Grades 7, 8, and 9.* Report from the Project on Individually Guided Instruction in English Language, Composition, and Literature. Madison, Wis.: Research and Development Center for Cognitive Learning, November 1969. ED 038 421.

Quilling, M. R., et al. *Individual Goal-Setting Conferences Related to Subject Matter Learning: A Report of the Field Test.* Technical report no. 190. Madison, Wis.: Research and Development Center for Cognitive Learning, 1971.

Rendfrey, Kaye, D. A. Frayer, and M. R. Quilling. *Individually Guided Motivation: Setting Individual Goals for Learning.* Practical paper no. 11. Madison, Wis.: Research and Development Center for Cognitive Learning, 1971.

Rendfrey, Kaye, et al. *Individually Guided Motivation: Setting Individual Goals for Learning.* Report from the Project on Situational Variables and Efficiency of Concept Learning. Madison, Wis.: Research and Development Center for Cognitive Learning, January 1971. ED 057 412.

Schwenn, E. A., J. S. Sorenson, and J. L. Bavry. *The Effect of Individual Adult-Child Conferences on the Independent Reading of Elementary School Children.* Technical report no. 125. Madison, Wis.: Research and Development Center for Cognitive Learning, 1970.

Sorenson, J., E. A. Schwenn, and H. J. Klausmeier. *The Individual Conference: A Motivational Device for Increasing Independent Reading in the Elementary Grades.* Practical paper no. 8. Madison, Wis.: Research and Development Center for Cognitive Learning, 1969.

Sorenson, J., E. A. Schwenn, and J. L. Bavry. *The Use of Individual and Group Goal Setting Conferences as a Motivational Device to Improve Student Conduct and Increase Student Self-Direction: A Preliminary Study.* Technical report no. 123. Madison, Wis.: Research and Development Center for Cognitive Learning, 1970.

Thomas, George I., and Joseph Crescimbeni. *Individualizing Instruction in the Elementary School.* New York: Random House, 1967.

Wade, Serena E. *Individualizing Instruction: An Annotated Bibliography.* A Series One paper from ERIC at Stanford. Stanford, Calif.: ERIC Clearinghouse on Educational Media and Technology, December 1968. ED 029 519.

MULTIUNIT SCHOOLS

Arends, Richard, and Don M. Essig. *The Role of the Principal and Curriculum Associate in the Unitized, Differentiated Staffing, Elementary School.* DSP Progress Report no. 3: Leadership. Eugene, Ore.: Eugene School District 4, 1972. ED 060 513.

Behrendt, David. "Away with Tradition." *American Education* 6, no. 1 (January-February 1970): 18-22.

Cook, Doris M., et al. *Research and Development Activities in R & I Units of Two Elementary Schools of Janesville, Wisconsin, 1966-67.* Report from Project Models. Madison, Wis.: Research and Development Center for Cognitive Learning, March 1968. ED 023 175.

DiPego, Gerald. *Unit Operation and Roles.* Dayton, Ohio: Institute for Development of Educational Activities, 1970.

Eidell, Terry L., Ronald Little, and Jon Thorlacius. "Uniformity and Variability in the Organizational Characteristics of Elementary Schools." Paper for the American Educational Research Association. Los Angeles, February 1969.

Feit, Donald. "Making It Work: The IIC." *Multiunit Newsletter* (February 1971): 6-7.

Graham, Richard A. "School as a Learning Community: Multiunit Schools." *Theory into Practice* 11, no. 1 (February 1972): 4-8.

Individually Guided Education in the Multiunit School. Madison, Wis.: Research and Development Center for Cognitive Learning, February 1972. ED 062 728.

Klausmeier, Herbert J. "The Multiunit Elementary School and Individually Guided Education." *Phi Delta Kappan* 53, no. 3 (November 1971): 181-184.

——————, et al. "Instructional Programming for the Individual Pupil in the Multiunit Elementary School." *Elementary School Journal* 72, no. 2 (November 1971): 88-101.

——————, and Mary R. Quilling. *An Alternative to Self-Contained, Age-Graded Classes.* Madison, Wis.: Research and Development Center for Cognitive Learning, 1967. ED 016 010.

——————, et al. *The Development and Evaluation of the Multiunit Elementary School, 1966-1970.* Report from the Project on Variables and Processes in Cognitive Learning. Madison, Wis.: Research and Development Center for Cognitive Learning, 1971. ED 051 589.

——————, et al. *Individualizing Instruction in Language Arts through Development and Research in R and I Units of Local Schools, 1965-1966.* Madison, Wis.: Research and Development Center for Cognitive Learning, February 1967. ED 013 255.

——————, et al. *The Multiunit Organization (I & R Units) and Elementary Education in the Decades Ahead.* Madison, Wis.: Research and Development Center for Cognitive Learning, 1968. ED 027 238.

——————, et al. *Project Models: A Facilitative Environment for Increasing Efficiency of Pupil Learning and for Conducting Educational Research and Development.* Madison, Wis.: Research and Development Center for Cognitive Learning, June 1967. ED 016 004.

——————, et al. *Project Models: Maximizing Opportunities for*

Development and Experimentation in Learning in the Schools.
Occasional paper no. 3. Madison, Wis.: Research and Development Center for Cognitive Learning, 1966.

——————, et al. *Research and Development Activities in R & I
Units of Five Elementary Schools of Racine, Wisconsin,
1966-1967.* Report from Project Models. Madison, Wis.: Research and Development Center for Cognitive Learning, 1968.
ED 023 176.

Morrow, Richard, Juanita Sorenson, and George Glasrud. *Evaluation
Procedures for Use with Multiunit Elementary School Personnel.* Working paper no. 21. Madison, Wis.: Research and Development Center for Cognitive Learning, 1969.

"MUS-E and IGE: More Alphabet Soup or Valid Change?" *NJEA
Review* 45 (January 1972): 28-31, 54.

Nussel, Edward J., et al. *The Ohio Model and the Multiunit School,
Educational Comment, 1971.* Toledo, Ohio: The University of
Toledo, 1971.

Packard, John S. "Changing to a Multiunit School." In *Contrasts in
the Process of Planned Change of the School's Instructional
Organization,* edited by W. W. Charters et al. Eugene, Ore.: University of Oregon, Center for the Advanced Study of Educational Administration, 1973.

Pellegrin, Roland J. *Professional Satisfaction and Decision Making in
the Multiunit School.* Eugene, Ore.: University of Oregon, Center for Advanced Study of Educational Administration, 1969.
ED 049 552.

——————. *Some Organizational Characteristics of Multiunit
Schools.* Eugene, Ore.: University of Oregon, Center for the
Advanced Study of Educational Administration, 1969. ED 049
553.

"Planning for a Statewide Network of Multiunit Schools, Competency-Based Teacher Education, and Performance-Based Teacher Education: A Proposal." Columbus, Ohio: Ohio Department
of Education, 1971.

Quilling, Mary R., and Herbert J. Klausmeier. "Alternative School
Organization." *Wisconsin Journal of Education* 100 (February
1968): 9-11.

Quilling, Mary R., et al. *Research and Development Activities in R & I
Units of Two Elementary Schools of Milwaukee, Wisconsin,*

1966-1967. Madison, Wis.: Research and Development Center for Cognitive Learning, 1968. ED 020 911.

Quilling, Mary R. *Summaries of Research and Development Activities Performed in Racine R and I Units during the 1966-1967 School Year*. Madison, Wis.: Research and Development Center for Cognitive Learning, 1967. ED 016 012.

Saxe, Richard W. "The Multiunit Principal: His New Role." *Ohio Association of Elementary School Principals Quarterly* 9, no. 4 (spring 1973): 13-16.

————, and Alfred H. Mackey. "The Principal—Communication Director." In *Field-Based Teacher Education: Emerging Relationships, Educational Comment*, edited by Joan D. Inglis. Toledo, Ohio: The University of Toledo, 1972.

Smith, Richard J., and Herbert J. Klausmeier. *The Development of a Facilitative Environment for Learning and Research through R and I Units in the Secondary School, 1966-1967*. Madison, Wis.: Research and Development Center for Cognitive Learning, 1967. ED 016 005.

Sowers, Paul C. *Open-End Elementary Education*. NASEC Monograph Series, Spectrum. Flagstaff, Ariz.: Northern Arizona Supplementary Education Center, 1968. ED 030 942.

Walter, James E., and Mary Horn. *Dissemination of the Multiunit Elementary School. Final Report*. Madison, Wis.: Research and Development Center for Cognitive Learning, 1967. ED 062 727.

Wardrop, James L., et al. *A Plan for Field Testing R and I Units*. Madison, Wis.: Research and Development Center for Cognitive Learning, 1967. ED 016 011.

Weber, Laurence J. "Principal Happy to Make Room Out on the Limb." *D & R Report* 2, no. 3 (April 1973): 6-7.